ABOUT THIS PUBLICATION

FOR SERVICE ASSISTANCE

Customer Service
1.704.898.0770

North Carolina General Statues is published by The Muliti-Media Group of Greater Charlotte in Charlotte, North Carolina. Copyright 2015 by the Multi-Media Group of Greater Charlotte. This book or parts thereof may not be reproduced in any form, stored in a retrieval system, or transmitted in any form by any means—electronic, mechanical, photocopy, recording or otherwise—without prior written permission of the publisher, except as provided by United States of America copyright law.

The records required by U.S. Code 2257(a) through (c) and the pertinent regulations 28 C.F.R. Cli. 1, Part 75 with respect to this publication and all materials associated with such records are maintained by The Multi-Media Group of Greater Charlotte, Publisher and available for review by Attorney General.

www.visionbooks.org

Copyright © 2015 by MMGGC
All rights reserved!

TID: 5107841
ISBN (10) digit: 1503243915
ISBN (13) digit: 978-1503243910

123-4-56789-01239-Paperback
123-4-56789-01239-Hardback

First Edition

090520140547

Printed in the United States of America

2015 EDITION

North Carolina Criminal Law And Procedure-Pamphlet # 79

Printed In conjunction with the Administration of the Courts

North Carolina Criminal Law and Procedure
Pamphlet Reference Guide

Chapters	Pamphlet
Chapter 1 Civil Procedure	1
Chapter 1 Civil Procedure (Continue)	2
Chapter 1A Rules of Civil Procedure	2
Chapter 1B Contribution.	2
Chapter 1C Enforcement of Judgments.	2
Chapter 1D Punitive Damages.	2
Chapter 1E Eastern Band of Cherokee Indians.	2
Chapter 1F North Carolina Uniform Interstate Depositions and Discovery Act.	2
Chapter 2 - Clerk of Superior Court [Repealed and Transferred.]	3
Chapter 3 - Commissioners of Affidavits and Deeds [Repealed.]	3
Chapter 4 - Common Law	3
Chapter 5 - Contempt [Repealed.]	3
Chapter 5A - Contempt	3
Chapter 6 - Liability for Court Costs	3
Chapter 7 - Courts [Repealed and Transferred.]	3
Chapter 7A – Judicial Department	3
Chapter 7A – Continuation (Judicial Department)	4
Chapter 7A – Continuation (Judicial Department)	5
Chapter 7B - Juvenile Code	5
Chapter 8 - Evidence	6
Chapter 8A - Interpreters for Deaf Persons [Recodified.]	6
Chapter 8B - Interpreters for Deaf Persons	6
Chapter 8C - Evidence Code	6
Chapter 9 - Jurors	6
Chapter 10 - Notaries [Repealed.]	6
Chapter 10A - Notaries [Recodified.]	6
Chapter 10B - Notaries	6
Chapter 11 - Oaths	6
Chapter 12 - Statutory Construction	6
Chapter 13 - Citizenship Restored	6
Chapter 14 - Criminal Law	7
Chapter 14 –Criminal Law (Continuation)	8
Chapter 15 - Criminal Procedure	9
Chapter 15A - Criminal Procedure Act (Continuation)	10
Chapter 15A - Criminal Procedure Act (Continuation)	11
Chapter 15B - Victims Compensation	11
Chapter 15C - Address Confidentiality Program	11
Chapter 16 - Gaming Contracts and Futures	11
Chapter 17 - Habeas Corpus	11

Chapter 17A - Law-Enforcement Officers [Recodified.]	11
Chapter 17B - North Carolina Criminal Justice Education and Training System [Recodified.] Chapter 17C - North Carolina Criminal Justice Education and Training Standards Commission	11
	11
Chapter 17D - North Carolina Justice Academy	11
Chapter 17E - North Carolina Sheriffs' Education and Training Standards Commission	11
Chapter 18 - Regulation of Intoxicating Liquors [Repealed.]	12
Chapter 18A - Regulation of Intoxicating Liquors [Repealed.]	12
Chapter 18B - Regulation of Alcoholic Beverages	12
Chapter 18C - North Carolina State Lottery	12
Chapter 19 - Offenses against Public Morals	12
Chapter 19A - Protection of Animals	12
Chapter 20 - Motor Vehicles	13
Chapter 20 - Motor Vehicles (Continuation)	14
Chapter 20 - Motor Vehicles (Continuation)	15
Chapter 20 - Motor Vehicles (Continuation)	16
Chapter 21 - Bills of Lading	17
Chapter 22 - Contracts Requiring Writing	17
Chapter 22A - Signatures	17
Chapter 22B - Contracts Against Public Policy	17
Chapter 22C - Payments to Subcontractors	17
Chapter 23 - Debtor and Creditor	17
Chapter 24 – Interest	17
Chapter 25 – Uniform Commercial Code	18
Chapter 25 – Uniform Commercial Code (Continuation)	19
Chapter 25A – Retail Installment Sales Act	20
Chapter 25B - Credit	20
Chapter 25C - Sales of Artwork	20
Chapter 26 - Suretyship	20
Chapter 27 - Warehouse Receipts [Repealed.]	20
Chapter 28 - Administration [Repealed.]	20
Chapter 28A - Administration of Decedents' Estates	20
Chapter 28B - Estates of Absentees in Military Service	20
Chapter 28C - Estates of Missing Persons	20
Chapter 29 - Intestate Succession	21
Chapter 30 - Surviving Spouses	21
Chapter 31 - Wills	21
Chapter 31A - Acts Barring Property Rights	21
Chapter 31B - Renunciation of Property and Renunciation of Fiduciary Powers Act	21
Chapter 31C - Uniform Disposition of Community Property Rights at Death Act	21
Chapter 32 - Fiduciaries	21
Chapter 32A - Powers of Attorney	21
Chapter 33 - Guardian and Ward [Repealed and Recodified.]	21

Chapter 33A - North Carolina Uniform Transfers to Minors Act	21
Chapter 33B - North Carolina Uniform Custodial Trust Act	21
Chapter 34 - Veterans' Guardianship Act	22
Chapter 35 - Sterilization Procedures	22
Chapter 35A - Incompetency and Guardianship	22
Chapter 36 - Trusts and Trustees [Repealed.]	22
Chapter 36A - Trusts and Trustees	22
Chapter 36B - Uniform Management of Institutional Funds Act [Repealed.]	22
Chapter 36C - North Carolina Uniform Trust Code	22
Chapter 36D - North Carolina Community Third Party Trusts, Pooled Trusts	23
Chapter 36E - Uniform Prudent Management of Institutional Funds Act	23
Chapter 37 - Allocation of Principal and Income [Repealed.]	23
Chapter 37A - Uniform Principal and Income Act	23
Chapter 38 - Boundaries	23
Chapter 38A - Landowner Liability	23
Chapter 39 - Conveyances	23
Chapter 39A - Transfer Fee Covenants Prohibited	23
Chapter 40 - Eminent Domain [Repealed.]	23
Chapter 40A - Eminent Domain	23
Chapter 41 - Estates	23
Chapter 41A - State Fair Housing Act	23
Chapter 42 - Landlord and Tenant	23
Chapter 42A - Vacation Rental Act	23
Chapter 43 - Land Registration	23
Chapter 44 - Liens	24
Chapter 44A - Statutory Liens and Charges	24
Chapter 45 - Mortgages and Deeds of Trust	24
Chapter 45A - Good Funds Settlement Act	24
Chapter 46 - Partition	24
Chapter 47 - Probate and Registration	25
Chapter 47A - Unit Ownership	25
Chapter 47B - Real Property Marketable Title Act	25
Chapter 47C - North Carolina Condominium Act	25
Chapter 47D - Notice of Settlement Act [Expired.]	25
Chapter 47E - Residential Property Disclosure Act	25
Chapter 47F - North Carolina Planned Community Act	25
Chapter 47G - Option to Purchase Contracts	25
Chapter 47H - Contracts for Deed	25
Chapter 48 - Adoptions	26
Chapter 48A - Minors	26
Chapter 49 - Bastardy	26
Chapter 49A - Rights of Children	26
Chapter 50 - Divorce and Alimony	26
Chapter 50A - Uniform Child-Custody Jurisdiction and	

Enforcement Act	26
Chapter 50B - Domestic Violence	26
Chapter 50C - Civil No-Contact Orders	26
Chapter 51 - Marriage	26
Chapter 52 - Powers and Liabilities of Married Persons	27
Chapter 52A - Uniform Reciprocal Enforcement of Support Act [Repealed.]	27
Chapter 52B - Uniform Premarital Agreement Act	27
Chapter 52C - Uniform Interstate Family Support Act	27
Chapter 53 - Banks	27
Chapter 53A - Business Development Corporations and North Carolina Capital Resource Corporations	28
Chapter 53B - Financial Privacy Act	28
Chapter 54 - Cooperative Organizations	28
Chapter 54A - Capital Stock Savings and Loan Associations [Repealed.]	28
Chapter 54B - Savings and Loan Associations	29
Chapter 54C - Savings Banks	29
Chapter 55 - North Carolina Business Corporation Act	30
Chapter 55A - North Carolina Nonprofit Corporation Act	31
Chapter 55B - Professional Corporation Act	31
Chapter 55C - Foreign Trade Zones	31
Chapter 55D - Filings, Names, and Registered Agents for Corporations, Nonprofit Corporations, and Partnerships	31
Chapter 56 - Electric, Telegraph and Power Companies [Repealed.]	31
Chapter 57 - Hospital, Medical and Dental Service Corporations [Recodified.]	31
Chapter 57A - Health Maintenance Organization Act [Recodified.]	31
Chapter 57B - Health Maintenance Organization Act [Recodified.]	31
Chapter 57C - North Carolina Limited Liability Company Act.	31
Chapter 58 - Insurance.	32
Chapter 58A - North Carolina Health Insurance Trust Commission [Recodified.]	32
Chapter 58A - North Carolina Health Insurance Trust Commission [Recodified.] (Continuation)	33
Chapter 58A - North Carolina Health Insurance Trust Commission [Recodified.] (Continuation)	34
Chapter 58A - North Carolina Health Insurance Trust Commission [Recodified.] (Continuation)	35
Chapter 58A - North Carolina Health Insurance Trust Commission [Recodified.] (Continuation)	36
Chapter 58A - North Carolina Health Insurance Trust Commission [Recodified.] (Continuation)	37
Chapter 58A - North Carolina Health Insurance Trust	

Commission [Recodified.] (Continuation)	38
Chapter 59 - Partnership.	39
Chapter 59B - Uniform Unincorporated Nonprofit Association Act.	39
Chapter 60 - Railroads and Other Carriers [Repealed and Transferred.]	39
Chapter 61 - Religious Societies	39
Chapter 62 - Public Utilities	39
Chapter 62 - Public Utilities (Continuation)	40
Chapter 62A - Public Safety Telephone Service And Wireless Telephone Service	40
Chapter 63 - Aeronautics	40
Chapter 63A - North Carolina Global TransPark Authority	40
Chapter 64 - Aliens	40
Chapter 65 – Cemeteries	40
Chapter 66 - Commerce and Business	41
Chapter 67 - Dogs	41
Chapter 68 - Fences and Stock Law	41
Chapter 69 - Fire Protection	41
Chapter 70 - Indian Antiquities, Archaeological Resources and Unmarked Human Skeletal Remains Protection	42
Chapter 71 - Indians [Repealed.]	42
Chapter 71A - Indians	42
Chapter 72 - Inns, Hotels and Restaurants	42
Chapter 73 - Mills	42
Chapter 74 - Mines and Quarries	42
Chapter 74A - Company Police [Repealed.]	42
Chapter 74B - Private Protective Services Act [Repealed.]	42
Chapter 74C - Private Protective Services	42
Chapter 74D - Alarm Systems	42
Chapter 74E - Company Police Act	42
Chapter 74F - Locksmith Licensing Act	42
Chapter 74G - Campus Police Act	42
Chapter 75 - Monopolies, Trusts and Consumer Protection	42
Chapter 75A - Boating and Water Safety	43
Chapter 75B - Discrimination in Business	43
Chapter 75C - Motion Picture Fair Competition Act	43
Chapter 75D - Racketeer Influenced and Corrupt Organizations	43
Chapter 75E - Unlawful Activities in Connection With Certain Corporate Transactions	43
Chapter 76 - Navigation	43
Chapter 76A - Navigation and Pilotage Commissions	43
Chapter 77 - Rivers, Creeks, and Coastal Waters	43
Chapter 78 - Securities Law [Repealed.]	43
Chapter 78A - North Carolina Securities Act	43
Chapter 78B - Tender Offer Disclosure Act [Repealed.]	43
Chapter 78C - Investment Advisers	43
Chapter 78D - Commodities Act	43

Chapter 79 - Strays [Repealed.]	43
Chapter 80 - Trademarks, Brands, etc.	44
Chapter 81 - Weights and Measures [Recodified.]	44
Chapter 81A - Weights and Measures Act of 1975.	44
Chapter 82 - Wrecks [Repealed.]	44
Chapter 83 - Architects [Recodified.]	44
Chapter 83A - Architects	44
Chapter 84 - Attorneys-at-Law	44
Chapter 84A - Foreign Legal Consultants	44
Chapter 85 - Auctions and Auctioneers [Repealed.]	44
Chapter 85A - Bail Bondsmen and Runners [Recodified.]	44
Chapter 85B - Auctions and Auctioneers	44
Chapter 85C - Bail Bondsmen and Runners [Recodified.]	44
Chapter 86 - Barbers [Recodified.]	44
Chapter 86A - Barbers	44
Chapter 87 - Contractors	44
Chapter 88 - Cosmetic Art [Repealed.]	44
Chapter 88A - Electrolysis Practice Act	44
Chapter 88B - Cosmetic Art	45
Chapter 89 - Engineering and Land Surveying [Recodified.]	45
Chapter 89A - Landscape Architects	45
Chapter 89B - Foresters	45
Chapter 89C - Engineering and Land Surveying	45
Chapter 89D - Landscape Contractors	45
Chapter 89E - Geologists Licensing Act	45
Chapter 89F - North Carolina Soil Scientist Licensing Act	45
Chapter 89G - Irrigation Contractors	45
Chapter 90 - Medicine and Allied Occupations	45
Chapter 90 - Medicine and Allied Occupations (Continuation)	46
Chapter 90 - Medicine and Allied Occupations (Continuation)	47
Chapter 90 - Medicine and Allied Occupations (Continuation)	48
Chapter 90A - Sanitarians and Water and Wastewater Treatment Facility Operators	48
Chapter 90B - Social Worker Certification and Licensure Act	48
Chapter 90C - North Carolina Recreational Therapy Licensure Act	48
Chapter 90D - Interpreters and Transliterators	48
Chapter 91 - Pawnbrokers [Repealed.]	48
Chapter 91A - Pawnbrokers Modernization Act of 1989	48
Chapter 92 - Photographers [Deleted.]	48
Chapter 93 - Certified Public Accountants	48
Chapter 93A - Real Estate License Law	49
Chapter 93B - Occupational Licensing Boards	49
Chapter 93C - Watchmakers [Repealed.]	49
Chapter 93D - North Carolina State Hearing Aid Dealers and Fitters Board.	49
Chapter 93E - North Carolina Appraisers Act	49

Chapter 94 - Apprenticeship	49
Chapter 95 - Department of Labor and Labor Regulations	49
Chapter 95 - Department of Labor and Labor Regulations (Continuation)	50
Chapter 96 - Employment Security	50
Chapter 97 - Workers' Compensation Act	50
Chapter 97 - Workers' Compensation Act (Continuation)	51
Chapter 98 - Burnt and Lost Records	51
Chapter 99 - Libel and Slander	51
Chapter 99A - Civil Remedies for Criminal Actions	51
Chapter 99B - Products Liability	51
Chapter 99C - Actions Relating to Winter Sports Safety and Accidents	51
Chapter 99D - Civil Rights	51
Chapter 99E - Special Liability Provisions	51
Chapter 100 - Monuments, Memorials and Parks	51
Chapter 101 - Names of Persons	51
Chapter 102 - Official Survey Base	51
Chapter 103 - Sundays, Holidays and Special Days	51
Chapter 104 - United States Lands	51
Chapter 104A - Degrees of Kinship	51
Chapter 104B - Hurricanes or Other Acts of Nature	51
Chapter 104C - Atomic Energy, Radioactivity and Ionizing Radiation [Repealed and Recodified.]	51
Chapter 104D - Southern States Energy Compact	51
Chapter 104E - North Carolina Radiation Protection Act	51
Chapter 104F - Southeast Interstate Low-Level Radioactive Waste Management Compact [Repealed]	51
Chapter 104G - North Carolina Low-Level Radioactive Waste Management Authority Act of 1987 [Repealed]	51
Chapter 105 - Taxation	51
Chapter 105 - Taxation (Continuation)	52
Chapter 105 - Taxation (Continuation)	53
Chapter 105 - Taxation (Continuation)	54
Chapter 105A - Setoff Debt Collection Act	55
Chapter 105B - Defaulted Student Loan Recovery Act	55
Chapter 106 - Agriculture	55
Chapter 106 - Agriculture (Continue)	56
Chapter 106 - Agriculture (Continue)	57
Chapter 107 - Agricultural Development Districts [Repealed.]	57
Chapter 108 - Social Services [Repealed and Recodified.]	57
Chapter 108A - Social Services	57
Chapter 108B - Community Action Programs	58
Chapter 108C Medicaid and Health Choice Provider Requirements.	58
Chapter 108D Medicaid Managed Care for Behavioral Health Services.	58
Chapter 109 - Bonds [Recodified.]	58

Chapter 110 - Child Welfare	58
Chapter 111 - Aid to the Blind	58
Chapter 112 - Confederate Homes and Pensions [Repealed.]	58
Chapter 113 - Conservation and Development	58
Chapter 113 - Conservation and Development (Continuation)	59
Chapter 113A - Pollution Control and Environment	59
Chapter 113A - Pollution Control and Environment (Continuation)	60
Chapter 113B - North Carolina Energy Policy Act of 1975	60
Chapter 114 - Department of Justice	60
Chapter 115 - Elementary and Secondary Education [Repealed.]	60
Chapter 115A - Community Colleges, Technical Institutes, and Industrial Education Centers [Repealed.]	60
Chapter 115B - Tuition and Fee Waivers	60
Chapter 115C - Elementary and Secondary Education	60
Chapter 115C - Elementary and Secondary Education (Continuation)	61
Chapter 115C - Elementary and Secondary Education (Continuation)	62
Chapter 115C - Elementary and Secondary Education (Continuation)	63
Chapter 115D - Community Colleges	63
Chapter 115E - Private Educational Facilities Finance Act [Recodified]	63
Chapter 116 - Higher Education	63
Chapter 116 - Higher Education (Continuation)	63
Chapter 116A - Escheats and Abandoned Property [Repealed.]	64
Chapter 116B - Escheats and Abandoned Property	64
Chapter 116C - Continuum of Education Programs	64
Chapter 116D - Higher Education Bonds	64
Chapter 116E - Education Longitudinal Data System	64
Chapter 117 - Electrification	64
Chapter 118 - Firemen's and Rescue Squad Workers' Relief and Pension Funds [Recodified.]	64
Chapter 118A - Firemen's Death Benefit Act [Repealed.]	64
Chapter 118B - Members of a Rescue Squad Death Benefit Act [Repealed.]	64
Chapter 119 - Gasoline and Oil Inspection and Regulation	64
Chapter 120 - General Assembly	65
Chapter 120 - General Assembly (Continuation)	66
Chapter 120 - General Assembly (Continuation)	67
Chapter 120C - Lobbying	67
Chapter 121 - Archives and History	67
Chapter 122 - Hospitals for the Mentally Disordered [Repealed.]	67
Chapter 122A - North Carolina Housing Finance Agency	67
Chapter 122B - North Carolina Agricultural Facilities	

Finance Act [Repealed.]	67
Chapter 122C - Mental Health, Developmental Disabilities, and Substance Abuse Act of 1985	67
Chapter 122C - Mental Health, Developmental Disabilities, and Substance Abuse Act of 1985 (Continuation)	68
Chapter 122D - North Carolina Agricultural Finance Act	68
Chapter 122E - North Carolina Housing Trust and Oil Overcharge Act	68
Chapter 123 - Impeachment	69
Chapter 123A - Industrial Development [Repealed.]	69
Chapter 124 - Internal Improvements	69
Chapter 125 - Libraries	69
Chapter 126 - State Personnel System	69
Chapter 127 - Militia [Repealed.]	69
Chapter 127A - Militia	69
Chapter 127B - Military Affairs	69
Chapter 127C - Advisory Commission on Military Affairs	69
Chapter 128 - Offices and Public Officers	69
Chapter 128 - Offices and Public Officers (Continuation)	70
Chapter 129 - Public Buildings and Grounds	70
Chapter 130 - Public Health [Repealed.]	70
Chapter 130A - Public Health	70
Chapter 130A - Public Health (Continuation)	71
Chapter 130A - Public Health (Continuation)	72
Chapter 130B - Hazardous Waste Management Commission [Repealed.]	72
Chapter 131 - Public Hospitals [Repealed.]	72
Chapter 131A - Health Care Facilities Finance Act	72
Chapter 131B - Licensing of Ambulatory Surgical Facilities [Repealed.]	72
Chapter 131C - Charitable Solicitation Licensure Act [Repealed.]	72
Chapter 131D - Inspection and Licensing of Facilities	72
Chapter 131E - Health Care Facilities and Services	72
Chapter 131E - Health Care Facilities and Services (Continuation)	73
Chapter 131F - Solicitation of Contributions	73
Chapter 132 - Public Records	73
Chapter 133 - Public Works	74
Chapter 134 - Youth Development [Recodified.]	74
Chapter 134A - Youth Services [Repealed.]	74
Chapter 135 - Retirement System for Teachers and State Employees; Social Security; Health Insurance Program for Children	74
Chapter 135 - Retirement System for Teachers and State Employees; Social Security; Health Insurance Program for Children	75

Chapter 136 - Transportation	75
Chapter 136 - Transportation (Continuation)	76
Chapter 137 - Rural Rehabilitation [Repealed.]	76
Chapter 138 - Salaries, Fees and Allowances	76
Chapter 138A - State Government Ethics Act	76
Chapter 139 - Soil and Water Conservation Districts	76
Chapter 140 - State Art Museum; Symphony and Art Societies	76
Chapter 140A - State Awards System	76
Chapter 141 - State Boundaries	76
Chapter 142 - State Debt	76
Chapter 143 - State Departments, Institutions, and Commissions	77
Chapter 143 - State Departments, Institutions, and Commissions (Continuation)	78
Chapter 143 - State Departments, Institutions, and Commissions (Continuation)	79
Chapter 143 - State Departments, Institutions, and Commissions (Continuation)	80
Chapter 143A - State Government Reorganization	80
Chapter 143B - Executive Organization Act of 1973	80
Chapter 143B - Executive Organization Act of 1973 (Continuation)	81
Chapter 143B - Executive Organization Act of 1973 (Continuation)	82
Chapter 143C - State Budget Act	83
Chapter 143D - The State Governmental Accountability and Internal Control Act	83
Chapter 144 - State Flag, Official Governmental Flags, Motto, and Colors	83
Chapter 145 - State Symbols and Other Official Adoptions.	83
Chapter 146 - State Lands	83
Chapter 147 - State Officers	83
Chapter 148 - State Prison System	84
Chapter 149 - State Song and Toast	84
Chapter 150 - Uniform Revocation of Licenses [Repealed.]	84
Chapter 150A - Administrative Procedure Act [Recodified.]	84
Chapter 150B - Administrative Procedure Act	84
Chapter 151 - Constables [Repealed.]	84
Chapter 152 - Coroners	84
Chapter 152A - County Medical Examiner [Repealed.]	84
Chapter 153 - Counties and County Commissioners [Repealed.]	84
Chapter 153A - Counties	84
Chapter 153A - Counties (Continue)	85

Chapter 153B - Mountain Resources Planning Act	85
Chapter 153C - Uwharrie Regional Resources Act	85
Chapter 154 - County Surveyor [Repealed.]	85
Chapter 155 - County Treasurer [Repealed.]	85
Chapter 156 - Drainage	85
Chapter 156 – Drainage (Continuation)	86
Chapter 157 - Housing Authorities and Projects	86
Chapter 157A - Historic Properties Commissions [Transferred.]	86
Chapter 158 - Local Development	86
Chapter 159 - Local Government Finance	86
Chapter 159 - Local Government Finance (Continuation)	87
Chapter 159A - Pollution Abatement and Industrial Facilities Financing Act [Unconstitutional.]	87
Chapter 159B - Joint Municipal Electric Power and Energy Act	87
Chapter 159C - Industrial and Pollution Control Facilities Financing Act	87
Chapter 159D - The North Carolina Capital Facilities Financing Act	87
Chapter 159E - Registered Public Obligations Act	87
Chapter 159F - North Carolina Energy Development Authority [Repealed.]	87
Chapter 159G - Water Infrastructure	87
Chapter 159H - [Reserved.]	87
Chapter 159I - Solid Waste Management Loan Program and Local Government Special Obligation Bonds	87
Chapter 160 - Municipal Corporations [Repealed And Transferred.]	87
Chapter 160A - Cities and Towns	88
Chapter 160A - Cities and Towns (Continuation)	89
Chapter 160B - Consolidated City-County Act	89
Chapter 160C - Baseball Park Districts [Repealed.]	90
Chapter 161 - Register of Deeds	90
Chapter 162 - Sheriff	90
Chapter 162A - Water and Sewer Systems	90
Chapter 162B Continuity of Local Government in Emergency.	90
Chapter 163 Elections and Election Laws.	90
Chapter 163 Elections and Election Laws. (Continuation)	91
Chapter 164 Concerning the General Statutes of North Carolina.	92
Chapter 165 Veterans.	92
Chapter 166 Civil Preparedness Agencies [Repealed.]	92
Chapter 166A North Carolina Emergency Management Act.	92
Chapter 167 State Civil Air Patrol [Repealed.]	92
Chapter 168 Persons with Disabilities.	92
Chapter 168A Persons With Disabilities Protection Act.	92

§ 143-215.87. Oil or Other Hazardous Substances Pollution Protection Fund.

There is hereby established under the control and direction of the Department an Oil or Other Hazardous Substances Pollution Protection Fund which shall be a nonlapsing, revolving fund consisting of any moneys appropriated for such purpose by the General Assembly or that shall be available to it from any other source. The moneys shall be used to defray the expenses of any project or program for the containment, collection, dispersal or removal of oil or other hazardous substances discharged to the land or waters of this State, or discharged into waters outside the territorial limits of the State which affect land and waters or related uses within the State; to assess damages for injury to, destruction of, or loss of use of natural resources; and to develop and implement plans for restoration, rehabilitation, replacement, or acquisition of the equivalent of the natural resources injured by the discharge. In addition to any moneys that shall be appropriated or otherwise made available to it, the fund shall be maintained by fees, charges, or other moneys except for the clear proceeds of civil penalties paid to or recovered by or on behalf of the Department under the provisions of this Part. Any moneys paid to or recovered by or on behalf of the Department as fees, charges, or other payments as damages authorized by this Part except for the clear proceeds of civil penalties shall be paid to the Oil or Other Hazardous Substances Pollution Protection Fund in an amount equal to the sums expended from the fund for the project or activity.

The clear proceeds of civil penalties provided for in this section shall be remitted to the Civil Penalty and Forfeiture Fund in accordance with G.S. 115C-457.2. (1973, c. 534, s. 1; c. 1262, s. 23; 1979, c. 535, s. 20; 1989, c. 656, s. 4; 1993, c. 402, s. 10; 1998-215, s. 67(b).)

§ 143-215.88. Payment to State agencies or State-designated local agencies.

Upon completion of any oil or other hazardous substances removal or restoration project or activity conducted pursuant to the provisions of this Part, each agency of the State or any State-designated local agency that has participated by furnishing personnel, equipment or material shall deliver to the Department a record of the expenses incurred by the agency. The amount of incurred expenses shall be disbursed by the Secretary to each such agency from the Oil or Other Hazardous Substances Pollution Protection Fund. Upon completion of any oil or other hazardous substances removal or restoration project or activity, the Secretary shall prepare a statement of all expenses and costs of the project or activity expended by the State and shall make demand for payment upon the person having control over the oil or other hazardous substances discharged to the land or waters of the State, unless the Commission shall determine that the discharge occurred due to any of the reasons stated in G.S. 143-215.83(b). Any person having control of oil or other hazardous substances discharged to the land or waters of the State in violation of the provisions of this Part and any other person causing or contributing to the discharge of oil or other hazardous substances shall be directly liable to the State for the necessary expenses of oil or other hazardous substances cleanup projects and activities arising from such discharge and the State shall have a cause of action to recover from any or all such persons. If the person having control over the oil or other hazardous substances discharged shall fail or refuse to pay the sum expended by the State, the Secretary shall refer the matter to the Attorney General of North Carolina, who shall institute an action in the name of the State in the Superior Court of Wake County, or in his discretion, in the superior court of the county in which the discharge occurred, to recover such cost and expenses. (1973, c. 534, s. 1; c. 1262, s. 23; 1977, c. 858, s. 2; 1979, c. 535, ss. 21, 22; 1987, c. 827, s. 154.)

§ 143-215.88A. Enforcement procedures: civil penalties.

(a) Any person who intentionally or negligently discharges oil or other hazardous substances, or knowingly causes or permits the discharge of oil in violation of this Part or fails to report a discharge as required by G.S. 143-215.85 or who fails to comply with the requirements of G.S. 143-215.84(a) or orders issued by the Commission as a result of violations thereof, shall incur, in addition to any other penalty provided by law, a penalty in an amount not to exceed five thousand dollars ($5,000) for every such violation, the amount to be determined by the Secretary after taking into consideration the factors set out in G.S. 143B-282.1(b), the amount expended by the violator in complying with the provisions of G.S. 143-215.84, and the estimated damages attributed to the violator under G.S. 143-215.90. Every act or omission which causes, aids or abets a violation of this subsection shall be considered a violation under the provisions of this subsection and subject to the penalty herein provided. The procedures set out in G.S. 143-215.6 and G.S. 143B-282.1 shall apply to civil penalties assessed under this section. The penalty herein provided for shall become due and payable when the person incurring the penalty receives a notice in writing from the Commission describing the violation with reasonable particularity and advising such person that the penalty is due. A person may contest a penalty by filing a petition for a contested case under G.S. 150B-23 within 30 days after receiving notice of the penalty. If any civil penalty has not been paid within 30 days after notice of assessment has been served on the violator, the Secretary shall request the Attorney General to institute a civil action in the Superior Court of any county in which the violator resides or has his or its principal place of business to recover the amount of the assessment, unless the violator contests the assessment as provided in this subsection, or requests remission of the assessment in whole or in part. If any civil penalty has not been paid within 30 days after the final agency decision or court order has been served on the violator, the Secretary shall request the Attorney General to institute a civil action in the Superior Court of any county in which the violator resides or has his or its principal place of business to recover the amount of the assessment. Notification received pursuant to this subsection or information obtained by the exploitation of such notification shall not be used against any person in any criminal case, except as prosecution for perjury or for giving a false statement.

(b) The civil penalties provided by this section, except the civil penalty for failure to report, shall not apply to the discharge of a pesticide regulated by the North Carolina Pesticide Board, if such discharge would constitute a violation of the North Carolina Pesticide Law and if such discharge has not entered the surface waters of the State.

(c) The clear proceeds of civil penalties provided for in this section shall be remitted to the Civil Penalty and Forfeiture Fund in accordance with G.S. 115C-457.2. (1973, c. 534, s. 1; 1973, c. 1262, s. 23; 1979, c. 535, ss. 25, 26; 1987, c. 270; c. 827, ss. 154, 197; 1989 (Reg. Sess., 1990), c. 1036, s. 6; c. 1045, s. 7; c. 1075, s. 8; 1998-215, s. 67(a).)

§ 143-215.88B. Enforcement procedures: criminal penalties.

(a) No proceeding shall be brought or continued under this section for or on account of a violation by any person who has previously been convicted of a federal violation based upon the same set of facts.

(b) In proving the defendant's possession of actual knowledge, circumstantial evidence may be used, including evidence that the defendant took affirmative steps to shield himself from relevant information. Consistent with the principles of common law, the subjective mental state of defendants may be inferred from their conduct.

(c) For the purposes of the felony provisions of this section, a person's state of mind shall not be found "knowingly and willfully" or "knowingly" if the conduct that is the subject of the prosecution is the result of any of the following occurrences or circumstances:

(1) A natural disaster or other act of God which could not have been prevented or avoided by the exercise of due care or foresight.

(2) An act of third parties other than agents, employees, contractors, or subcontractors of the defendant.

(3) An act done in reliance on the written advice or emergency on-site direction of an employee of the Department. In emergencies, oral advice may be relied upon if written confirmation is delivered to the employee as soon as practicable after receiving and relying on the advice.

(4) An act causing no significant harm to the environment or risk to the public health, safety, or welfare and done in compliance with other conflicting environmental requirements or other constraints imposed in writing by environmental agencies or officials after written notice is delivered to all relevant agencies that the conflict exists and will cause a violation of the identified standard.

(5) Violations of permit limitations causing no significant harm to the environment or risk to the public health, safety, or welfare for which no enforcement action or civil penalty could have been imposed under any written civil enforcement guidelines in use by the Department at the time, including but not limited to, guidelines for the pretreatment permit civil penalties. This subdivision shall not be construed to require the Department to develop or use written civil enforcement guidelines.

(d) All general defenses, affirmative defenses, and bars to prosecution that may apply with respect to other criminal offenses under State criminal offenses may apply to prosecutions brought under this section or other criminal statutes that refer to this section and shall be determined by the courts of this State according to the principles of common law as they may be applied in the light of reason and experience. Concepts of justification and excuse applicable under this section may be developed in the light of reason and experience.

(e) Any person who knowingly and willfully discharges or causes or permits the discharge of oil or other hazardous substances in violation of this Part shall be guilty of a Class H felony which may include a fine to be not more than one hundred thousand dollars ($100,000) per day of violation, provided that this fine shall not exceed a cumulative total of five hundred thousand dollars ($500,000) for each period of 30 days during which a violation continues. For the purposes of this subsection, the phrase "knowingly and willfully" shall mean intentionally and consciously as the courts of this State, according to the principles of common law interpret the phrase in the light of reason and experience.

(f) (1) Any person who knowingly discharges or causes or permits the discharge of oil or other hazardous substances in violation of this Part, and who knows at that time that he places another person in imminent danger of death or serious bodily injury shall be guilty of a Class C felony which may include a fine not to exceed two hundred fifty thousand dollars ($250,000) per day of violation, provided that this fine shall not exceed a cumulative total of one million dollars ($1,000,000) for each period of 30 days during which a violation continues.

(2) For the purposes of this subsection, a person's state of mind is knowing with respect to:

a. His conduct, if he is aware of the nature of his conduct;

b. An existing circumstance, if he is aware or believes that the circumstance exists; or

c. A result of his conduct, if he is aware or believes that his conduct is substantially certain to cause danger of death or serious bodily injury.

(3) Under this subsection, in determining whether a defendant who is a natural person knew that his conduct placed another person in imminent danger of death or serious bodily injury:

a. The person is responsible only for actual awareness or actual belief that he possessed; and

b. Knowledge possessed by a person other than the defendant but not by the defendant himself may not be attributed to the defendant.

(4) It is an affirmative defense to a prosecution under this subsection that the conduct charged was conduct consented to by the person endangered and that the danger and conduct charged were reasonably foreseeable hazards of an occupation, a business, or a profession; or of medical treatment or medical or scientific experimentation conducted by professionally approved methods and such other person had been made aware of the risks involved prior to giving consent. The defendant may establish an affirmative defense under this subdivision by a preponderance of the evidence.

(g) The criminal penalties provided by this section shall not apply to the discharge of a pesticide regulated by the North Carolina Pesticide Board, if such discharge would constitute a violation of the North Carolina Pesticide Law and if such discharge has not entered the surface waters of the State.

(h) Any person who knowingly and willfully makes any false statement, representation, or certification in any application, record, report, plan, or other document filed or required to be maintained under this Article or rules adopted under this Article; or who knowingly and willfully makes a false statement of a material fact in a rule-making proceeding or contested case under this Article; or who falsifies, tampers with, or knowingly and willfully renders inaccurate any recording or monitoring device or method required to be operated or maintained under this Article or rules adopted under this Article is guilty of a Class I felony, which may include a fine not to exceed one hundred thousand dollars ($100,000) per day of violation, provided that the fine shall not exceed a cumulative total of five hundred thousand dollars ($500,000) for each period of 30 days during which a violation continues. (1973, c. 534, s. 1; 1973, c. 1262, s. 23; 1979, c. 535, ss. 25, 26; 1987, c. 270; c. 827, ss. 154, 197; 1989 (Reg. Sess., 1990), c. 1045, s. 8; 1993, c. 539, ss. 1316, 1317; 1994, Ex. Sess., c. 24, s. 14(c); 1997-394, s. 6.)

§ 143-215.89. Multiple liability for necessary expenses; limit on State recovery.

(a) Any person liable for costs of cleanup of oil or other hazardous substances under this Part shall have a cause of action to recover such costs in part or in whole from any other person causing or contributing to the discharge of oil or other hazardous substances into the waters of the State, including any amount recoverable by the State as necessary expenses.

(b) The total recovery by the State for damage to the public resources pursuant to G.S. 143-215.90 and for the cost of oil or other hazardous substances cleanup, arising from any discharge, shall not exceed the applicable limits prescribed by federal law with respect to the United States government on account of such discharge. The limitations on recovery referenced in this subsection shall not apply to damages recoverable pursuant to G.S. 143-215.94CC. (1973, c. 534, s. 1; 1979, c. 535, s. 23; 1989 (Reg. Sess., 1990), c. 1045, s. 12; 2010-179, s. 1(a).)

§ 143-215.90. Liability for damage to public resources.

(a) Any person who discharges oil or other hazardous substances in violation of this Article or violates any order or rule of the Commission adopted pursuant to this Article, or fails to perform any duty imposed by this Article, or violates an order or other determination of the Commission made pursuant to the provisions of this Article, including the provisions of a discharge permit issued pursuant to G.S. 143-215.1, and in the course thereof causes the death of, or injury to fish, animals, vegetation or other resources of the State or otherwise causes a reduction in the quality of the waters of the State below the standards set by the Commission, shall be liable to pay the State damages. Such damages shall be an amount equal to the cost of all reasonable and necessary investigations made or caused to be made by the Commission in connection with such violation and the sum of money necessary to restock such waters, replenish such resources, or otherwise restore the rivers, streams, bays, tidal flats, beaches, estuaries or coastal waters and public lands adjoining the seacoast to their condition prior to the injury as such condition is determined by the Commission in conference with the Wildlife Resources Commission, and any other State agencies having an interest affected by such violation (or by the designees of any such boards, commissions, and agencies).

(b) Upon receipt of the estimate of damages caused, the Department shall give written notice by registered or certified mail to the person responsible for the death, killing, or injury to fish, animals, vegetation, or other resources of the State, or any reduction in quality of the waters of the State, describing the damages and their causes with reasonable specificity, and shall request payment from such person. Damages shall become due and payable upon receipt of such notice. A person may contest an assessment of damages by filing a petition for a contested case under G.S. 150B-23 within 30 days after receiving notice of the damages. In a contested case hearing, the estimate of the replacement cost of fish or animals or vegetation destroyed, and the estimate of costs of replacing or restoring other resources of the State, and the estimate of the cost of restoring the quality of waters of the State shall be prima facie evidence of the actual replacement of cost of fish, animals, vegetation or other resources of the State, and of the actual cost of restoring the quality of the waters of the State; provided, that such evidence is rebuttable. In arriving at such estimate, any reasonably accurate method may be used and it shall not be necessary for any agent of the Department or Wildlife Resources Commission to collect, handle, or weigh numerous specimens of dead or injured fish, animals, vegetation or other resources of the State, or to calculate the costs of restoring the quality of the waters using any technology other than that which is existing and practicable, as found to be such by the Secretary. Provided, that the Department may effect such mitigation of the amount of damages as the Commission may deem proper and reasonable. If a person fails to pay damages assessed against him, the Commission shall refer the matter to the Attorney General for collection. Any money recovered by the Attorney General or by payment of damages by the person charged therewith by the Department shall be transferred by the Commission to appropriate funds administered by the State agencies affected by the violation for use in such activities as food fish or shellfish management programs, wildlife and waterfowl management programs, water quality improvement programs and such other uses as may best mitigate the damage incurred as a result of the violation. No action shall be authorized under the provisions of this section against any person operating in compliance with the conditions of a waste discharge permit issued pursuant to G.S. 143-215.1 and the provisions of this Part.

(c) For the purpose of carrying out its duties under this Article, the Commission shall have the power to direct the investigation of any death, killing, or injury to fish, animals, vegetation or other resources of the State, or any reduction in quality of the waters of the State, which in the opinion of the Commission is of sufficient magnitude to justify investigation. (1973, c. 534, s. 1; c. 1262, s. 23; 1979, c. 535, s. 24; 1987, c. 827, ss. 154, 196.)

§ 143-215.91: Recodified as §§ 143-215.88A, 143-215.88B.

§ 143-215.91A. Limited liability for volunteers in oil and hazardous substance abatement.

Part 5 of this Article shall apply to the determination of civil liability or penalty pursuant to this Article. (1987, c. 269, s. 3.)

§ 143-215.92. Lien on vessel.

Any vessel (other than one owned or operated by the State of North Carolina or its political subdivisions or the United States government) from which oil or other hazardous substances is discharged in violation of this Part or any rule prescribed pursuant thereto, shall be liable for the pecuniary penalty and costs of oil or other hazardous substances removal specified in this Part and such penalty and costs shall constitute a lien on such vessel; provided, however, that said lien shall not attach if a surety bond is posted with the Commission in an amount and with sureties acceptable to the Commission, or a cash deposit is made with the Commission in an amount acceptable to the Commission. Provided further, that such lien shall not have priority over any existing perfected lien or security interest. The Commission may adopt rules providing for such conditions, limitations, and requirements concerning the bond or deposit prescribed by this section as the Commission deems necessary. (1973, c. 534, s. 1; c. 1262, s. 23; 1979, c. 535, s. 27; 1987, c. 827, ss. 154, 198.)

§ 143-215.93. Liability for damage caused.

Any person having control over oil or other hazardous substances which enters the waters of the State in violation of this Part shall be strictly liable, without regard to fault, for damages to persons or property, public or private, caused by such entry, subject to the exceptions enumerated in G.S. 143-215.83(b). (1973, c. 534, s. 1; 1979, c. 535, s. 28.)

§ 143-215.93A. Limitation on liability of persons engaged in removal of oil discharges.

(a)   Except as provided in subsection (b) of this section, a person is not liable under this Part, Part 2C of this Article, Articles 21 and 21B of this Chapter, other provisions of the General Statutes relating to protection of the environment or public health, Chapter 1B of the General Statutes, or common law causes of action in tort for removal costs or damages which result from, arise out of, or are related to the discharge or threatened discharge of oil, when such removal costs or damages result from acts or omissions in the course of rendering care, assistance, or advice consistent with the National Contingency Plan or as otherwise directed by the President of the United States, the Federal On-Scene Coordinator, the Governor, the Secretary, the Secretary of Public Safety, or any person designated to direct oil discharge removal activities by the President of the United States, the Governor, the Secretary, or the Secretary of Public Safety.

(b)   The limitation on liability under subsection (a) of this section does not apply:

(1)   To a responsible party;

(2)   To a response under CERCLA/SARA or under Part 4 of Article 9 of Chapter 130A of the General Statutes;

(3)   To a response under Part 3 of Article 9 of Chapter 130A of the General Statutes;

(4)   To a cleanup under Part 2A of this Article;

(5)   With respect to personal injury or wrongful death; or

(6)   If the person is grossly negligent or engages in willful misconduct.

(c)   A responsible party is liable for any removal costs and damages that another person is relieved of under this section.

(d)   Nothing in this section affects the obligation of an owner or operator to respond immediately to a discharge, or the threat of a discharge, of oil.

(e)   As used in this section:

(1)   "CERCLA/SARA" means the Comprehensive Environmental Response, Compensation, and Liability Act of 1980, Pub. L. No. 96-510, 94 Stat. 2767, 42 U.S.C. § 9601 et seq., as amended, and the Superfund Amendments and Reauthorization Act of 1986, Pub. L. No. 99-499, 100 Stat. 1613, as amended.

(2) "Damages" has the same meaning as in the Oil Pollution Act of 1990, 33 U.S.C. § 2701, and G.S. 143-215.94BB.

(3) "Federal On-Scene Coordinator" means a person designated as such in the National Contingency Plan.

(4) "National Contingency Plan" has the same meaning as in 33 U.S.C. § 1321, as amended.

(5) "Oil Pollution Act of 1990" means the Oil Pollution Act of 1990, Pub. L. No. 101-380, 104 Stat. 484, which appears generally as 33 U.S.C. § 2701 et seq., as amended.

(6) "Remove" or "removal" has the same meaning as in the Oil Pollution Act of 1990, 33 U.S.C. § 2701.

(7) "Removal costs" has the same meaning as in the Oil Pollution Act of 1990, 33 U.S.C. § 2701.

(8) "Responsible party" means a person who is a "responsible party" as defined in the Oil Pollution Act of 1990, 33 U.S.C. § 2701, and who is liable for removal costs or damages which result from, arise out of, or are related to the discharge or threatened discharge of oil. (1991, c. 432, s. 1; 2011-145, s. 19.1(g).)

§ 143-215.94. Joint and several liability.

In order to provide maximum protection for the public interest, any actions brought pursuant to G.S. 143-215.88 through 143-215.91(a), 143-215.93 or any other section of this Article, for recovery of cleanup costs or for civil penalties or for damages, may be brought against any one or more of the persons having control over the oil or other hazardous substances or causing or contributing to the discharge of oil or other hazardous substances. All said persons shall be jointly and severally liable, but ultimate liability as between the parties may be determined by common-law principles. (1973, c. 534, s. 1; 1977, c. 858, s. 3; 1979, c. 535, s. 29.)

Part 2A. Leaking Petroleum Underground Storage Tank Cleanup.

§ 143-215.94A. Definitions.

Unless a different meaning is required by the context, the following definitions shall apply throughout this Part and Part 2B of this Article:

(1a)   "Affiliate" has the same meaning as in 17 Code of Federal Regulations § 240.12(b)-2 (1 April 1994 Edition), which defines "affiliate" as a person that directly, or indirectly through one or more intermediaries, controls, is controlled by, or is under common control of another person.

(1b)   "Commercial Fund" means the Commercial Leaking Petroleum Underground Storage Tank Cleanup Fund established pursuant to this Part.

(2)   "Commercial underground storage tank" means any one or combination of tanks (including underground pipes connected thereto) used to contain an accumulation of petroleum products, the volume of which (including the volume of the underground pipes connected thereto) is ten percent (10%) or more beneath the surface of the ground. The term "commercial underground storage tank" does not include any:

a.   Farm or residential underground storage tank of 1,100 gallons or less capacity used for storing motor fuel for noncommercial purposes;

b.   Underground storage tank of 1,100 gallons or less capacity used for storing heating oil for consumptive use on the premises where stored;

c.   Underground storage tank of more than 1,100 gallon capacity used for storing heating oil for consumptive use on the premises where stored by four or fewer households;

d.   Septic tank;

e.   Pipeline facility (including gathering lines) regulated under:

1.   The Natural Gas Pipeline Safety Act of 1968 (49 U.S.C. § 1671 et seq.);

2.   The Hazardous Liquid Pipeline Safety Act of 1979 (49 U.S.C. § 2001 et seq.); or

3. Any intrastate pipeline facility regulated under State laws comparable to the provisions of the Natural Gas Pipeline Safety Act of 1968 or the Hazardous Liquid Pipeline Safety Act of 1979;

f. Surface impoundment, pit, pond, or lagoon;

g. Storm water or waste water collection system;

h. Flow-through process tank;

i. Liquid trap or associated gathering lines directly related to oil or gas production and gathering operations; or

j. Storage tank situated in an underground area (such as a basement, cellar, mineworking, drift, shaft, or tunnel) if the storage tank is situated upon or above the surface of the floor.

(2a) "Cost-effective cleanup" means the cleanup method that meets all of the following criteria:

a. Addresses imminent threats to human health or the environment.

b. Provides for the cleanup or removal of all contaminated soil except in circumstances where it is impractical to remove contaminated soil.

c. Is approved by the Commission for remediation of the site.

d. Is the least expensive cleanup based on total cost, including costs not eligible for reimbursement from the Commercial Fund or the Noncommercial Fund.

(3) Repealed by Session Laws 2011-266, s. 1.20(b), effective July 1, 2011.

(3a) "Facility" means an underground storage tank, or two or more underground storage tanks located in close proximity to each other and having the same owner or operator, that are located on a single tract of land or on contiguous tracts of land that are owned or controlled by the same person. As used in this subdivision, the terms "owner", "operator", and "person" include any affiliate, parent, and subsidiary of the owner, operator, or person, respectively. The owner or person having control of the land on which an underground storage tank is located, or on which two or more underground storage tanks are located, need not be the owner or operator of the underground storage tank or underground storage tanks. The term "facility", as defined in this subdivision, does not apply to a "pipeline facility", as that phrase is used in subdivisions (2) and (7) of this section.

(4)   "Heating oil" means petroleum that is No. 1, No. 2, No. 4-light, No. 4-heavy, No. 5-light, No. 5-heavy, or No. 6 technical grades of fuel oil; other residual fuel oils, including Navy Special Fuel Oil and Bunker C; and other fuels when used as substitutes for one of these fuel oils for the purpose of heating.

(5)   "Loan Fund" means the Groundwater Protection Loan Fund.

(6)   "Noncommercial Fund" means the Noncommercial Leaking Petroleum Underground Storage Tank Cleanup Fund established pursuant to this Part.

(7)   "Noncommercial underground storage tank" means any one or combination of tanks (including underground pipes connected thereto) used to contain an accumulation of petroleum products, the volume of which (including the volume of the underground pipes connected thereto) is ten percent (10%) or more beneath the surface of the ground. The term "noncommercial storage tank" does not include any:

a.   Commercial underground storage tanks;

b.   Septic tank;

c.   Pipeline facility (including gathering lines) regulated under:

1.   The Natural Gas Pipeline Safety Act of 1968 (49 U.S.C. § 1671 et seq.);

2.   The Hazardous Liquid Pipeline Safety Act of 1979 (49 U.S.C. § 2001 et seq.); or

3.   Any intrastate pipeline facility regulated under State laws comparable to the provisions of the Natural Gas Pipeline Safety Act of 1968 or the Hazardous Liquid Pipeline Safety Act of 1979;

d.   Surface impoundment, pit, pond, or lagoon;

e.   Storm water or waste water collection system;

f. Flow-through process tank;

g. Liquid trap or associated gathering lines directly related to oil or gas production and gathering operations; or

h. Storage tank situated in an underground area (such as a basement, cellar, mineworking, drift, shaft, or tunnel) if the storage tank is situated upon or above the surface of the floor.

(8) "Operator" means any person in control of, or having responsibility for, the operation of an underground storage tank.

(9) "Owner" means:

a. In the case of an underground storage tank in use on 8 November 1984, or brought into use after that date, any person who owns an underground storage tank used for the storage, use, or dispensing of petroleum products; and

b. In the case of an underground storage tank in use before 8 November 1984, but no longer in use on or after that date, any person who owned such tank immediately before the discontinuation of its use.

(9a) "Parent" has the same meaning as in 17 Code of Federal Regulations § 240.12(b)-2 (1 April 1994 Edition), which defines "parent" as an affiliate that directly, or indirectly through one or more intermediaries, controls another person.

(10) "Petroleum" or "petroleum product" means crude oil or any fraction thereof which is a liquid at standard conditions of temperature and pressure (60 degrees Fahrenheit and 14.7 pounds per square inch absolute), including any such liquid which consists of a blend of petroleum and alcohol and which is intended for use as a motor fuel. The terms "petroleum" and "petroleum product" do not include any hazardous substance as defined in Section 101(14) of the Comprehensive Environmental Response, Compensation, and Liability Act of 1980, Pub. L. No. 96-510, 94 Stat. 2767, 42 U.S.C. § 9601(14) as amended; any substance regulated as a hazardous waste under Subtitle C of Title II of the Resource Conservation and Recovery Act of 1976, Pub. L. 94-580, 90 Stat. 2806, 42 U.S.C. § 6921 et seq., as amended; or any mixture of petroleum or a petroleum product containing any such hazardous substance or hazardous waste in greater than de minimis quantities.

(11) "Subsidiary" has the same meaning as in 17 Code of Federal Regulations § 240.12(b)-2 (1 April 1994 Edition), which defines "subsidiary" as an affiliate that is directly, or indirectly through one or more intermediaries, controlled by another person. (1987 (Reg. Sess., 1988), c. 1035, s. 1; 1989, c. 652, s. 3; 1991, c. 538, s. 1; 1995, c. 377, s. 4; 1997-456, s. 27; 2003-352, s. 1; 2011-266, s. 1.20(b).)

§ 143-215.94B. Commercial Leaking Petroleum Underground Storage Tank Cleanup Fund.

(a) There is established under the control and direction of the Department the Commercial Leaking Petroleum Underground Storage Tank Cleanup Fund. This Commercial Fund shall be a nonreverting revolving fund consisting of any monies appropriated for such purpose by the General Assembly or available to it from grants, other monies paid to it or recovered on behalf of the Commercial Fund, and fees paid pursuant to this Part.

(b) The Commercial Fund shall be used for the payment of the following costs up to an aggregate maximum of one million dollars ($1,000,000) per occurrence resulting from a discharge or release of a petroleum product from a commercial underground storage tank:

(1) For discharges or releases discovered or reported between 30 June 1988 and 31 December 1991 inclusive, the cleanup of environmental damage as required by G.S. 143-215.94E(a) in excess of fifty thousand dollars ($50,000) per occurrence.

(2) For discharges or releases discovered on or after 1 January 1992 and reported between 1 January 1992 and 31 December 1993 inclusive, the cleanup of environmental damage as required by G.S. 143-215.94E(a) in excess of twenty thousand dollars ($20,000) per occurrence.

(2a) For discharges or releases discovered and reported on or after 1 January 1994 and prior to 1 January 1995, the cleanup of environmental damage as required by G.S. 143-215.94E(a) in excess of twenty thousand dollars ($20,000) if the owner or operator (i) notifies the Department prior to 1 January 1994 of its intent to permanently close the tank in accordance with applicable regulations or to upgrade the tank to meet the requirements that existing underground storage tanks must meet by 22 December 1998, (ii) commences closure or upgrade of the tank prior to 1 July 1994, and (iii) completes closure or upgrade of the tank prior to 1 January 1995.

(3)   For discharges or releases reported on or after 1 January 1994, the cleanup of environmental damage as required by G.S. 143-215.94E(a) in excess of twenty thousand dollars ($20,000) if, prior to the discharge or release, the commercial underground storage tank from which the discharge or release occurred met the performance standards applicable to tanks installed after 22 December 1988 or met the requirements that existing underground storage tanks must meet by 22 December 1998.

(4)   For discharges or releases reported on or after 1 January 1994 from a commercial underground storage tank that does not qualify under subdivision (2a) of this subsection or does not meet the standards in subdivision (3) of this subsection, sixty percent (60%) of the costs per occurrence of the cleanup of environmental damage as required by G.S. 143-215.94E(a) that exceeds twenty thousand dollars ($20,000) but is not more than one hundred fifty-seven thousand five hundred dollars ($157,500) and one hundred percent (100%) of the costs above this amount, up to the limits established in this section.

(5)   Compensation to third parties for bodily injury and property damage in excess of one hundred thousand dollars ($100,000) per occurrence.

(6)   Reimbursing the State for damages or other costs incurred as a result of a loan from the Loan Fund. The per occurrence limit does not apply to reimbursements to the State under this subdivision.

(7)   Recordation of residual petroleum as required by G.S. 143B-279.11 if the Commercial Fund is responsible for the payment of costs under subdivisions (1) through (4) of this subsection.

(8)   The costs of a site investigation required by the Department for the purpose of determining whether a release from a tank system has occurred, whether or not the investigation confirms that a release has occurred. This subdivision shall not be construed to allow reimbursement for costs of investigations that are part of routine leak detection procedures required by statute or rule.

(b1)   In the event that two or more discharges or releases at any one facility, the first of which was discovered or reported on or after 30 June 1988, result in more than one plume of soil, surface water, or groundwater contamination, the

Commercial Fund shall be used for the payment of the costs of the cleanup of environmental damage as required by G.S. 143-215.94E(a) in excess of the multiple discharge amount up to the applicable aggregate maximum specified in subsections (b) and (b2) of this section. The multiple discharge amount shall be calculated as follows:

(1) Each discharge or release shall be considered separately as if it were the only discharge or release, and the cost for which the owner or operator is responsible under subdivisions (1), (2), (2a), or (3) of subsection (b) of this section, whichever are applicable, shall be determined for each discharge or release. For each discharge or release for which subdivision (4) of subsection (b) of this section is applicable, the cost for which the owner or operator is responsible, for the purpose of this subsection, shall be seventy-five thousand dollars ($75,000). For purposes of this subsection, two or more discharges or releases that result in a single plume of soil, surface water, or groundwater contamination shall be considered as a single discharge or release.

(2) The multiple discharge amount shall be the lesser of:

a. The sum of all the costs determined as set out in subdivision (1) of this subsection; or

b. The product of the highest of the costs determined as set out in subdivision (1) of this subsection multiplied by one and one-half (1 1/2).

(3) If an owner or operator elects to cleanup a separate discharge or release for which the owner or operator is not responsible, the responsible party for the other discharge cannot be identified, and the discharges are commingled, the owner or operator shall only be responsible for those costs applicable to the discharge for which the owner or operator is actually the responsible party.

(b2) In the event that the aggregate costs per occurrence described in subsection (b) or (b1) of this section exceed one million dollars ($1,000,000), the Commercial Fund shall be used for the payment of eighty percent (80%) of the costs in excess of one million dollars ($1,000,000) up to a maximum of one million five hundred thousand dollars ($1,500,000). The Department shall not pay or reimburse costs under this subsection unless the owner, operator, or landowner eligible for reimbursement under G.S. 143-215.94E(b1) submits proof that the owner, operator, or landowner eligible for reimbursement under

G.S. 143-215.94E(b1) has paid at least twenty percent (20%) of the costs for which reimbursement is sought.

(b3)   For purposes of subsections (b) and (b1) of this section, the cleanup of environmental damage includes connection of a third party to a public water system if the Department determines that connection of the third party to a public water system is a cost-effective measure, when compared to other available measures, to reduce risk to human health or the environment. A payment or reimbursement under this subsection is subject to the requirements and limitations of this section. This subsection shall not be construed to limit any right or remedy available to a third party under any other provision of law. This subsection shall not be construed to require a third party to connect to a public water system. Except as provided by this subsection, connection to a public water system does not constitute cleanup under Part 2 of this Article, G.S. 143-215.94E, G.S. 143-215.94V, any other applicable statute, or at common law.

(b4)   The Commercial Fund shall pay any claim made after 1 September 2001 for compensation to third parties pursuant to subdivision (5) of subsection (b) of this section only if the owner, operator, or other party responsible for the discharge or release has complied with the requirements of G.S. 143B-279.9 and G.S. 143B-279.11, unless compliance is prohibited by another provision of law.

(b5)   The Commercial Fund may be used by the Department for the payment of costs necessary to render harmless any commercial underground storage tank from which a discharge or release has not occurred but which poses an imminent hazard to the environment if the owner or operator cannot be identified or located, or if the owner or operator fails to take action to render harmless the underground storage tank within 90 days of having been notified of the imminent hazard posed by the underground storage tank. The Secretary shall seek to recover the costs of the action from any owner or operator as provided in G.S. 143-215.94G.

(c)   The Commercial Fund is to be available on an occurrence basis, without regard to number of occurrences associated with tanks owned or operated by the same owner or operator.

(d)   The Commercial Fund shall not be used for:

(1) Costs incurred as a result of a discharge or release from an aboveground tank, aboveground pipe or fitting not connected to an underground storage tank, or vehicle.

(2) The removal or replacement of any tank, pipe, fitting or related equipment.

(3) Costs incurred as a result of a discharge or release of petroleum from a transmission pipeline.

(4) Costs intended to be paid by the Noncommercial Fund.

(5) Costs associated with the administration of any underground storage tank program other than the program administered pursuant to this Part.

(6) Costs paid or reimbursed by or from any source other than the Commercial Fund, including but not limited to, any payment or reimbursement made under a contract of insurance.

(7) Costs incurred as a result of the cleanup of environmental damage to groundwater to a more protective standard than the risk-based standard required by the Department unless the cleanup of environmental damage to groundwater to a more protective standard is necessary to resolve a claim for compensation by a third party for property damage.

(8) Costs in excess of those required to achieve the most cost-effective cleanup.

(e) The Commercial Fund shall be treated as a special trust fund and shall be credited with interest by the State Treasurer pursuant to G.S. 147-69.2 and G.S. 147-69.3.

(f) Expired October 1, 2011, pursuant to Session Laws 2001-442, s. 8, as amended by Session Laws 2008-195, s. 11.

(g) The Commercial Fund may be used to support the administrative functions of the program for underground storage tanks under this Part and Part 2B of this Article up to the amounts allowed by law, which amounts may be changed from time to time. In the case of a legislated increase or decrease in salaries and benefits, the administrative allowance existing at the time of the increase or decrease shall be correspondingly increased or decreased an amount equal to the legislated increase or decrease in salaries and benefits.

(h)   The Commercial Fund may be used to reimburse the owner or operator of a commercial petroleum underground storage tank for annual operating fees that were paid under protest pursuant to G.S. 143-215.94C(f) to the extent the Department has recovered the fees from the previous owner or operator from whom the annual operating fees were due. The Commercial Fund may be used only to reimburse those fees that the owner or operator paid to eliminate an unpaid annual operating fees balance that had been accrued by and was the obligation of a previous owner or operator.

(i)   During each fiscal year, the Department shall use up to one million dollars ($1,000,000) of the funds in the Commercial Fund to fund necessary assessment and cleanup to be conducted by the Department of discharges or releases for which a responsible party has been identified but for which the responsible party can demonstrate that undertaking the costs of assessment and cleanup will impose a severe financial hardship. Any portion of the $1,000,000 designated each fiscal year, which is not used during that fiscal year to address situations of severe financial hardship, shall revert to the Commercial Fund for the uses otherwise provided by this section. The Commission shall adopt rules to define severe financial hardship; establish criteria for assistance due to severe financial hardship pursuant to this section; and establish a process for evaluation and determinations of eligibility with respect to applications for assistance due to severe financial hardship. The Commission shall create a subcommittee of the Commission's Committee on Civil Penalty Remissions as established by G.S. 143B-282.1 to render determinations of eligibility under this subsection. (1987 (Reg. Sess., 1988), c. 1035, s. 1; 1989, c. 652, ss. 4, 16; 1991, c. 538, ss. 2, 3; 1991 (Reg. Sess., 1992), c. 817, s. 1; 1993, c. 400, s. 15; c. 402, s. 1; 1995, c. 377, s. 5; 1998-161, s. 2; 2001-384, ss. 4, 5, 8; 2001-442, s. 1; 2003-352, ss. 2, 3; 2007-323, s. 12.1(a); 2008-195, s. 11; 2008-198, s. 7(a); 2011-394, ss. 11.1, 11.2, 11.3(a); 2012-200, s. 13(a).)

§ 143-215.94C. Commercial leaking petroleum underground storage tank cleanup fees.

(a)   For purposes of this subsection, each compartment of a commercial underground storage tank that is designed to independently contain a petroleum product is a separate petroleum commercial underground storage tank. The owner or operator of a commercial petroleum underground storage tank shall pay to the Secretary for deposit into the Commercial Fund an annual operating fee of four-hundred twenty dollars ($420.00) for each petroleum commercial underground storage tank.

(b) The annual operating fee shall be determined on a calendar year basis. For petroleum commercial underground storage tanks in use on 1 January and remaining in use on or after 1 December of that year, the annual operating fee due for that year shall be as specified in subsection (a) of this section. For a petroleum commercial underground storage tank that is first placed in service in any year, the annual operating fee due for that year shall be determined by multiplying one-twelfth (1/12) of the amount specified in subsection (a) of this section by the number of months remaining in the calendar year. For a petroleum commercial underground storage tank that is permanently removed from service in any year, the annual operating fee due for that year shall be determined by multiplying one-twelfth (1/12) of the amount specified in subsection (a) of this section by the number of months in the calendar year preceding the permanent removal from use. In calculating the pro rata annual operating fee for a tank that is first placed in use or permanently removed during a calendar year under the preceding two sentences, a partial month shall count as a month, except that where a tank is permanently removed and replaced by another tank, the total of the annual operating fee for the tank that is removed and the replacement tank shall not exceed the annual operating fee for the replacement tank. Except as provided in this subsection, the annual operating fee shall be due and payable on the first day of the month in accordance with a staggered schedule established by the Department. The Department shall implement a staggered schedule to the end that the total amount of fees to be collected by the Department is approximately the same each quarter. A person who owns or operates more than one petroleum commercial underground storage tank may request that the fee for all tanks be due at the same time. A person may request that the total of all fees be paid in four equal payments to be due on the first day of each calendar quarter.

(c) Beginning no later than sixty days before the first due date of the annual operating fee imposed by this section, any person who deposits a petroleum product in a commercial underground storage tank that would be subject to the annual operating fee shall, at least once in each calendar year during which such deposit of a petroleum product is made, notify the owner or operator of the duty to pay the annual operating fee. The requirement to notify pursuant to this subsection does not constitute a duty owed by the person depositing a petroleum product in a commercial underground storage tank to the owner or operator and the person depositing a petroleum product in an underground storage tank shall not incur any liability to the owner or operator for failure to give notice of the duty to pay the operating fee.

(d)   Repealed by Session Laws 1991, c. 538, s. 3.1.

(e)   An owner or operator of a commercial underground storage tank who fails to pay an annual operating fee due under this section within 30 days of the date that the fee is due shall pay, in addition to the fee, a late penalty of five dollars ($5.00) per day per commercial underground storage tank, up to a maximum equal to the annual operating fee due. The Department may waive a late penalty in whole or in part if:

(1)   The late penalty was incurred because of the late payment or nonpayment of an annual operating fee by a previous owner or operator.

(2)   The late penalty was incurred because of a billing error for which the Department is responsible.

(3)   Where the late penalty was incurred because the annual operating fee was not paid by the owner or operator due to inadvertence or accident.

(4)   Where payment of the late penalty will prevent the owner or operator from complying with any substantive law, rule, or regulation applicable to underground storage tanks and intended to prevent or mitigate discharges or releases or to facilitate the early detection of discharges or releases.

(f)   A person who becomes the owner or operator of a commercial petroleum underground storage tank may pay, under protest, unpaid annual operating fees that were the obligation of a previous owner or operator for the purpose of obtaining an operating permit for the underground storage tanks. An owner or operator who pays unpaid operating fees that were due from a previous owner or operator may request reimbursement of those fees as provided in G.S. 143-215.94B(h). In collecting unpaid annual operating fees, the Department shall diligently seek to collect unpaid annual operating fees from the person who was the owner or operator of the commercial petroleum underground storage tank at the time the fee first became due notwithstanding the fact that those fees were paid under protest as provided in this subsection. (1987 (Reg. Sess., 1988), c. 1035, s. 1; 1989, c. 652, ss. 5, 16; 1991, c. 538, ss. 3.1, 4, 5; 1993, c. 400, s. 15; c. 402, s. 2; 1995, c. 377, s. 6; 1995 (Reg. Sess., 1996), c. 648, s. 2; 2008-195, s. 1; 2008-198, s. 7(b); 2011-394, s. 11.3(c).)

§ 143-215.94D. Noncommercial Leaking Petroleum Underground Storage Tank Cleanup Fund.

(a)   There is established under the control and direction of the Department the Noncommercial Leaking Petroleum Underground Storage Tank Cleanup Fund. This Noncommercial Fund shall be a nonreverting revolving fund consisting of any monies appropriated for such purpose by the General Assembly or available to it from grants, or other monies paid to it or recovered on behalf of the Noncommercial Fund.

(b)   The Noncommercial Fund shall be used for the payment of the costs set out in subsection (b1) of this section, up to an aggregate maximum of one million dollars ($1,000,000) per occurrence resulting from a discharge or release of a petroleum product from:

(1)   Noncommercial underground storage tanks if the discharge or release meets the minimum priority criteria for corrective action established by the Department.

(2)   Commercial underground storage tanks if the owner or operator cannot be identified or fails to proceed with the cleanup.

(3)   Commercial underground storage tanks that were taken out of operation prior to 1 January 1974 if, at the time the discharge or release is discovered, neither the owner or operator owns or leases the lands on which the tank is located.

(4)   Commercial underground storage tanks if the owner of the commercial underground storage tank is the owner only as a result of owning the land on which the commercial underground storage tank is located, the owner did not know or have reason to know that the underground storage tank was located on the property, and the land was not transferred to the owner to avoid liability for the commercial underground storage tank.

(b1)   The Noncommercial Fund shall be used for the payment of the costs of:

(1)   For releases discovered or reported to the Department prior to August 1, 2013, the cleanup of environmental damage as required by G.S. 143-215.94E(a).

(1a) For releases discovered or reported to the Department on or after August 1, 2013, the cleanup of environmental damage as required by G.S.143-215.94E(a) in excess of two thousand dollars ($2,000) or the sum of the following amounts, whichever is less:

a. A deductible of one thousand dollars ($1,000) per occurrence.

b. A co-payment equal to ten percent (10%) of the costs of the cleanup of environmental damage, per occurrence.

(2) Compensation to third parties for bodily injury and property damage in excess of one hundred thousand dollars ($100,000) per occurrence.

(3) Reimbursing the State for damages or other costs incurred as a result of a loan from the Loan Fund. The per occurrence limit does not apply to reimbursements to the State under this subdivision.

(4) Recordation of residual petroleum as required by G.S. 143B-279.11 if the Noncommercial Fund is responsible for the payment of costs under subdivisions (1) through (3) of this subsection and subsection (b) of this section.

(b2) The Noncommercial Fund may be used by the Department for the payment of costs necessary to render harmless any noncommercial underground storage tank from which a discharge or release has not occurred but which poses an imminent hazard to the environment if the owner or operator cannot be identified or located, or if the owner or operator fails to take action to render harmless the underground storage tank within 90 days after having been notified of the imminent hazard posed by the underground storage tank. The Secretary shall seek to recover the costs of the action from the owner or operator as provided in G.S. 143-215.94G.

(b3) For purposes of subsection (b1) of this section, the cleanup of environmental damage includes connection of a third party to a public water system if the Department determines that connection of the third party to a public water system is a cost-effective measure, when compared to other available measures, to reduce risk to human health or the environment. A payment or reimbursement under this subsection is subject to the requirements and limitations of this section. This subsection shall not be construed to limit any right or remedy available to a third party under any other provision of law. This subsection shall not be construed to require a third party to connect to a public water system. Except as provided by this subsection, connection to a public water system does not constitute cleanup under Part 2 of this Article, G.S. 143-215.94E, G.S. 143-215.94V, any other applicable statute, or at common law.

(b4) The Noncommercial Fund shall pay any claim made after 1 September 2001 for compensation to third parties pursuant to subdivision (2) of subsection (b1) of this section only if the owner, operator, or other party responsible for the discharge or release has complied with the requirements of G.S. 143B-279.9 and G.S. 143B-279.11, unless compliance is prohibited by another provision of law.

(c) The Noncommercial Fund is to be available on an occurrence basis, without regard to number of occurrences associated with tanks owned or operated by the same owner or operator.

(d) The Noncommercial Fund shall not be used for:

(1) Costs incurred as a result of a discharge or release from an aboveground tank, aboveground pipe or fitting not connected to an underground storage tank, or vehicle.

(2) The removal or replacement of any tank, pipe, fitting or related equipment.

(3) Costs incurred as a result of a discharge or release of petroleum from a transmission pipeline.

(4) Costs intended to be paid for by the Commercial Fund.

(5) Costs associated with the administration of any underground storage tank program other than the program administered pursuant to this Part.

(6) Costs paid or reimbursed by or from any source other than the Noncommercial Fund, including, but not limited to, any payment or reimbursement made under a contract of insurance.

(7) Costs incurred as a result of the cleanup of environmental damage to groundwater to a more protective standard than the risk-based standard required by the Department unless the cleanup of environmental damage to groundwater to a more protective standard is necessary to resolve a claim for compensation by a third party for property damage.

(8) Costs in excess of those required to achieve the most cost-effective cleanup.

(e) The Noncommercial Fund shall be treated as a special trust fund and shall be credited with interest by the State Treasurer pursuant to G.S. 147-69.2 and G.S. 147-69.3.

(f) Expired October 1, 2011, pursuant to Session Laws 2001-442, s. 8, as amended by Session Laws 2008-195, s. 11.

(g) The Noncommercial Fund may be used to support the administrative functions of the program for underground storage tanks under this Part and Part 2B of this Article up to the amounts allowed by law, which amounts may be changed from time to time. In the case of a legislated increase or decrease in salaries and benefits, the administrative allowance existing at the time of the increase or decrease shall be correspondingly increased or decreased an amount equal to the legislated increase or decrease in salaries and benefits.

(h) During each fiscal year, the Department shall use up to one hundred thousand ($100,000) of the funds in the Noncommercial Fund to fund necessary assessment and cleanup to be conducted by the Department of discharges or releases for which a responsible party has been identified but for which the responsible party can demonstrate that undertaking the costs of assessment and cleanup will impose a severe financial hardship. Any portion of the $100,000 designated each fiscal year, which is not used during that fiscal year to address situations of severe financial hardship, shall revert to the Noncommercial Fund for the uses otherwise provided by this section. The Commission shall adopt rules to define severe financial hardship; establish criteria for assistance due to severe financial hardship pursuant to this section; and establish a process for evaluation and determinations of eligibility with respect to applications for assistance due to severe financial hardship. The Commission shall create a subcommittee of the Commission's Committee on Civil Penalty Remissions as established by G.S. 143B-282.1 to render determinations of eligibility under this subsection. (1987 (Reg. Sess., 1988), c. 1035, s. 1; 1989, c. 652, ss. 6, 16; 1991, c. 538, s. 6; 1991 (Reg. Sess., 1992), c. 890, s. 17; 1993, c. 400, s. 15; 1995, c. 377, s. 7; 1998-161, ss. 3, 11(a); 2001-384, ss. 6, 7, 9; 2001-442, s. 2; 2003-352, ss. 4, 5; 2007-323, s. 12.1(b); 2008-195, s. 11; 2011-394, s. 11.3(b); 2012-200, s. 13(b); 2013-360, s. 14.15(a).)

§ 143-215.94E. Rights and obligations of the owner or operator.

(a) Upon a determination that a discharge or release of petroleum from an underground storage tank has occurred, the owner or operator of the underground storage tank shall notify the Department pursuant to G.S. 143-215.85. The owner or operator of the underground storage tank shall immediately undertake to collect and remove the discharge or release and to restore the area affected in accordance with the requirements of this Article.

(a1) If a spill or overfill associated with a petroleum underground storage tank results in a release of petroleum to the environment of 25 gallons or more or causes a sheen on nearby surface water, the owner or operator of the petroleum underground storage tank shall immediately clean up the spill or overfill, report the spill or overfill to the Department within 24 hours of the spill or overfill, and begin to restore the area affected in accordance with the requirements of this Article. The owner or operator of a petroleum underground storage tank shall immediately clean up a spill or overfill of less than 25 gallons of petroleum that does not cause a sheen on nearby surface water. If a spill or overfill of less than 25 gallons of petroleum cannot be cleaned up within 24 hours of the spill or overfill or causes a sheen on nearby surface water, the owner or operator of the petroleum underground storage tank shall immediately notify the Department.

(b) In the case of a discharge or release from a commercial underground storage tank where the owner or operator has been identified and has proceeded with cleanup, the owner or operator may elect to have the Commercial Fund pay or reimburse the owner or operator for any costs described in subsection (b) or (b1) of G.S. 143-215.94B that exceed the amounts for which the owner or operator is responsible under that subsection. The sum of payments by the owner or operator and the payments from the Commercial Fund shall not exceed one million dollars ($1,000,000) per discharge or release except as provided in G.S. 143-215.94B(b2).

(b1) In the case of a discharge or release from a commercial underground storage tank where the owner and operator cannot be identified or located, or where the owner and operator fail to proceed as required by subsection (a) of this section, if the current landowner of the land in which the commercial underground storage tank is located notifies the Department in accordance with G.S. 143-215.85 and undertakes to collect and remove the discharge or release and to restore the area affected in accordance with the requirements of this Article and applicable federal and State laws, regulations, and rules, the current landowner may elect to have the Commercial Fund pay or reimburse the current landowner for any costs described in subdivisions (1), (2), (2a), (3), and (4) of G.S. 143-215.94B(b) or G.S. 143-215.94B(b1) that exceed the amounts for which the owner or operator is responsible under that subsection. The current landowner is not eligible for payment or reimbursement until the current landowner has paid the costs described in subdivisions (1), (2), (2a), (3), and (4) of G.S. 143-215.94B(b) or G.S. 143-215.94B(b1) for which the owner or operator is responsible. Eligibility for reimbursement under this subsection may be transferred from a current landowner who has paid the costs described in subdivisions (1), (2), (2a), (3), and (4) of G.S. 143-215.94B(b) or G.S. 143-215.94B(b1) to a subsequent landowner. The sum of payments from the Commercial Fund and from all other sources shall not exceed one million dollars ($1,000,000) per discharge or release except as provided in G.S. 143-215.94B(b2). This subsection shall not be construed to require a current landowner to cleanup a discharge or release of petroleum from an underground storage tank for which the current landowner is not otherwise responsible. This subsection does not alter any right, duty, obligation, or liability of a current landowner, former landowner, subsequent landowner, owner, or operator under other provisions of law. This subsection shall not be construed to limit the authority of the Department to engage in a cleanup under this Article or any other provision of law. In the event that an owner or operator is subsequently identified or located, the Secretary shall seek reimbursement as provided in G.S. 143-215.94G(d). The current landowner shall submit documentation of all expenditures as required by G.S. 143-215.94G(b).

(c)   In the case of a discharge or release from a noncommercial underground storage tank or a commercial underground storage tank eligible for the Noncommercial Fund in accordance with G.S. 143-215.94D(b), where the owner or operator has been identified and has proceeded with the cleanup, the owner or operator may elect to have the Noncommercial Fund pay or reimburse the owner or operator for any costs described in G.S. 143-215.94D(b1) up to a maximum of one million dollars ($1,000,000) per discharge or release.

(c1)   In the case of a discharge or release from a noncommercial underground storage tank where the owner and operator cannot be identified or located, or where the owner and operator fail to proceed as required by subsection (a) of this section, if the current landowner of the land in which the noncommercial underground storage tank is located notifies the Department in accordance with G.S. 143-215.85 and undertakes to collect and remove the discharge or release and to restore the area affected in accordance with the requirements of this Article and applicable federal and State laws, regulations, and rules, the current landowner may elect to have the Noncommercial Fund pay or reimburse the current landowner for any costs described in G.S. 143-215.94D(b1). Eligibility for reimbursement under this subsection may be transferred to a subsequent landowner from a current landowner. The sum of payments from the Noncommercial Fund and from all other sources shall not exceed one million dollars ($1,000,000) per discharge or release. This subsection shall not be construed to require a current landowner to clean up a discharge or release of petroleum from an underground storage tank for which the current landowner is not otherwise responsible. This subsection does not alter any right, duty, obligation, or liability of a current landowner, former landowner, subsequent landowner, owner, or operator under other provisions of law. This subsection shall not be construed to limit the authority of the Department to engage in a cleanup under this Article or any other provision of law. The current landowner shall submit documentation of all expenditures as required by G.S. 143-215.94G(b).

(d) In any case where the costs described in G.S. 143-215.94B(b), 143-215.94B(b1), or 143-215.94D(b1) exceed one million dollars ($1,000,000), or one million five hundred thousand dollars ($1,500,000) if G.S. 143-215.94B(b2) applies, the provisions of Article 21A of this Chapter or any other applicable statute or common law principle regarding liability shall apply for the amount in excess of one million dollars ($1,000,000) or, if G.S. 143-215.94B(b2) applies, one million five hundred thousand dollars ($1,500,000). Nothing contained in this Part shall limit or modify any liability that any party may have pursuant to Article 21A of this Chapter, any other applicable statute, or at common law.

(e) When an owner, operator, or landowner pays the costs described in G.S. 143-215.94B(b), 143-215.94B(b1), or 143-215.94D(b1) resulting from a discharge or release of petroleum from an underground storage tank, the owner, operator, or landowner may seek reimbursement from the appropriate fund for any costs that the owner, operator, or landowner may elect to have either the Commercial Fund or the Noncommercial Fund pay in accordance with the applicable subsections of this section.

(e1) The Department may contract for any services necessary to evaluate any claim for reimbursement or compensation from either the Commercial Fund or the Noncommercial Fund, may contract for any expert witness or consultant services necessary to defend any decision to pay or deny any claim for reimbursement, and may pay the cost of these services from the fund against which the claim is made; provided that in any fiscal year the Department shall not expend from either fund more than one percent (1%) of the unobligated balance of the fund on 30 June of the previous fiscal year. The cost of contractual services to evaluate a claim or for expert witness or consultant services to defend a decision with respect to a claim shall be included as costs under G.S. 143-215.94B(b), 143-215.94B(b1), and 143-215.94D(b1).

(e2)   An owner or operator whose claim for reimbursement is denied may appeal a decision of the Department as provided in Article 3 of Chapter 150B of the General Statutes. If the owner or operator is eligible for reimbursement under this section and the cleanup extends beyond a period of three months, the owner or operator may apply to the Department for interim reimbursements to which he is entitled under this section on a quarterly basis. If the Department fails to notify an owner or operator of its decision on a claim for reimbursement under this section within 90 days after the date the claim is received by the Department, the owner or operator may elect to consider the claim to have been denied, and may appeal the denial as provided in Article 3 of Chapter 150B of the General Statutes.

(e3)   The Department shall not pay any third party or reimburse any owner or operator who has paid any third party pursuant to any settlement agreement or consent judgment relating to a claim by or on behalf of a third party for compensation for bodily injury or property damage unless the Department has approved the settlement agreement or consent judgment prior to entry into the settlement agreement or consent judgment by the parties or entry of a consent judgment by the court. The approval or disapproval by the Department of a proposed settlement agreement or consent judgment shall be subject to challenge only in a contested case filed under Chapter 150B of the General Statutes.

(e4)   (1)   If the owner or operator takes initial steps to collect and remove the discharge or release as required by the Department and completes the initial assessment required to determine degree of risk, the owner or operator shall not be subject to any violation or penalty for any failure to proceed with further assessment or cleanup under G.S. 143-215.84 or this section before the owner or operator is authorized to proceed with further assessment or cleanup as provided in subsection (e5) of this section. The lack of availability of funds in the Commercial Fund or the Noncommercial Fund shall not relieve an owner or operator of responsibility to immediately undertake to collect and remove the discharge or release or to conduct any assessment or cleanup ordered by the Department or be a defense against any violations and penalties issued to the owner or operator for failure to conduct required assessment or cleanup.

(2) The Department shall establish the degree of risk to human health and the environment posed by a discharge or release of petroleum from a commercial underground storage tank and shall determine a schedule for further assessment and cleanup that is based on the degree of risk to human health and the environment posed by the discharge or release and that gives priority to the assessment and cleanup of discharges and releases that pose the greatest risk. If any of the costs of assessment and cleanup of the discharge or release from a commercial underground storage tank are eligible to be paid or reimbursed from the Commercial Fund, the Department shall also consider the availability of funds in the Commercial Fund and the order in which the discharge or release was reported in determining the schedule.

(3) The Department shall establish the degree of risk to human health and the environment posed by a discharge or release of petroleum from a noncommercial underground storage tank and shall determine a schedule for further assessment and cleanup that is based on the degree of risk to human health and the environment posed by the discharge or release and that gives priority to the assessment and cleanup of discharges and releases that pose the greatest risk. If any of the costs of assessment or cleanup of the discharge or release from a noncommercial underground storage tank are eligible to be paid or reimbursed from the Noncommercial Fund, the Department shall also consider the availability of funds in the Noncommercial Fund and the order in which the discharge or release was reported in determining the schedule.

(4) The Department may revise the schedules that apply to the assessment and cleanup of any discharge or release at any time based on its reassessment of any of the foregoing factors.

(e5) (1) As used in this subsection:

a. "Authorization" means a determination by the Department that a person may proceed with one or more tasks associated with the assessment or cleanup of a discharge or release from a petroleum underground storage tank. To "authorize" means to make such a determination.

b. "Preapproval" means a determination by the Department that:

1. The nature and scope of a task is reasonable and necessary to be performed under G.S. 143-215.94B(b), 143-215.94B(b1), or 143-215.94D(b1) in order to achieve the purposes of this Part.

2. The amount estimated for the cost of a task does not exceed the amount or rate that is reasonable for that task.

(2) The Department may require an owner, operator, or landowner to obtain preapproval before proceeding with any task. The Department shall specify those tasks for which preapproval is required. The Department shall deny any request for payment or reimbursement of the cost of any task for which preapproval is required if the owner, operator, or landowner failed to obtain preapproval of the task. Preapproval of a task by the Department does not guarantee payment or reimbursement in the amount estimated for the cost of the task at the time preapproval is requested. The Department shall pay or reimburse the cost of a task only if all of the following apply:

a. The cost is eligible to be paid under G.S. 143-215.94B(b), 143-215.94B(b1), or 143-215.94D(b1).

b. Payment is in accordance with G.S. 143-215.94B(d) or G.S. 143-215.94D(d).

c. The Department determines that the cost is reasonable and necessary.

(3) The Commission may adopt rules governing payment or reimbursement of reasonable and necessary costs and, consistent with any rules adopted by the Commission, the Department shall develop, implement, and periodically revise a schedule of costs that the Department determines to be reasonable and necessary costs for specific tasks. Statements that specify tasks for which preapproval is required and schedules of reasonable and necessary costs for specific tasks are statements within the meaning of G.S. 150B-2(8a)g. This subsection shall not be construed to invalidate any rule of the Commission related to preapproval of tasks that will result in a cost that is eligible to be paid or reimbursed under G.S. 143-215.94B(b), 143-215.94B(b1), or 143-215.94D(b1), provided, however, that the Department may specify additional tasks for which preapproval is required.

(4) In all cases, the Department shall require an owner, operator, or landowner to submit documentation sufficient to establish that a claim is eligible to be paid or reimbursed under this Part before the Department pays or reimburses the claim.

(5) The Department shall authorize a task the cost of which is to be paid or reimbursed from the Commercial Fund or the Noncommercial Fund only when

the task is scheduled to be performed on the basis of a priority determination pursuant to subsection (e4) of this section. The Department shall not pay or reimburse the cost of any task for which authorization is required under this subsection until the Department has preapproved and authorized the task.

(6) Except as provided in subdivisions (8) and (9) of this subsection, the Department shall not authorize any task the cost of which is to be paid or reimbursed from the Commercial Fund or the Noncommercial Fund unless the Department determines, based on the scope of the work to be performed and the schedule of reasonable and necessary costs, that sufficient funds will be available in the Commercial Fund or the Noncommercial Fund, whichever applies, to pay or reimburse the cost of that task within 90 days after the Department determines that the owner, operator, or landowner has submitted a claim with documentation sufficient to establish that the claim is eligible to be paid under this Part.

(7) This subsection shall not be construed to establish a cause of action against the Commission or the Department for any failure to pay or reimburse any cost within any specific period of time. This subsection shall not be construed to establish a defense to any action to enforce the requirements of either G.S. 143-215.84 or subsection (a) of this section.

(8) The Department may preapprove and authorize a task the cost of which is to be paid or reimbursed from the Commercial Fund or the Noncommercial Fund that has not been authorized pursuant to subdivisions (5) and (6) of this subsection if the owner, operator, or landowner specifically requests that the task be authorized and agrees that the claim for payment or reimbursement of the cost will not be paid until after the Department has paid all claims for payment or reimbursement of costs for tasks that the Department has authorized pursuant to subdivisions (5) and (6) of this subsection.

(9) The Department may preapprove and authorize a task the cost of which is to be paid or reimbursed from the Commercial Fund or the Noncommercial Fund that has not been authorized pursuant to subdivisions (5) and (6) of this subsection if the discharge or release creates an emergency situation. An emergency situation exists when a discharge or release of petroleum results in an imminent threat to human health or the environment. A claim for payment or reimbursement of costs for tasks that are authorized under this subdivision shall be paid or reimbursed on the same basis as tasks that are authorized under subdivisions (5) and (6) of this subsection.

(f)   Repealed by Session Laws 2003-352, s. 6, effective July 27, 2003.

(f1)   Any person seeking payment or reimbursement from either the Commercial Fund or the Noncommercial Fund shall certify to the Department that the costs to be paid or reimbursed by the Commercial Fund or the Noncommercial Fund are not eligible to be paid or reimbursed by or from any other source, including any contract of insurance. If any cost paid or reimbursed by the Commercial Fund or the Noncommercial Fund is eligible to be paid or reimbursed by or from another source, that cost shall not be paid from, or if paid shall be repaid to, the Commercial Fund or the Noncommercial Fund. As used in this Part, the phrase "any other source including any contract of insurance" does not include self-insurance.

(g)   No owner or operator shall be reimbursed pursuant to this section, and the Department shall seek reimbursement of the appropriate fund or of the Department for any monies disbursed from the appropriate fund or expended by the Department if any of the following apply:

(1)   The owner or operator has willfully violated any substantive law, rule, or regulation applicable to underground storage tanks and intended to prevent or mitigate discharges or releases or to facilitate the early detection of discharges or releases.

(2)   The discharge or release is the result of the owner's or operator's willful or wanton misconduct.

(3)   The owner or operator has failed to pay any annual tank operating fee due pursuant to G.S. 143-215.94C.

(h)   Subdivision (1) of subsection (g) of this section shall not be construed to limit the right of an owner or operator to contest notices of violation or orders issued by the Department. Subdivision (1) of subsection (g) of this section shall not apply to a payment or reimbursement pursuant to this section if, at the time of the discharge or release, the owner or operator holds a valid operating permit as required by G.S. 143-215.94U.

(i)   Repealed by Session Laws 2005-365, s. 1, effective September 8, 2005.

(j)   An owner, operator, or landowner shall request that the Department determine whether any of the costs of assessment and cleanup of a discharge or release from a petroleum underground storage tank are eligible to be paid or reimbursed from either the Commercial Fund or the Noncommercial Fund within one year after completion of any task that is eligible to be paid or reimbursed under G.S. 143-215.94B(b), 143-215.94B(b1), or 143-215.94D(b1).

(k) An owner, operator, or landowner shall request payment or reimbursement from the Commercial Fund or the Noncommercial Fund for the cost of a task within one year after the completion of the task. The Department shall deny any request for payment or reimbursement of the cost of any task that would otherwise be eligible to be paid or reimbursed if the request is not received within 12 months after the later of the date on which the:

(1) Department determines that the cost is eligible to be paid or reimbursed.

(2) Task is completed. (1987 (Reg. Sess., 1988), c. 1035, s. 1; 1989, c. 652, ss. 7, 16; 1991, c. 538, ss. 7, 22; 1991 (Reg. Sess., 1992), c. 817, s. 2; 1993, c. 400, s. 15; c. 402, s. 3; 1995, c. 377, s. 8; 1995 (Reg. Sess., 1996), c. 648, ss. 3, 4; 1998-161, ss. 4, 5, 8(a), (b), 11(b); 1998-215, s. 68; 2000-172, s. 7.1; 2003-352, ss. 6, 7; 2004-124, s. 30.10(d); 2005-365, ss. 1, 2; 2008-195, s. 2(a); 2010-154, ss. 5, 6; 2011-398, s. 51.)

§ 143-215.94F. Limited amnesty.

Any owner or operator who reports a suspected discharge or release from an underground storage tank prior to 1 October 1989 shall not be liable for any civil penalty that might otherwise be imposed pursuant to G.S. 143-215.88A(a) for violations of G.S. 143-215.83(a) and G.S. 143-215.85. The limited amnesty provided by this section shall not apply upon a finding by the Commission that the discharge or release was the result of gross negligence or an intentional act. (1987 (Reg. Sess., 1988), c. 1035, s. 1; 1989, c. 652, s. 8.)

§ 143-215.94G. Authority of the Department to engage in cleanups; actions for fund reimbursement.

(a) The Department may use staff, equipment, or materials under its control or provided by other cooperating federal, State, or local agencies and may contract with any agent or contractor it deems appropriate to investigate a release, to develop and implement a cleanup plan, to provide interim alternative sources of drinking water to third parties, and to pay the initial costs for providing permanent alternative sources of drinking water to third parties, and shall pay the costs resulting from commercial underground storage tanks from the Commercial Fund and shall pay the costs resulting from noncommercial underground storage tanks from the Noncommercial Fund, whenever there is a discharge or release of petroleum from any of the following:

(1) A noncommercial underground storage tank.

(2) An underground storage tank whose owner or operator cannot be identified or located.

(3) An underground storage tank whose owner or operator fails to proceed as required by G.S. 143-215.94E(a).

(4) A commercial underground storage tank taken out of operation prior to 1 January 1974 if, when the discharge or release is discovered, neither the owner nor operator owns or leases the land on which the underground storage tank is located.

(a1) Every State agency shall provide to the Department to the maximum extent feasible such staff, equipment, and materials as may be available and useful to the development and implementation of a cleanup program.

(a2) The cost of any action authorized under subsection (a) of this section shall be paid, to the extent funds are available, from the following sources in the order listed:

(1) Any funds to which the State is entitled under any federal program providing for the cleanup of petroleum discharges or releases from underground storage tanks, including, but not limited to, the Leaking Underground Storage Tank Trust Fund established pursuant to 26 U.S.C. § 4081 and 42 U.S.C. § 6991b(h).

(2) The Commercial Fund or the Noncommercial Fund.

(a3) Expired October 1, 2011, pursuant to Session Laws 2001-442, s. 8, as amended by Session Laws 2008-195, s. 11.

(b) Whenever the discharge or release of a petroleum product is from a commercial underground storage tank, the Department may supervise the cleanup of environmental damage required by G.S. 143-215.94E(a). If the owner or operator elects to have the Commercial Fund reimburse or pay for any costs allowed under subsection (b) or (b1) of G.S. 143-215.94B, the Department shall require the owner or operator to submit documentation of all expenditures claimed for the purposes of establishing that the owner or operator has spent the amounts required to be paid by the owner or operator pursuant to and in accordance with G.S. 143-215.94E(b). The Department shall allow credit for all expenditures that the Department determines to be reasonable and necessary. The Department may not pay for any costs for which the Commercial Fund was established until the owner or operator has paid the amounts specified in G.S. 143-215.94E(b).

(c) The Secretary shall keep a record of all expenses incurred for the services of State personnel and for the use of the State's equipment and material.

(d) The Secretary shall seek reimbursement through any legal means available, for:

(1) Any costs not authorized to be paid from either the Commercial or the Noncommercial Fund;

(2) The amounts provided for in G.S. 143-215.94B(b) or G.S. 143-215.94B(b1) required to be paid for by the owner or operator pursuant to G.S. 143-215.94E(b) where the owner or operator of a commercial underground storage tank is later identified or located;

(3) The amounts provided for in G.S. 143-215.94B(b) or G.S. 143-215.94B(b1) required to be paid for by the owner or operator pursuant to G.S. 143-215.94E(b) where the owner or operator of a commercial underground storage tank failed to proceed as required by G.S. 143-215.94E(a);

(3a) The amounts provided for by G.S. 143-215.94B(b)(5) required to be paid by the owner or operator to third parties for the cost of providing interim alternative sources of drinking water to third parties and the initial cost of providing permanent alternative sources of drinking water to third parties;

(4) Any funds due under G.S. 143-215.94E(g); and

(5) Any funds to which the State is entitled under any federal program providing for the cleanup of petroleum discharges or releases from underground storage tanks; [and]

(6) The amounts provided for in G.S. 143-215.94B(b5) and G.S. 143-215.94D(b2).

(e) In the event that a civil action is commenced to secure reimbursement pursuant to subdivisions (1) through (4) of subsection (d) of this section, the Secretary may recover, in addition to any amount due, the costs of the action, including but not limited to reasonable attorney's fees and investigation expenses. Any monies received or recovered as reimbursement shall be paid into the appropriate fund or other source from which the expenditures were made.

(f) In the event that a recovery equal to or in excess of the amounts required to be paid for by the owner or operator pursuant to G.S. 143-215.94E(b) is recovered pursuant to subdivisions (2) and (3) of subsection (d) of this section for the costs described in G.S. 143-215.94B(b) or G.S. 143-215.94B(b1), the Department shall transfer funds from the Commercial Fund that would have been paid from the Commercial Fund pursuant to subsection (b) or (b2) of G.S. 143-215.94B if the owner or operator had proceeded with the cleanup, but which were paid from the Noncommercial Fund, into the Noncommercial Fund.

(g) If the Department paid or reimbursed costs that are not authorized to be paid or reimbursed under G.S. 143-215.94B or G.S. 143-215.94D as a result of a misrepresentation by an agent who acted on behalf of an owner, operator, or landowner, the Department shall first seek reimbursement, pursuant to subdivision (1) of subsection (d) of this section, from the agent of monies paid to or retained by the agent.

(h) The Department shall take administrative action to recover costs or bring a civil action pursuant to subdivision (1) of subsection (d) of this section to seek reimbursement of costs in accordance with the time limits set out in this subsection.

(1) The Department shall take administrative action to recover costs or bring a civil action to seek reimbursement of costs that are not authorized to be paid from the Commercial Fund under subdivision (1), (2), or (3) of G.S. 143-

215.94B(d) or from the Noncommercial Fund under subdivision (1), (2), or (3) of G.S. 143-215.94D(d) within five years after payment.

(2)   The Department shall take administrative action to recover costs or bring a civil action to seek reimbursement of costs other than those described in subdivision (1) of this subsection within three years after payment.

(3)   Notwithstanding the time limits set out in subdivisions (1) and (2) of this subsection, the Department may take administrative action to recover costs or bring a civil action to seek reimbursement of costs paid as a result of fraud or misrepresentation at any time.

(i)   An administrative action or civil action that is not commenced within the time allowed by subsection (h) of this section is barred.

(j)   Except with the consent of the claimant, the Department may not withhold payment or reimbursement of costs that are authorized to be paid from the Commercial Fund or the Noncommercial Fund in order to recover any other costs that are in dispute unless the Department is authorized to withhold payment by a final decision of the Commission pursuant to G.S. 150B-36 or an order or final decision of a court. (1987 (Reg. Sess., 1988), c. 1035, s. 1; 1989, c. 652. ss. 9, 16; 1991, c. 538, ss. 8, 23; 1993, c. 400, s. 15; c. 402, s. 4; 1995, c. 377, s. 9; 2001-442, s. 3; 2008-195, ss. 3, 11; 2012-200, s. 13(c).)

§ 143-215.94H. Financial responsibility.

(a)   The Department shall require each owner and operator of a petroleum underground storage tank who is required to demonstrate financial responsibility under rules promulgated by the United States Environmental Protection Agency pursuant to 42 U.S.C. § 6991b(d) to maintain evidence of financial responsibility that is the lesser of:

(1)   The full amount of the financial responsibility that an owner or operator is required to demonstrate under rules promulgated by the United States Environmental Protection Agency pursuant to 42 U.S.C. § 6991b(d).

(2)   The amounts required to be paid for by the owner or operator pursuant to G.S. 143-215.94E(b) per occurrence for costs described in G.S. 143-

215.94B(b) and G.S. 143-215.94B(b1) if costs are eligible to be paid under those subsections.

(b)   Financial responsibility may be established in accordance with rules adopted by the Commission which shall provide that financial responsibility may be established by either insurance, guarantee, surety bond, letter of credit, qualification as a self-insurer, or any combination thereof. The compliance date schedule for demonstrating financial responsibility shall conform to the schedule adopted by the Environmental Protection Agency. (1987 (Reg. Sess., 1988), c. 1035, s. 1; 1989, c. 652, s. 10; 1993, c. 402, s. 5; 2008-195, s. 4; 2009-570, s. 19.)

§ 143-215.94I. Insurance pools authorized; requirements.

(a)   As used in this section, "Commissioner" means the Commissioner of Insurance of the State of North Carolina.

(b)   Owners and operators of underground storage tanks may demonstrate financial responsibility by establishing insurance pools which provide insurance coverage to pool members in at least the minimum amounts specified in G.S. 143-215.94H. Each such pool shall be operated by a board of trustees consisting of at least five persons who are elected or appointed officials of pool members. The board of trustees of each pool shall:

(1)   Establish terms and conditions of coverage within the pool, including underwriting criteria, applicable deductible levels, the maximum level of claims that the pool will self-insure, and exclusions of coverage;

(2)   Ensure that all valid claims are paid promptly;

(3)   Take all necessary precautions to safeguard the assets of the pool;

(4)   Maintain minutes of its meetings and make those minutes available to the Commissioner;

(5)   Designate an administrator to carry out the policies established by the board of trustees and to provide continual management of the pool, and delineate in written minutes of its meetings the areas of authority it delegates to the pool's administrator;

(6) Establish the amount of insurance to be purchased by the pool to provide coverage over and above the claims that are not to be satisfied directly from the pool's resources;

(7) Establish the amount, if any, of aggregate excess insurance coverage to be purchased and maintained in the event that the pool's resources are exhausted in a given fiscal period; and

(8) Establish guidelines for membership in the pool, including the amount of money to be collected from each pool member to form and fund the pool.

(c) The board of trustees may not:

(1) Extend credit to individual members for payment of a premium, except pursuant to payment plans approved by the Commissioner; or

(2) Borrow any monies from the pool or in the name of the pool, except in the ordinary course of business, without first advising the Commissioner of the nature and purpose of the loan and obtaining prior approval from the Commissioner.

(d) A contract or agreement made pursuant to this section must contain provisions:

(1) For a system or program of loss control;

(2) For termination of membership including both:

a. Cancellation of individual membership in the pool by the pool; and

b. Election by an individual member of the pool to terminate its participation;

(3) That a pool or a terminating member must provide at least 90 days' written notice of cancellation or termination;

(4) Requiring the pool to pay all claims for which each member incurs liability during each member's period of membership, except:

a. Where a member has individually retained the risk;

b. Where the risk is not covered; or

c. For amounts of claims above the coverage provided by the pool;

(5) For the maintenance of claim reserves equal to known incurred losses and loss adjustment expenses and to an estimate of incurred but not reported losses;

(6) For compliance with any applicable federal requirements regarding financial responsibility for underground storage tanks;

(7) For a final accounting and settlement of the obligations of or refunds to a terminating member to occur when all incurred claims are concluded, settled, or paid;

(8) That the pool may establish offices where necessary in this State and employ necessary staff to carry out the purposes of the pool;

(9) That the pool may retain legal counsel, actuaries, claims adjusters, auditors, engineers, private consultants, and advisors, and other persons as the board of trustees or the administrator deems to be necessary;

(10) That the pool may make and alter bylaws and rules pertaining to the exercise of its purpose and powers;

(11) That the pool may purchase, lease, or rent real and personal property it deems to be necessary; and

(12) That the pool may enter into financial services agreements with financial institutions and that it may issue checks in its own name.

(e) In the event that either the pool or an individual pool member gives notice of an intent to cancel or terminate participation in the pool as provided by subdivision (4) of subsection (d) of this section, the pool shall so notify both the Commissioner and the Secretary within five business days of the issuance or receipt of such notice by the pool. In addition, the pool shall notify both the Commissioner and the Secretary within five business days of the date such cancellation or termination becomes effective, unless notice of cancellation or termination is rescinded.

(f) The formation and operation of an insurance pool under this section shall be subject to approval by the Commissioner who shall, after notice and hearing, establish reasonable requirements and rules for the approval and monitoring of such pools, including prior approval of pool administrators and provisions for periodic examinations of financial condition. The Commissioner may disapprove an application for the formation of an insurance pool, and may suspend or withdraw such approval whenever he finds that such applicant or pool:

(1) Has refused to submit its books, papers, accounts, or affairs to the reasonable inspection of the Commissioner or his representative;

(2) Has refused, or its officers, agents, or administrators have refused, to furnish satisfactory evidence of its financial and business standing or solvency;

(3) Is insolvent, or is in such condition that its further transaction of business in this State is hazardous to its members and creditors in this State and to the public;

(4) Has refused or neglected to pay a valid final judgment against it within 60 days after its rendition;

(5) Has violated any law of this State or has violated or exceeded the powers granted by its members;

(6) Has failed to pay any taxes, fees, or charges imposed in this State within 60 days after they are due and payable, or within 60 days after final disposition or any legal contest with respect to liability therefor; or

(7) Has been found insolvent by a court of any other state, by the insurance regulator or other proper officer or agency of any other state, and has been prohibited from doing business in such state.

(g) Each pool shall be audited annually at the expense of the pool by a certified public accounting firm, with a copy of the report available to the governing body or chief executive officer of each member of the pool and to the Commissioner. The board of trustees of the pool shall obtain an appropriate actuarial evaluation of the loss and loss adjustment expense reserves of the pool, including an estimate of losses and loss adjustment expenses incurred but not reported. The provisions of G.S. 58-2-131, 58-2-132, 58-2-133, 58-2-134, 58-2-150, 58-2-155, 58-2-165, 58-2-180, 58-2-185, 58-2-190, 58-2-200, and 58-6-5 apply to each pool and to persons that administer the pools. Annual financial statements required by G.S. 58-2-165 shall be filed by each pool within 60 days after the end of the pool's fiscal year. All financial statements required by this section shall be prepared in accordance with generally accepted statutory accounting principles.

(h)   If, as a result of the annual audit or an examination by the Commissioner, it appears that the assets of a pool are insufficient to enable the pool to discharge its legal liabilities and other obligations, the Commissioner shall notify the administrator and the board of trustees of the pool of the deficiency and his list of recommendations to abate the deficiency, including a recommendation not to add any new members until the deficiency is abated. If the pool fails to comply with the recommendations within 30 days after the date of the notice, the Commissioner may apply to the Superior Court of Wake County for an order requiring the pool to abate the deficiency and authorizing the Commissioner to appoint one or more special deputy commissioners, counsel, clerks, or assistants to oversee the implementation of the Court's order. The Commissioner has all of the powers granted to him under Article 17A of General Statute Chapter 58 relating to rehabilitation and liquidation of insurers; and the provisions of that Article apply to this section to the extent they are not in conflict with this section. The compensation and expenses of such persons shall be fixed by the Commissioner, subject to the approval of the Court, and shall be paid out of the funds or assets of the pool.

(i)   Each pool contract shall provide that the members of the pool shall be assessed on a pro rata basis as calculated by the amount of each member's average annual contribution in order to satisfy the amount of any deficiency where a pool is determined to be insolvent, financially impaired, or is otherwise found to be unable to discharge its legal liabilities and other obligations.

(j)   In the event that the Commissioner finds that a pool is insolvent, financially impaired, or otherwise, unable to discharge its legal liabilities or obligations, or if the Commissioner at any time has reason to believe that any owner or operator is unable to demonstrate financial responsibility as required by G.S. 143-215.94H and rules adopted by the Commission as a result of the financial condition of the pool or for any other reason, the Commissioner shall so notify the Secretary.

(k)   The provisions of Article 48 of Chapter 58 do not apply to any risks retained by any pool.

(l)   The Department of Insurance, in consultation with the Department of Environment and Natural Resources, shall provide guidance and technical assistance for the formation of an insurance pool pursuant to G.S. 143-215.94I to any responsible entity that requests assistance. (1987 (Reg. Sess., 1988), c. 1035, s. 1; 1989, c. 652, s. 11; 1995, c. 193, s. 66; 1999-132, s. 11.11; 2008-195, s. 10; 2011-266, s. 1.20(c).)

§ 143-215.94J. Limitation of liability of the State of North Carolina.

(a)   No claim filed against either the Commercial Fund or the Noncommercial Fund shall be paid except from assets of the respective fund as provided for in this Part or as may otherwise be authorized by law.

(b)   This Part shall not be construed to obligate the General Assembly to make any appropriation to implement the provisions of this Part; nor shall it be construed to obligate the Secretary to take any action pursuant to this Part for which funds are not available from appropriations or otherwise.

(c)   The Secretary may budget anticipated receipts as needed to implement this Part.

(d)   Should the Secretary find that the Noncommercial Fund balance is insufficient to satisfy all claims and other obligations of the Noncommercial Fund incurred pursuant to this Part, the Secretary may transfer funds which would otherwise revert to the General Fund to the Noncommercial Fund in order to meet such claims and obligations.

(e)   If at any time either fund balance is insufficient to pay all valid claims against it, the claims shall be paid in full in the order in which they are finally determined. The Secretary may retain not more than five hundred thousand dollars ($500,000) in the Noncommercial Fund as a contingency reserve and not apply the reserve to the claims. The Department may use the contingency reserve to conduct cleanups in accordance with G.S. 143-215.94G when an imminent hazard poses a threat to human health or to significant natural resources. (1987 (Reg. Sess., 1988), c. 1035, s. 1; 1989, c. 652, s. 16; 1991, c. 538, s. 9; 1993, c. 400, s. 15.)

§ 143-215.94K. Enforcement.

The provisions of G.S. 143-215.94W through G.S. 143-215.94Y shall apply to this Part. (1987 (Reg. Sess., 1988), c. 1035, s. 1; 1993, c. 400, s. 15; 1995, c. 377, s. 10.)

§ 143-215.94L. Definitions.

(a) The Commission may adopt rules necessary to implement the provisions of this Part. Except as may be otherwise specifically provided, the provisions of Chapter 150B of the General Statutes apply to this Part.

(b) This Part shall be administered by the Department consistent with the provisions of Title VI, § 601 of the Hazardous and Solid Waste Amendments of 1984, Pub. L. No. 98-616, 42 U.S.C. § 6991 et seq., as amended. The provisions of 40 Code of Federal Regulations Part 280, Subpart I - Lender Liability (1 July 1997 Edition) apply to this Part and Part 2B of this Article.

(c) The provisions of this Part and of Part 2 of this Article are intended to be complementary. This Part shall not be construed to limit the liability under G.S. 143-215.84(a) of any person or to limit the authority of the Department to take any action pursuant to G.S. 143-215.84(b).

(d) This Part shall be known and may be cited as the Leaking Petroleum Underground Storage Tank Cleanup Act of 1988.

(e) The Department of Environment and Natural Resources shall establish a process to provide informal notice of any proposed policy change or rule interpretation that is not a rule, as defined in G.S. 150B-2, to interested parties. Except in a situation that requires immediate action, the Department shall receive and consider oral and written comment from interested parties before the Department implements the proposed policy change or rule interpretation. Except in a situation that requires immediate action, the Department shall provide written notice of a policy change or rule interpretation to interested parties at least 30 days prior to its implementation. (1987 (Reg. Sess., 1988), c. 1035, s. 1; 1991, c. 538, ss. 10, 16; 1993, c. 400, s. 15; 1998-161, s. 9; 2008-195, s. 9.)

§ 143-215.94M. Reports.

(a) The Secretary shall present an annual report to the Environmental Review Commission, the Fiscal Research Division, the Senate Appropriations Subcommittee on Natural and Economic Resources, and the House Appropriations Subcommittee on Natural and Economic Resources which shall include at least the following:

(1) A list of all discharges or releases of petroleum from underground storage tanks.

(2) A list of all cleanups requiring State funding through the Noncommercial Fund and a comprehensive budget to complete such cleanups.

(3) A list of all cleanups undertaken by tank owners or operators and the status of these cleanups.

(4) A statement of receipts and disbursements for both the Commercial Fund and the Noncommercial Fund.

(5) A statement of all claims against both the Commercial Fund and the Noncommercial Fund, including claims paid, claims denied, pending claims, anticipated claims, and any other obligations.

(6) The adequacy of both the Commercial Fund and the Noncommercial Fund to carry out the purposes of this Part together with any recommendations as to measures that may be necessary to assure the continued solvency of the Commercial Fund and the Noncommercial Fund.

(7) Repealed by Session Laws 2012-200, s. 23, effective August 1, 2012.

(b) The report required by this section shall be made by the Secretary on or before November 1 of each year. (1987 (Reg. Sess., 1988), c. 1035, s. 1; 1989, c. 652, ss. 12, 16; 1991, c. 538, s. 11; 1993, c. 400, s. 15; c. 402, s. 6; 2002-148, s. 7; 2012-200, s. 23.)

§ 143-215.94N. Applicability.

(a)   The provisions of this Part as they relate to costs paid from the Commercial Fund apply only to discharges or releases that are discovered or reported on or after 30 June 1988 from a commercial underground storage tank.

(b)   The provisions of this Part as they relate to costs paid from the Noncommercial Fund apply to discharges or releases without regard to the date discovered or reported; however, reimbursement of costs under G.S. 143-215.94G(d)(1), (2), (3), (3a), and (4) shall be for the full amount of the costs paid for from the Noncommercial Fund and shall not be limited pursuant to G.S. 143-215.94E(b) for discharges or releases from commercial underground storage tanks discovered or reported on or before 30 June 1988. (1989, c. 652, s. 13; 1993, c. 400, s. 15; 1995, c. 377, s. 11.)

§ 143-215.94O: Repealed by Session Laws 2011-266, s. 1.20(a), effective July 1, 2011.

§ 143-215.94P. Groundwater Protection Loan Fund.

(a)   There is established under the control and direction of the Department the Groundwater Protection Loan Fund. This Loan Fund shall be a nonreverting revolving fund consisting of any monies appropriated to it by the General Assembly or available to it from grants, and other monies paid to it or recovered on behalf of the Loan Fund. The Loan Fund shall be credited with interest on the Loan Fund by the State Treasurer pursuant to G.S. 147-69.2 and G.S. 147-69.3.

(b)   The Loan Fund shall be used to provide loans to the owners of commercial petroleum underground storage tanks who are creditworthy but may be unable to secure conventional loans to upgrade or replace commercial underground storage tanks in use on 1 July 1991 so as to meet the performance standards applicable to tanks installed after 22 December 1988 or the requirements that existing underground storage tanks must meet by 22 December 1998. All applications for loans under this section must be received by the Department prior to 1 January 1995.

(c)   The Department shall adopt rules for use in managing the Loan Fund. Rules for managing the Loan Fund shall be based on generally accepted standards prevailing among commercial lending institutions with such modifications as may be necessary to achieve the purpose of this section to make loans available to creditworthy applicants. The Department shall administer the loan program through existing commercial lending institutions. In the event that the Department is unable to arrange for the administration of the loan program through existing commercial institutions in all or any part of the State, the Department may administer the loan program through the Office of State Budget and Management. Each commercial institution or agency that administers any part of the loan program shall collect all charges for securing and administering each loan, including but not limited to application fees, recording costs, collection costs, and attorneys' fees from the borrower. Receipt of a loan from the Loan Fund is not a right, duty, or privilege; therefore, Article 3 of Chapter 150B of the General Statutes does not apply to the grant or denial of a loan from the Loan Fund.

(d)   Funds received in repayment of loans made from the Loan Fund shall be deposited into the Loan Fund until the proceeds of all approved loans are disbursed to the borrowers. Thereafter, funds received in repayment of loans made from the Loan Fund and any other funds remaining in the Loan Fund shall be deposited in the Commercial Fund.

(e)   In the event of a default on a loan from the Loan Fund or a violation of a loan agreement, the Secretary may request the Attorney General to bring a civil action for collection of the amount owed or other appropriate relief. An action shall be filed in the superior court of the county where the loan recipient resides, where the loan recipient does business, or where the tanks replaced or upgraded by the loan are located. In an action, the Attorney General may recover all costs of litigation, including attorneys' fees.

(f)   If the State incurs liability in extending credit from the Loan Fund and, as a result of the liability, the State is ordered to pay or, as part of a settlement agreement, agrees to pay damages or other costs, the State shall seek reimbursement for the amount of the damages or other costs from the following sources in the order listed:

(1)   Any funds to which the State is entitled under any federal program providing for the cleanup of petroleum discharges or releases from underground storage tanks, including but not limited to the Leaking Underground Storage Tank Trust Fund established pursuant to 26 U.S.C. § 4081 and 42 U.S.C. § 6991b(h).

(2)   The Noncommercial Fund.

(3) The Commercial Fund. (1989, c. 652, s. 16; 1991, c. 538, ss. 13, 21; 1993, c. 400, s. 15; c. 402, s. 7; 2000-140, s. 93.1(a); 2001-424, s. 12.2(b).)

§§ 143-215.94Q through 143-215.94S. Reserved for future codification purposes.

Part 2B. Underground Storage Tank Regulation.

§ 143-215.94T. Adoption and implementation of regulatory program.

(a) The Commission shall adopt, and the Department shall implement and enforce, rules relating to underground storage tanks as provided by G.S. 143-215.3(a)(15) and G.S. 143B-282(a)(2)h. These rules shall include standards and requirements applicable to both existing and new underground storage tanks and tank systems, may include different standards and requirements based on tank capacity, tank location, tank age, and other relevant factors, and shall include, at a minimum, standards and requirements for:

(1) Design, construction, and installation, including monitoring systems.

(2) Notification to the Department, inspection, and registration.

(3) Recordation of tank location.

(4) Modification, retrofitting, and upgrading.

(5) General operating requirements.

(6) Release detection.

(7) Release reporting, investigation, and confirmation.

(8) Corrective action.

(9) Repair.

(10) Closure.

(11) Financial responsibility.

(12) Tank tightness testing procedures and certification of persons who conduct tank tightness tests.

(13) Secondary containment for all components of petroleum underground storage tank systems.

(b) Rules adopted pursuant to subsection (a) of this section that apply only to commercial underground storage tanks shall not apply to any:

(1) Farm or residential underground storage tank of 1,100 gallons or less capacity used for storing motor fuel for noncommercial purposes.

(2) Underground storage tank of 1,100 gallons or less capacity used for storing heating oil for consumptive use on the premises where stored.

(3) Underground storage tank of more than 1,100 gallon capacity used for storing heating oil for consumptive use on the premises where stored by four or fewer households.

(c) Rules adopted pursuant to subdivision (13) of subsection (a) of this section shall require secondary containment for all components of underground storage tank systems, including, but not limited to, tanks, piping, fittings, pump heads, and dispensers. Secondary containment requirements shall include standards for double wall tanks, piping, and fittings and for sump containment for pump heads and dispensers. The rules shall provide for monitoring of double wall interstices and sump containments. The rules shall apply to any underground storage tank system that is installed on or after the date on which the rules become effective and to the replacement of any component of an underground storage tank system on or after that date. This section shall not be construed to limit the right of an owner or operator to repair any existing component of an underground storage tank system. If an existing underground storage tank is replaced, the secondary containment and interstitial monitoring requirements shall apply only to the replaced underground tank. Likewise, if existing piping is replaced, the secondary containment and interstitial monitoring requirements shall apply only to the replaced piping.

(d) The Department shall allow non-tank metallic components that are unprotected from corrosion, including flex connectors and other metal fittings and connectors at the ends of piping runs, to have corrosion protection added as an alternative to replacement of these components if the component does not have visible corrosion and passes a tightness test. (1989, c. 652, s. 14;

1998-161, s. 10; 1999-328, s. 4.12; 2003-352, s. 8; 2008-195, s. 5; 2009-570, s. 20; 2011-394, s. 11.4.)

§ 143-215.94U. Registration of petroleum commercial underground storage tanks; operation of petroleum underground storage tanks; operating permit required.

(a)   The owner or operator of each petroleum commercial underground storage tank shall annually obtain an operating permit from the Department for the facility at which the tank is located. The Department shall issue an operating permit only if the owner or operator has done all of the following:

(1)   Notified the Department of the existence of all tanks as required by 40 Code of Federal Regulations § 280.22 (1 July 1994 Edition) or 42 U.S.C. § 6991a, if applicable, at the facility.

(2)   Paid all fees required under G.S. 143-215.94C for all commercial petroleum underground storage tanks located at the facility.

(3)   Complies with applicable release detection, spill and overfill protection, and corrosion protection requirements set out in rules adopted pursuant to this Chapter, notifies the Department of the method or combination of methods of leak detection, spill and overfill protection, and corrosion protection in use, and certifies to the Department that all applicable release detection, spill and overfill protection, and corrosion protection requirements are being met for all petroleum underground storage tanks located at the facility.

(4)   If applicable, complies with the Stage I vapor control requirements set out in 15A North Carolina Administrative Code 2D.0928, effective 1 March 1991, notifies the Department of the method or combination of methods of vapor control in use, and certifies to the Department that all Stage I vapor control requirements are being met for all petroleum underground storage tanks located at the facility.

(5)   Substantially complied with the air quality, groundwater quality, and underground storage tank standards applicable to any activity in which the applicant has previously engaged and has been in substantial compliance with federal and State laws, regulations, and rules for the protection of the environment. In determining substantial compliance, the compliance history of

the owner or operator and any parent, subsidiary, or other affiliate of the owner, operator, or parent may be considered.

(6)   Demonstrated financial responsibility as required by G.S. 143-215.94H.

(b)   The operating permit shall be issued at the time the commercial underground storage annual tank operating fee required under G.S. 143-215.94C(a) is paid and shall be valid from the first day of the month in which the fee is due through the last day of the last month for which the fee is paid in accordance with the schedule established by the Department under G.S. 143-215.94C(b).

(c)   No person shall place a petroleum product, and no owner or operator shall cause a petroleum product to be placed, into an underground storage tank at a facility for which the owner or operator does not hold a currently valid operating permit.

(d)   The Department shall issue an operating permit certificate for each facility that meets the requirements of subsection (a) of this section. The operating permit certificate shall identify the number of tanks at the facility and shall conspicuously display the date on which the permit expires. Except for the owner or operator, no person shall be liable under subsection (c) of this section if an unexpired operating permit certificate is displayed at the facility, unless the person knows or has reason to know that the owner or operator does not hold a currently valid operating permit for the facility.

(e)   The Department may revoke an operating permit only if the owner or operator fails to continuously meet the requirements set out in subsection (a) of this section. If the Department revokes an operating permit, the owner or operator of the facility for which the operating permit was issued shall immediately surrender the operating permit certificate to the Department, unless the revocation is stayed pursuant to G.S. 150B-33. An owner or operator may challenge a decision by the Department to deny or revoke an operating permit by filing a contested case under Article 3 of Chapter 150B of the General Statutes. (1995, c. 377, s. 2; 1998-161, s. 6; 2008-195, s. 6; 2011-398, s. 52.)

§ 143-215.94V. Standards for petroleum underground storage tank cleanup.

(a)   Legislative findings and intent.

(1) The General Assembly finds that:

a. The goals of the underground storage tank program are to protect human health and the environment. Maintaining the solvency of the Commercial Fund and the Noncommercial Fund is essential to these goals.

b. The sites at which discharges or releases from underground storage tanks occur vary greatly in terms of complexity, soil types, hydrogeology, other physical and chemical characteristics, current and potential future uses of groundwater, and the degree of risk that each site may pose to human health and the environment.

c. Risk-based corrective action is a process that recognizes this diversity and utilizes an approach where assessment and remediation activities are specifically tailored to the conditions and risks of a specific site.

d. Risk-based corrective action gives the State flexibility in requiring different levels of cleanup based on scientific analysis of different site characteristics, and allowing no action or no further action at sites that pose little risk to human health or the environment.

e. A risk-based approach to the cleanup of environmental damage can adequately protect human health and the environment while preventing excessive or unproductive cleanup efforts, thereby assuring that limited resources are directed toward those sites that pose the greatest risk to human health and the environment.

(2) The General Assembly intends:

a. To direct the Commission to adopt rules that will provide for risk-based assessment and cleanup of discharges and releases from petroleum underground storage tanks. These rules are intended to combine groundwater standards that protect current and potential future uses of groundwater with risk-based analysis to determine the appropriate cleanup levels and actions.

b. That these rules apply to all discharges or releases that are reported on or after the date the rules become effective in order to ascertain whether cleanup is necessary, and if so, the appropriate level of cleanup.

c.   That these rules may be applied to any discharge or release that has been reported at the time the rules become effective at the discretion of the Commission.

d.   That these rules and decisions of the Commission and the Department in implementing these rules facilitate the completion of more cleanups in a shorter period of time.

e.   That neither the Commercial Fund nor the Noncommercial Fund be used to clean up sites where the Commission has determined that a discharge or release poses a degree of risk to human health or the environment that is no greater than the acceptable level of risk established by the Commission.

f.   Repealed by Session Laws 1998-161, s. 11(c), effective retroactively to January 1, 1998.

g.   That the Commercial Fund and the Noncommercial Fund be used to perform the most cost-effective cleanup that addresses imminent threats to human health and the environment.

(b)   The Commission shall adopt rules to establish a risk-based approach for the assessment, prioritization, and cleanup of discharges and releases from petroleum underground storage tanks. The rules shall address, at a minimum, the circumstances where site-specific information should be considered, criteria for determining acceptable cleanup levels, and the acceptable level or range of levels of risk to human health and the environment. Rules that use the distance between a source area of a confirmed discharge or release to a water supply well or a private drinking water well, as those terms are defined under G.S. 87-85, shall include a determination whether a nearby well is likely to be affected by the discharge or release as a factor in determining levels of risk.

(c)   The Commission may require an owner or operator or a landowner eligible for payment or reimbursement under subsections (b), (b1), (c), and (c1) of G.S. 143-215.94E to provide information necessary to determine the degree of risk to human health and the environment that is posed by a discharge or release from a petroleum underground storage and to identify the most cost-effective cleanup that addresses imminent threats to human health and the environment.

(d)   If the Commission concludes that a discharge or release poses a degree of risk to human health or the environment that is no greater than the acceptable level of risk established by the Commission, the Commission shall notify an owner, operator, or landowner who provides the information required by subsection (c) of this section that no cleanup, further cleanup, or further action will be required unless the Commission later determines that the discharge or release poses an unacceptable level of risk or a potentially unacceptable level of risk to human health or the environment. If the Commission concludes that a discharge or release poses a degree of risk to human health or the environment that requires further cleanup, the Commission shall notify the owner, operator, or landowner who provides the information required by subsection (c) of this section of the cleanup method approved by the Commission as the most cost-effective cleanup method for the site. This section shall not be construed to prohibit an owner, operator, or landowner from selecting a cleanup method other than the cost-effective cleanup method approved by the Commission so long as the Commission determines that the alternative cleanup method will address imminent threats to human health and the environment.

(e) If the Commission concludes under subsection (d) of this section that no cleanup, no further cleanup, or no further action will be required, the Department shall not pay or reimburse any costs otherwise payable or reimbursable under this Article from either the Commercial or Noncommercial Fund, other than reasonable and necessary to conduct the risk assessment required by this section, unless:

(1) Cleanup is ordered or damages are awarded in a finally adjudicated judgment in an action against the owner or landowner.

(2) Cleanup is required or damages are agreed to in a consent judgment approved by the Department prior to its entry by the court.

(3) Cleanup is required or damages are agreed to in a settlement agreement approved by the Department prior to its execution by the parties.

(4) The payment or reimbursement is for costs that were incurred prior to or as a result of notification of a determination by the Commission that no cleanup, no further cleanup, or no action is required.

(5) The payment or reimbursement is for costs that were incurred as a result of a later determination by the Commission that the discharge or release poses a threat or potential threat to human health or the environment as provided in subsection (d) of this section.

(e1) If the Commission concludes under subsection (d) of this section that further cleanup is required and notifies the owner, operator, or landowner of the cleanup method approved by the Commission as the most cost-effective cleanup method for the site, the Department shall not pay or reimburse any costs otherwise payable or reimbursable under this Article from either the Commercial Fund or Noncommercial Fund, other than those costs that are reasonable and necessary to conduct the risk assessment and to implement the cost-effective cleanup method approved by the Commission. If the owner, operator, or landowner selects a cleanup method other than the one identified by the Commission as the most cost-effective cleanup, the Department shall not pay or reimburse for costs in excess of the cost of implementing the approved cost-effective cleanup.

(f) This section shall not be construed to limit the authority of the Commission to require investigation, initial response, and abatement of a discharge or release pending a determination by the Commission under subsection (d) of this section as to whether cleanup, further cleanup, or further action will be required.

(g) Subsections (c) through (e1) of this section apply only to assessments and cleanups in progress or begun on or after 2 January 1998.

(h) If a discharge or release of petroleum from an underground storage tank results in contamination in soil or groundwater that becomes commingled with contamination that is the result of a discharge or release of petroleum from a source of contamination other than an underground storage tank, the cleanup of petroleum may proceed under rules adopted pursuant to this section. The Department shall not pay or reimburse any costs associated with the assessment or remediation of that portion of contamination that results from a release or discharge of petroleum from a source other than an underground storage tank from either the Commercial Fund or the Noncommercial Fund. (1995, c. 377, s. 1; 1998-161, s. 11(c); 2003-352, s. 9; 2011-394, s. 11.5.)

§ 143-215.94W. Enforcement procedures: civil penalties.

(a) A civil penalty of not more than ten thousand dollars ($10,000) may be assessed by the Secretary against any person who:

(1) Violates any provision of this Part or rule adopted pursuant to this Part.

(2)   Fails to apply for or to secure a permit required by this Part.

(3)   Violates or fails to act in accordance with the terms, conditions, or requirements of any permit issued pursuant to this Part.

(4)   Fails to file, submit, or make available, as the case may be, any documents, data, or reports required by this Part.

(5)   Violates or fails to act in accordance with the terms, conditions, or requirements of any special order or other appropriate document issued pursuant to G.S. 143-215.2 or fails to comply with the requirements of G.S. 143B-279.9 through G.S. 143B-279.11.

(6)   Falsifies or tampers with any recording or monitoring device or method required to be operated or maintained under this Part or rules implementing this Part.

(7)   Knowingly renders inaccurate any recording or monitoring device or method required to be operated or maintained under this Part or rules implementing this Part.

(8)   Knowingly makes any false statement, representation, or certification in any application, record, report, plan, or other document filed or required to be maintained under this Part or a rule implementing this Part.

(9)   Knowingly makes a false statement of a material fact in a rule-making proceeding or contested case under this Part.

(10)   Refuses access to the Commission or its duly designated representative to any premises for the purpose of conducting a lawful inspection provided for in this Part.

(b)   If any action or failure to act for which a penalty may be assessed under this section is continuous, the Secretary may assess a penalty not to exceed ten thousand dollars ($10,000) per day for so long as the violation continues. A penalty for a continuous violation shall not exceed two hundred thousand dollars ($200,000) for each period of 30 days during which the violation continues.

(c)   In determining the amount of the penalty, the Secretary shall consider the factors set out in G.S. 143B-282.1(b). The procedures set out in G.S. 143B-

282.1 shall apply to civil penalty assessments that are presented to the Commission for final agency decision.

(d) The Secretary shall notify any person assessed a civil penalty of the assessment and the specific reasons therefor by registered or certified mail, or by any means authorized by G.S. 1A-1, Rule 4. Contested case petitions shall be filed pursuant to G.S. 150B-23 within 30 days of receipt of the notice of assessment. The Secretary shall make the final decision regarding assessment of a civil penalty under this section.

(e) Requests for remission of civil penalties shall be filed with the Secretary. Remission requests shall not be considered unless made within 30 days of receipt of the notice of assessment. Remission requests must be accompanied by a waiver of the right to a contested case hearing pursuant to Chapter 150B and a stipulation of the facts on which the assessment was based. Consistent with the limitations in G.S. 143B-282.1(c) and (d), remission requests may be resolved by the Secretary and the violator. If the Secretary and the violator are unable to resolve the request, the Secretary shall deliver remission requests and his recommended action to the Committee on Civil Penalty Remissions of the Environmental Management Commission appointed pursuant to G.S. 143B-282.1(c).

(f) If any civil penalty has not been paid within 30 days after notice of assessment has been served on the violator, the Secretary shall request the Attorney General to institute a civil action in the superior court of any county in which the violator resides or has his or its principal place of business to recover the amount of the assessment, unless the violator contests the assessment as provided in subsection (d) of this section, or requests remission of the assessment in whole or in part as provided in subsection (e) of this section. If any civil penalty has not been paid within 30 days after the final agency decision or court order has been served on the violator, the Secretary shall request the Attorney General to institute a civil action in the superior court of any county in which the violator resides or has his or its principal place of business to recover the amount of the assessment. Such civil actions must be filed within three years of the date the final agency decision or court order was served on the violator.

(g) Repealed by Session Laws 1995 (Regular Session, 1996), c. 743, s. 17.

(h) The clear proceeds of civil penalties assessed pursuant to this section shall be remitted to the Civil Penalty and Forfeiture Fund in accordance with

G.S. 115C-457.2. (1995, c. 377, s. 3; 1995 (Reg. Sess., 1996), c. 743, s. 17; 1998-215, s. 69; 2002-90, s. 6.)

§ 143-215.94X. Enforcement procedures: criminal penalties.

(a) Any person who negligently commits any of the offenses set out in subdivisions (1) through (9) of G.S. 143-215.94W(a) shall be guilty of a Class 2 misdemeanor which may include a fine not to exceed fifteen thousand dollars ($15,000) per day of violation, provided that such fine shall not exceed a cumulative total of two hundred thousand dollars ($200,000) for each period of 30 days during which a violation continues.

(b) Any person who knowingly and willfully commits any of the offenses set out in subdivisions (1) through (5) of G.S. 143-215.94W(a) shall be guilty of a Class I felony, which may include a fine not to exceed one hundred thousand dollars ($100,000) per day of violation, provided that this fine shall not exceed a cumulative total of five hundred thousand dollars ($500,000) for each period of 30 days during which a violation continues. For the purposes of this subsection, the phrase "knowingly and willfully" shall mean intentionally and consciously as the courts of this State, according to the principles of common law interpret the phrase in the light of reason and experience.

(c) (1) Any person who knowingly commits any of the offenses set out in subdivisions (1) through (5) of G.S. 143-215.94W(a) and who knows at that time that he thereby places another person in imminent danger of death or serious bodily injury shall be guilty of a Class C felony, which may include a fine not to exceed two hundred fifty thousand dollars ($250,000) per day of violation, provided that this fine shall not exceed a cumulative total of one million dollars ($1,000,000) for each period of 30 days during which a violation continues.

(2) For the purposes of this subsection, a person's state of mind is knowing with respect to:

a. His conduct, if he is aware of the nature of his conduct;

b. An existing circumstance, if he is aware or believes that the circumstance exists; or

c. A result of his conduct, if he is aware or believes that his conduct is substantially certain to cause danger of death or serious bodily injury.

(3) Under this subsection, in determining whether a defendant who is a natural person knew that his conduct placed another person in imminent danger of death or serious bodily injury:

a. The person is responsible only for actual awareness or actual belief that he possessed; and

b. Knowledge possessed by a person other than the defendant but not by the defendant himself may not be attributed to the defendant.

(4) It is an affirmative defense to a prosecution under this subsection that the conduct charged was conduct consented to by the person endangered and that the danger and conduct charged were reasonably foreseeable hazards of an occupation, a business, or a profession; or of medical treatment or medical or scientific experimentation conducted by professionally approved methods and such other person had been made aware of the risks involved prior to giving consent. The defendant may establish an affirmative defense under this subdivision by a preponderance of the evidence.

(d) No proceeding shall be brought or continued under this section for or on account of a violation by any person who has previously been convicted of a federal violation based upon the same set of facts.

(e) In proving the defendant's possession of actual knowledge, circumstantial evidence may be used, including evidence that the defendant took affirmative steps to shield himself from relevant information. Consistent with the principles of common law, the subjective mental state of defendants may be inferred from their conduct.

(f) For the purposes of the felony provisions of this section, a person's state of mind shall not be found "knowingly and willfully" or "knowingly" if the conduct that is the subject of the prosecution is the result of any of the following occurrences or circumstances:

(1) A natural disaster or other act of God which could not have been prevented or avoided by the exercise of due care or foresight.

(2) An act of third parties other than agents, employees, contractors, or subcontractors of the defendant.

(3) An act done in reliance on the written advice or emergency on-site direction of an employee of the Department. In emergencies, oral advice may be relied upon if written confirmation is delivered to the employee as soon as practicable after receiving and relying on the advice.

(4) An act causing no significant harm to the environment or risk to the public health, safety, or welfare and done in compliance with other conflicting environmental requirements or other constraints imposed in writing by environmental agencies or officials after written notice is delivered to all relevant agencies that the conflict exists and will cause a violation of the identified standard.

(5) Violations causing no significant harm to the environment or risk to the public health, safety, or welfare for which no enforcement action or civil penalty could have been imposed under any written civil enforcement guidelines in use by the Department at the time. This subdivision shall not be construed to require the Department to develop or use written civil enforcement guidelines.

(6) Occasional, inadvertent, short-term violations causing no significant harm to the environment or risk to the public health, safety, or welfare. If the violation occurs within 30 days of a prior violation or lasts for more than 24 hours, it is not an occasional, short-term violation.

(g) All general defenses, affirmative defenses, and bars to prosecution that may apply with respect to other criminal offenses under State criminal offenses may apply to prosecutions brought under this section or other criminal statutes that refer to this section and shall be determined by the courts of this State according to the principles of common law as they may be applied in the light of reason and experience. Concepts of justification and excuse applicable under this section may be developed in the light of reason and experience. (1995, c. 377, s. 3.)

§ 143-215.94Y. Enforcement procedures; injunctive relief.

Whenever the Department has reasonable cause to believe that any person has violated or is threatening to violate any of the provisions of this Part, any of the terms of any permit issued pursuant to this Part, or a rule implementing this Part or has failed to comply with the requirements of G.S. 143B-279.9 through G.S. 143B-279.11, the Department may, either before or after the institution of any other action or proceeding authorized by this Part, request the Attorney General to institute a civil action in the name of the State upon the relation of the Department for injunctive relief to restrain the violation or threatened violation and for such other and further relief in the premises as the court shall deem proper. The Attorney General may institute such action in the superior court of the county in which the violation occurred or may occur or, in his discretion, in the superior court of the county in which the person responsible for the violation or threatened violation resides or has his or its principal place of business. Upon a determination by the court that the alleged violation of the provisions of this Part, the rules of the Commission, or the failure to comply with the requirements of G.S. 143B-279.9 through G.S. 143B-279.11 has occurred or is threatened, the court shall grant the relief necessary to prevent or abate the violation or threatened violation. Neither the institution of the action nor any of the proceedings thereon shall relieve any party to such proceedings from any penalty prescribed for violation of this Part or for failure to comply with the requirements of G.S. 143B-279.9 through G.S. 143B-279.11. (1995, c. 377, s. 3; 2002-90, s. 7.)

§ 143-215.94Z: Reserved for future codification purposes.

Part 2C. Offshore Oil and Gas Activities. Adverse Environmental Impact Protection.

§ 143-215.94AA. Declaration of public policy.

The General Assembly hereby finds and declares as follows:

(1)   The traditional uses of the seacoast of the State are public and private recreation, commercial and sports fishing, and habitat for natural resources;

(2)   The preservation of these uses is a matter of the highest urgency and priority, and such uses can only be preserved effectively by maintaining and enhancing the existing condition of the coastal waters, estuaries, wetlands, tidal flats, beaches, and public lands adjoining the seacoast;

(3) The coastal economy, including access to the coast of the State, depends, either directly or indirectly, upon a ready and continuous reserve of petroleum products and by-products, including that portion of the supply resulting from oil and gas activities on the Outer Continental Shelf;

(4) Offshore oil and natural gas exploration, production, processing, recovery, and transportation pose increased potential for damage to the State's coastal environment, to the traditional uses of the area, and to the beauty of the North Carolina coast;

(5) Spills, discharges, and escapes of pollutants occurring as a result of procedures involving offshore oil and natural gas related activities have occurred in the past, and future threats of potentially catastrophic proportions from such activities require adoption of this Part as mitigation against such events;

(6) The economic burdens imposed by the General Assembly upon those engaged in the offshore exploration, production, processing, recovery, and transportation of oil and natural gas are reasonable and necessary in light of the traditional uses and interests herein protected, which are expressly declared to be of grave public interest and concern to the State in promoting its general interest and welfare promoting the public health, preventing diseases, and providing for the public safety. (1989, c. 656, s. 5, c. 770, s. 75.5.)

§ 143-215.94BB. Definitions.

In addition to the definitions set out in G.S. 143-215.77, the following definitions shall apply to this Part:

(1) "Damages" are damages for any of the following:

a. Injury or harm to real or personal property, which includes the cost of restoring, repairing, or replacing any real or personal property damaged or destroyed by a discharge under this section, any income lost from the time such property is damaged to the time such property is restored, repaired, or replaced, and any reduction in value of such property caused by such discharge by comparison with its value prior thereto.

b. Business loss, including loss of income or impairment of earning capacity due to damage to real or personal property or to damage or destruction of natural resources upon which such income or earning capacity is reasonably dependent.

c. Interest on loans obtained or other financial obligations incurred by an injured party for the purpose of ameliorating the adverse effects of a discharge pending the payment of a claim in full as provided by this Article.

d. Costs of cleanup, removal, or treatment of natural gas, oil, or drilling waste discharges.

e. Costs of restoration, rehabilitation, and, where possible, replacement of wildlife or other natural resources damaged as a result of a discharge.

f. When the injured party is the State or one of its political subdivisions, in addition to any injury described in subparagraphs (a) to (e), inclusive, damages include all of the following:

1. Injury to natural resources or wildlife, including recreational or commercial fisheries, and loss of use and enjoyment of public beaches and other public resources or facilities within the jurisdiction of the State or one of its political subdivisions.

2. Costs to assess damages to natural resources, wildlife, or habitat.

3. Costs incurred to monitor the cleanup of the natural gas, oil, or drilling waste spilled.

4. Loss of State or local government tax revenues resulting from damages to real or personal property proximately resulting from a discharge.

(2) For the purposes of this Part, "oil" and "drilling wastes" include, but are not limited to: petroleum, refined or processed petroleum, petroleum by-products, oil sludge, oil refuse, oil mixed with wastes and chemicals, or other materials used in the exploration, recovery, or processing of oil. "Oil" does not include oil carried in a vessel for use as fuel in that vessel.

(3) "Natural gas" includes natural gas, liquified natural gas, and natural gas by-products. "Natural gas" does not include natural gas carried in a vessel for use as fuel in that vessel.

(4) "Exploration" means undersea boring, drilling, soil sampling, and any other technique employed to assess and evaluate the presence of subterranean oil and natural gas deposits.

(5) "Injured party" means any person who suffers damages from natural gas, oil, or drilling waste which is discharged or leaks into marine waters, or from offshore exploration. The State, or a county or municipality, may be an injured party.

(6) "Responsible person" means any of the following:

a. The owner or transporter of natural gas, oil, or drilling waste which causes an injury covered by this Part.

b. The owner, operator, lessee of, or person who charters by demise, any offshore well, undersea site, facility, oil rig, oil platform, vessel, or pipeline which is the source of natural gas, oil, drilling waste, or is the source or location of exploration which causes an injury covered by this Part.

"Responsible party" does not include the United States, the State, any county, municipality or public governmental agency; however, this exception to the definition of "responsible person" shall not be read to exempt utilities from the provisions of this Part.

(7) "Offshore waters" shall include both the territorial sea extending seaward from the coastline of North Carolina or any other coastal state bordering the Atlantic Ocean, including the Gulf of Mexico, and the exclusive economic zone extending seaward from the territorial sea of each such state.

(8) "Natural resources" shall include "marine and estuarine resources" and "wildlife resources" as those terms are defined in G.S. 113-129(11) and G.S. 113-129(17), respectively.

(9) "Coastal fishing waters" has the same meaning as in G.S. 113-129.

(10) "Exclusive economic zone" has the same meaning as in section 1001(8) of the Oil Pollution Act of 1990, 33 U.S.C. § 2701(8). (1989, c. 656, s. 5; c. 770, s. 75.5; 2010-179, s. 1(b).)

§ 143-215.94CC. Liability under this section; exceptions.

(a) Any responsible person shall be strictly liable, notwithstanding any language of limitation found in G.S. 143-215.89, for all cleanup and removal costs and all direct or indirect damages incurred within the territorial jurisdiction of the State by any injured party that arise out of, or are caused by any of the following:

(1) The discharge, as defined in G.S. 143-215.77, of natural gas, oil, or drilling waste into or onto coastal fishing waters or offshore waters, from any of the following sources wherever located:

a. Any well or undersea site at which there is exploration for or extraction or recovery of natural gas or oil.

b. Any facility, oil rig, or oil platform at which there is exploration for, or extraction, recovery, processing, or storage of, natural gas or oil.

c. Any vessel in which natural gas, oil, or drilling waste is transported, processed or stored other than for purposes of fuel for the vessel carrying it.

d. Any pipeline in which natural gas, oil, or drilling waste is transported.

(2) Any exploration in or upon coastal fishing waters.

(3) Any technique or method used for cleanup and removal of any discharge of natural gas, oil, or drilling waste from any source listed in subdivision (1) of this subsection into or onto coastal fishing waters, including, but not limited to, chemical dispersants.

(b) A responsible person is not liable to an injured party under this section for any of the following:

(1) Damages, other than costs of removal incurred by the State or a local government, caused solely by any act of war, hostilities, civil war, or insurrection or by an unanticipated grave natural disaster or other act of God of an exceptional, inevitable, and irresistible character, which could not have been prevented or avoided by the exercise of due care or foresight.

(2) Damages caused solely by the negligence or intentional malfeasance of that injured party.

(3) Damages caused solely by the criminal act of a third party other than the defendant or an agent or employee of the defendant. In any action arising under the provisions of this Article wherein this exception is raised as a defense to liability, the burden of proving that the alleged third-party intervention occurred in such a manner as to limit the liability of the person sought to be held liable shall be upon the person charged.

(4) Natural seepage not caused by a responsible person.

(5) Discharge of oil or natural gas from a private pleasure boat or commercial fishing vessel having a fuel capacity of less than 500 gallons.

(6) Damages which arise out of, or are caused by, a discharge that is authorized by and in compliance with a State or federal permit.

(7) Damages that could have been reasonably mitigated by the injured party in accordance with common law.

(c) A court of suitable jurisdiction in any action under this Part may award reasonable costs of the suit and attorneys' fees, and the costs of any necessary expert witnesses, to any prevailing plaintiff. The court may award reasonable costs of the suit and attorneys' fees to any prevailing defendant only if the court finds that the plaintiff commenced or prosecuted the suit under this Part in bad faith or solely for purposes of harassing the defendant. (1989, c. 656, s. 5; c. 770, ss. 75.4, 75.5; 2010-179, s. 1(c).)

§ 143-215.94DD. Joint and several liability; damages; personal injury.

(a) Liability under this Part shall be joint and several. However, this section does not bar a cause of action that a responsible person has or would have, by reason of subrogation or otherwise, against any person.

(b) This section does not prohibit any person from bringing an action for damages caused by natural gas, oil or drilling waste, or by exploration, under any other provisions or principle of law, including, but not limited to, common law. However, damages shall not be awarded pursuant to this section to an injured party for any loss or injury for which the party is or has been awarded damages under any other provisions or principles of law. G.S. 143-215.94CC(b) does not create any defense not otherwise available regarding any action brought under any other provision or principle of law, including, but not limited to, common law.

(c) This section shall not apply to claims for damages for personal injury or wrongful death, and does not limit the right of any person to bring such an action under any provision or theory of law. (1989, c. 656, s. 5, c. 770, s. 75.5.)

§ 143-215.94EE. Removal of prohibited discharges.

(a) The Department shall be authorized and empowered to proceed with the cleanup of discharges covered under this Part pursuant to the authority granted to the Department in G.S. 143-215.84(b) and G.S. 143-215.94HH(b)(2).

(b) Any unexplained discharge of oil, natural gas or drilling wastes occurring in waters beyond the jurisdiction of the State that for any reason penetrates within State jurisdiction shall be removed by or under the direction of the Department. Except for any expenses incurred by the responsible person, should such person become known, all expenses incurred in the removal of such discharges shall be paid promptly by the State from the Oil or Other Hazardous Substances Pollution Protection Fund established pursuant to G.S. 143-215.87 or from any other available sources. In the case of unexplained discharges, the matter shall be referred by the Secretary to the North Carolina Attorney General for collection of damages pursuant to G.S. 143-215.94FF of this Part. At his discretion, the Attorney General may refer the matter to the State Bureau of Investigation or other appropriate State or federal authority to determine the identity of the responsible person.

(c) Nothing in this section is intended to preclude cleanup and removal by any person threatened by such discharges, who, as soon as is reasonably possible, coordinates and obtains approval for such actions with ongoing State or federal operations and appropriate State and federal authorities.

(d) No action taken by any person to contain or remove an unlawful discharge shall be construed as an admission of liability for said discharge. (1989, c. 656, s. 5, c. 770, s. 75.5; 1991, c. 342, s. 13.)

§ 143-215.94FF. Authorization of the Attorney General; citizens' suits.

(a) For any violation of this Part, the Attorney General may, on behalf of the State and on behalf of affected citizens of the State as a class, bring a civil action in the Superior Court of Wake County against the alleged responsible person. The action may seek:

(1) Injunctive relief; or

(2) Damages caused by the violation; or

(3) Both damages and injunctive relief; or

(4) Such other and further relief in the premises as the Court shall deem proper.

(b) Any injured party under this Part may bring a civil action for damages against the alleged responsible person. Civil actions under this subsection shall be brought in the superior court of the county in which the alleged injury occurred or in which the alleged damaged property is located, or in the county in which the injured party resided.

(c) Nothing in this section shall restrict any right which any person (or class of persons) may have under any statute or common law to seek injunctive or other relief. (1989, c. 656, s. 5, c. 770, s. 75.5.)

§ 143-215.94GG. Notification by persons responsible for discharge.

(a) Any person responsible for an offshore discharge under this Part shall immediately notify the Division of Emergency Management pursuant to rules established by the Secretary of Public Safety, if any, but in no case later than two hours after the discharge. Failure to so notify the Division of Emergency Management shall make the responsible person liable to the penalties set out in subsection (b) of this section. No penalty shall be imposed under this section when the owner or operator has promptly reported the discharge to federal authorities designated pursuant to 33 U.S.C. § 1321.

(b) The civil penalty for failure to immediately report a discharge under this Part shall be determined by the Commission. In determining the amount of a penalty for failure to report under this section, the Commission shall take into consideration such circumstances as the gravity of the violation, the previous record of the responsible person in complying with the terms of this Article, whether the violator reported the discharge and if so after what period of time following the spill, the size of the business of the responsible person and the effect of the penalty on the violator's ability to continue in business, and other relevant factors; provided that the penalty assessed under this section shall not exceed the following daily maximum amounts, based upon the quantity of oil spilled:

(1)   Up to 50,000 gallons............................. $ 50,000

(2)   More than 50,000 gallons...................... 250,000

For purposes of this section, each day or any part thereof during which a discharge goes unreported by the responsible person shall constitute a separate offense.

(c)   The clear proceeds of penalties provided for in this section shall be remitted to the Civil Penalty and Forfeiture Fund in accordance with G.S. 115C-457.2. (1989, c. 656, s. 5; c. 770, s. 75.5; 1998-215, s. 70; 2011-145, s. 19.1(g).)

§ 143-215.94HH. Oil spill contingency plan.

(a)   The State Emergency Response Commission, in consultation with the Secretary of Administration or his designee in the Outer Continental Shelf Lands Office, shall develop a State oil spill contingency plan relating solely to the undersea exploration, extraction, production and transport of oil or natural gas in the marine environment off the North Carolina coast, including any such development on the Outer Continental Shelf seaward of the State's jurisdiction over its territorial waters.

(b)   The Secretary of Public Safety or his designee shall establish, pursuant to such a plan, an emergency oil spill control network which shall be comprised of available equipment from appropriate State, county and municipal governmental agencies. Such network shall be employed to provide an immediate response to an oil discharge into the offshore marine environment which is reasonably likely to affect the State's coastal waters. Furthermore, such network shall be employed in conjunction with the cleanup operations under this Article or any applicable federal law, required of the owner or operator of the discharging operation, vessel, or facility, the Department of Environment and Natural Resources, and any federal agency.

(1) The Secretary of Public Safety or his designee shall make an inventory, including its location and condition, of all equipment owned by the State, its counties and municipalities, and private equipment that is available to the State for leasing in the case of an oil spill including costs of leasing, that would be capable of participating in discharge cleanup operations.

(2) The Secretary of Public Safety shall at his discretion have the power to deploy such equipment in participating in a discharge cleanup operation.

(3) The Secretary of Environment and Natural Resources shall be authorized to reimburse such State agencies, counties, and municipalities for use of such equipment with such funds as may be available from the "Oil or Other Hazardous Substances Pollution Protection Fund" created pursuant to G.S. 143-215.87 or any other sources.

(4) The oil spill contingency plan and oil spill response network developed pursuant to this section shall be reviewed and evaluated for adequacy and continued feasibility every three years, or more often if deemed appropriate by the Secretary of Public Safety. (1989, c. 656, s. 5; c. 727, s. 218(111a); c. 770, s. 75.5; 1997-443, s. 11A.119(a); 2011-145, s. 19.1(g).)

§ 143-215.94II. Emergency proclamation; Governor's powers.

(a) Whenever any emergency exists or appears imminent, arising from the discharge of oil or other pollutants within the marine environment, the Governor shall by proclamation declare a state of emergency in the appropriate sections of the State. Upon such proclamation, the Governor shall have all powers enumerated in G.S. 166A-19.30(c) subject to the limitations contained in that subsection.

(b) If the Governor is unavailable, the Lieutenant Governor shall, by proclamation, declare a state of emergency in the appropriate sections of the State.

(c) In performing his duties under this section, the Governor is authorized and directed to cooperate with all departments and agencies of the federal government, the offices and agencies of other states and foreign countries and the political subdivisions thereof, and private agencies in all matters pertaining to an emergency described herein.

(d)   In addition to the powers enumerated in G.S. 166A-19.30(c), in the case of such an emergency described in subsection (a) of this section, the Governor is further authorized and empowered to transfer any funds available to him by statute for emergency use into the Oil or Other Hazardous Substances Pollution Protection Fund created pursuant to G.S. 143-215.87, to be utilized for the purposes specified therein. (1989, c. 656, s. 5; c. 770, s. 75.5; 1991, c. 342, s. 14; 2012-12, s. 2(ww).)

§ 143-215.94JJ. Federal law.

Nothing in this Part shall authorize State agencies to impose any duties or obligations in conflict with limitations on State authority established by federal law at the time such agency action is taken. Likewise, no additional liability is established by this Part to the extent that, at the time of the injury, federal law establishes limits on liability which preempt State law. The federal limits on liability established in the Oil Pollution Act of 1990, 33 U.S.C.A. §§ 2701 to 2762, shall not apply to discharges or pollution by oil within the territorial jurisdiction of the State. (1989, c. 656, s. 5; c. 770, s. 75.5; 2010-179, s. 1(d).)

§ 143-215.94KK: Reserved for future codification purposes.

§ 143-215.94LL: Reserved for future codification purposes.

§ 143-215.94MM: Reserved for future codification purposes.

Part 2D. Training of Underground Storage Tank Operators.

§ 143-215.94NN. Applicability.

The requirements of this Part apply to underground storage tank systems regulated under Subtitle I of the Resource Conservation and Recovery Act of 1976, Pub. L. 94-580, 90 Stat. 2795, 42 U.S.C. § 6901, et seq., as amended, except those excluded by regulation at 40 Code of Federal Regulations

280.10(b) (July 1, 2009 Edition) and those deferred by regulation at 40 Code of Federal Regulations 280.10(c) (July 1, 2009 Edition). (2010-154, s. 2.)

§ 143-215.94OO. Definitions.

Unless a different meaning is required by the context, the definitions in G.S. 143-212 and G.S. 143-215.94A apply in this Part.

(1) "Emergency response operator" means an on-site person whose responsibilities include addressing emergencies presented by a spill or release, or responding to alarms or releases from an underground storage tank system. For an unmanned facility, "emergency response operator" means the person responsible for responding to emergencies or alarms or releases at the facility.

(2) "Primary operator" means a person having primary responsibility for the daily on-site operation and maintenance of an underground storage tank system.

(3) "Underground storage tank" means: (i) any one or combination of tanks (including underground pipes connected thereto) that is used to contain an accumulation of regulated substances, and the volume of which (including the volume of the underground pipes connected thereto) is ten percent (10%) or more beneath the surface of the ground; and (ii) to which this Part applies pursuant to G.S. 143-215.94NN.

(4) "Underground storage tank system" or "tank system" means an underground storage tank, connected underground piping, underground ancillary equipment, dispenser, and containment system, if any. (2010-154, s. 2.)

§ 143-215.94PP. Designation of operators to be trained.

(a) The owner of an underground storage tank system shall designate the primary operator of the underground storage tank system. The person designated shall be the underground storage tank operator, as defined in 40 Code of Federal Regulations Part 280 (July 1, 2009 Edition), or an employee or agent of the underground storage tank operator. There shall be a designated primary operator of the underground storage tank system at all times, until the underground storage tank system has been permanently closed. If the owner fails to designate a primary operator, the owner shall be deemed to be the primary operator of the underground storage tank system for purposes of this Part.

(b) The primary operator shall designate one or more emergency response operators who are employees or agents of the primary operator and shall be on call to respond to emergencies or alarms at the facility. If an emergency response operator is not present at the facility at all times during which a regulated substance is being withdrawn from, or is capable of being withdrawn from, the underground storage tank system, the facility shall have an automated notification system in place that will alert the emergency response operator of an emergency or activated alarm at the facility. If the primary operator fails to designate one or more emergency response operators, the primary operator shall be deemed to be the emergency response operator of the underground storage tank system.

(c) A person may act as both the primary operator and the emergency response operator of the underground storage tank system. (2010-154, s. 2.)

§ 143-215.94QQ. Training requirements for primary operators.

(a) The Department shall develop and implement a training program for primary operators. The training program shall provide instruction on the proper operation and maintenance of the underground storage tank system at the facility, principles of construction and safety, and all regulatory requirements associated with the underground storage tank system. The training may consist of a combination of on-site instruction and on-site testing, as well as online instruction and online testing. In order to satisfactorily complete the training, a primary operator shall, at a minimum, demonstrate all of the following:

(1) Knowledge of the requirements for spill prevention, overfill prevention, release detection, corrosion protection, emergency response, and product compatibility.

(2) Site-specific knowledge of the equipment used at the facility and the components of the underground storage tank system, and the methods of

release detection and release prevention associated with the underground storage tank components.

(3) Knowledge of the requirements for demonstrating financial responsibility.

(4) Understanding of notification requirements associated with the underground storage tank system, including requirements for reporting releases and suspected releases.

(5) Understanding of the requirements for the temporary and permanent closure of underground storage tank systems.

(6) Knowledge of the emergency response operator training requirements, and the actions to be taken in response to emergencies and alarms.

(b) A primary operator shall be retrained if an inspection at the facility reveals that the underground storage tank system is not in substantial compliance with the requirements for: release detection, release prevention, financial responsibility, emergency response, suspected release reporting and investigation, the proximity of the underground storage tank system to water supply wells and surface water, and permitting. A primary operator who is required to be retrained shall complete the retraining within a reasonable time as determined by the Department. The retraining shall include training in the areas for which the underground storage tank system was not in compliance. The retraining may consist of a combination of on-site instruction and on-site testing, as well as in-class instruction and in-class testing, and, if available, the Department shall offer online instruction and online testing in lieu of in-class instruction and in-class testing. In-class instruction shall be provided by the Department at least once each quarter in each one of the regional offices of the Department. An operator required to be retrained pursuant to this subsection shall only be required to attend in-class instruction and in-class testing at the regional office closest to the facility for which the operator is designated.

(c) The primary operator shall maintain documentation to show that the operator has satisfactorily completed all training required by this section. (2010-154, s. 2.)

§ 143-215.94RR. Training requirements for emergency response operators.

(a) The Department shall develop a training program for emergency response operators. In order to satisfactorily complete the training, an emergency response operator shall, at a minimum, demonstrate all of the following:

(1) General understanding of the underground storage tank system at the facility, and knowledge of the location and proper operation of the safety and emergency response equipment.

(2) Understanding of the actions to be taken in response to an emergency, including situations posing an immediate danger or threat to the public or to the environment and requiring immediate action.

(3) Understanding of leak detection alarms and preparations needed to respond to alarms before a release has occurred.

(4) Recognition of unusual operating conditions, equipment failures, or environmental conditions that may indicate a release, and knowledge of the steps to take in response to a suspected release.

(5) Knowledge of immediate steps to take in response to a confirmed release to stop further release and to contain spills before they reach the environment.

(b) The primary operator is responsible for implementing the training program developed by the Department for emergency response operators. The primary operator shall train each emergency response operator of the underground storage tank system at the facility. Prior to training an emergency response operator, the primary operator shall have satisfactorily completed all training required by this section. The primary operator shall maintain documentation of training provided to emergency response operators. (2010-154, s. 2.)

§ 143-215.94SS. Tank systems for emergency power generators.

This section applies only to a facility that utilizes an underground storage tank system to store fuel solely for use by emergency power generators. A primary operator that has satisfactorily completed the training required by G.S. 143-215.94QQ at a facility shall be deemed trained as the primary operator at another facility that has identical spill prevention, overfill prevention, release detection, corrosion protection, emergency response, and product compatibility requirements as the facility for which the primary operator has satisfactorily completed training. (2010-154, s. 2.)

§ 143-215.94TT. Enforcement.

This Part may be enforced as provided in G.S. 143-215.94W, 143-215.94X, and 143-215.94Y. (2010-154, s. 2.)

§ 143-215.94UU. Effect on other laws.

The requirements of this Part are in addition to, and not in lieu of, any other requirements applicable to underground storage tank owners or operators, as defined in 40 Code of Federal Regulations Part 280 (July 1, 2009 Edition), under law. (2010-154, s. 2.)

§§ 143-215.94VV through 143-215.94ZZ: Reserved for future codification purposes.

Part 3. Oil Terminal Facilities.

§ 143-215.95. Duties of Secretary.

The Secretary shall administer the provisions for registration of oil terminal facilities contained in this Part. In addition, he shall engage in such study and research concerning oil terminal facilities and their regulation in this State and elsewhere as may be required to furnish the General Assembly with a thorough factual basis for his recommendations for further legislation pursuant to this Part. (1973, c. 534, s. 1; 1977, c. 771, s. 4; 1987, c. 827, s. 154(3).)

§ 143-215.96. Oil terminal facility registration.

(a) The owner or operator of every oil terminal facility in the State shall secure a registration certificate from the Secretary. The Secretary shall not issue a registration certificate until the owner or operator has furnished the following information:

(1) Complete name of the owner and operator of the oil terminal facility together with addresses and telephone numbers;

(2) Number of employees of the oil terminal facility and the principal officers;

(3) Maps or sketches, based on criteria developed by the Secretary, showing property lines of the oil terminal facility and location of nearby watercourses or bodies of water as specified by the Secretary; and

(4) Summary of present and proposed procedures, if any, for prevention of oil spills.

(b) The owner or operator of an oil terminal facility shall secure a registration certificate no later than 30 days after the oil terminal facility begins operation. (1973, c. 534, s. 1; 1995, c. 504, s. 11.)

§ 143-215.97. Rules.

The Secretary may adopt rules to implement this Part. (1973, c. 534, s. 1; 1975, 2nd Sess., c. 983, s. 82; 1977, c. 771, s. 4; 1987, c. 827, s. 199.)

§ 143-215.98. Violations.

Any person who shall be adjudged to have violated any provision of this Part or any rule of the Secretary adopted hereunder shall be guilty of a Class 3 misdemeanor. (1973, c. 534, s. 1; 1977, c. 771, s. 4; 1987, c. 827, ss. 154(3), 200; 1993, c. 539, s. 1024; 1994, Ex. Sess., c. 24, s. 14(c).)

§ 143-215.99. Repealed by Session Laws 1975, c. 521, s. 1.

Part 4. Oil Refining Facility Permits.

§ 143-215.100. Oil refining facility permits.

No facility which is to be used or is capable of being used for the purpose of refining oil shall be initiated or constructed after July 1, 1975, without a permit from the Secretary. (1975, c. 521, s. 2; 1977, c. 771, s. 4; 1987, c. 827, s. 154.)

§ 143-215.101. Powers of the Secretary.

The Secretary has the power to:

(1)   Adopt rules implementing this Part. Rules adopted under this Part may include the following matters:

a.   Requirements for submission of engineering reports, plans and specifications for the location and construction of oil terminal facilities.

b.   Establishment of procedures and methods of reporting discharges and other occurrences prohibited by this Article.

c.   Establishment of procedures, methods, means, and equipment to be used in the removal of oil pollutants.

(2)   To deny the issuance of a permit upon a finding that:

a.   The installation will have substantial adverse effects on wildlife or on fresh water, estuarine or marine fisheries; or

b.   The operation of the installation will violate standards of air or water quality promulgated or administered by the Commission; or

c.   The installation will have a substantial adverse effect on a publicly owned park, forest, or recreation area.

(3) To grant permits for the operation of existing or proposed oil refining facilities and to impose such terms and conditions therein as it shall deem necessary and appropriate to effectuate the purposes of this Article.

(4) To require the installation of such facilities and the employment of such protective measures and operating procedures as are deemed necessary to prevent, insofar as possible, any oil discharges to the waters or lands of the State.

(5) Repealed by Session Laws 1987, c. 827, s. 201. (1975, c. 521, s. 2; 1987, c. 827, ss. 154, 201.)

§ 143-215.102. Penalties.

(a) Civil Penalty. - Any person who violates any provision of this Part, or any rule, regulation or order made pursuant to this Part, shall incur, in addition to any other penalty provided by law, a civil penalty in an amount not to exceed ten thousand dollars ($10,000) for every such violation, the amount to be determined by the Secretary after taking into consideration the factors set out in G.S. 143B-282.1(b). The procedures set out in G.S. 143-215.6 and G.S. 143B-282.1 shall apply to civil penalties assessed under this section. The penalty herein provided for shall become due and payable when the person incurring the penalty receives a notice in writing from the Commission describing the violation with reasonable particularity and advising such person that the penalty is due. A person may contest a penalty by filing a petition for a contested case under G.S. 150B-23 within 30 days after receiving notice of the penalty. If any civil penalty has not been paid within 30 days after notice of assessment has been served on the violator, the Secretary shall request the Attorney General to institute a civil action in the Superior Court of any county in which the violator resides or has his or its principal place of business to recover the amount of the assessment, unless the violator contests the assessment, or requests remission of the assessment in whole or in part as provided in G.S. 143-215.6. If any civil penalty has not been paid within 30 days after the final agency decision or court order has been served on the violator, the Secretary shall request the Attorney General to institute a civil action in the Superior Court of any county in which the violator resides or has his or its principal place of business to recover the amount of the assessment.

The clear proceeds of civil penalties provided for in this section shall be remitted to the Civil Penalty and Forfeiture Fund in accordance with G.S. 115C-457.2.

(b) Criminal Penalties. - Any person who intentionally or knowingly or willfully violates any provision of this Part, or any rule, regulation or order made pursuant to this Part shall be guilty of a Class 2 misdemeanor which may include a fine to be not more than ten thousand dollars ($10,000). No proceeding shall be brought or continued under this subsection for or on account of a violation by any person who has previously been convicted of a federal violation or a local ordinance violation based upon the same set of facts. (1975, c. 521, s. 2; 1987, c. 827, s. 202; 1989 (Reg. Sess., 1990), c. 1036, s. 7; 1993, c. 539, s. 1025; 1994, Ex. Sess., c. 24, s. 14(c); 1998-215, s. 71.)

Part 5. Limitation On Liability For Hazardous Materials Abatement.

§ 143-215.103. Definitions.

As used in this Part, unless the context otherwise requires:

(1) "Discharge" shall mean leakage, seepage, or other release.

(2) "Hazardous materials" shall mean oil, low-level radioactive waste, and all materials and substances which are now or hereafter defined as toxic or hazardous by any State or federal law or by the regulations of any State or federal government agency.

(3) "Person" shall mean any individual, partnership, corporation, association, or other entity or employee thereof. (1987, c. 269, s. 1.)

§ 143-215.104. Limited liability for volunteers in hazardous material abatement.

Any person who provides assistance or advice in mitigating or attempting to mitigate the effects of an actual or threatened discharge of hazardous materials, or in preventing, cleaning up, or disposing of or in attempting to prevent, clean up or dispose of any such discharge, when the reasonably apparent circumstances indicate the need for prompt decisions and action, shall not be subject to civil liabilities of any type, unless:

(1) Prior to providing assistance or advice in mitigating or attempting to mitigate the effects of an actual or threatened discharge or in preventing, cleaning up, or disposal of or in attempting to prevent cleanup or disposal of any such discharge, he had incurred liability for the actual or threatened discharge;

(2) He receives compensation other than reimbursement for out-of-pocket expenses for his services in rendering assistance or advice, except that an individual receiving compensation for employment from his regular employer for services performed in preventing, cleaning up, or disposing of or in attempting to prevent, clean up or dispose of a discharge shall not be deemed to have received compensation if his employer is entitled to the protection afforded by this Part; or

(3) His act or omission led to damages resulting from his gross negligence, or from his reckless, wanton, or intentional misconduct.

The limited immunity provided herein shall not be applicable to any act or omission or occurrence involving the operation of a motor vehicle. The limited immunity provided herein is waived to the extent of any indemnification by insurance for damages caused by such volunteer. (1987, c. 269, s. 1.)

Part 6. Dry-Cleaning Solvent Cleanup.

(Expires January 1, 2022 - see notes)

§ 143-215.104A. (Expires January 1, 2022 - see notes) Title; sunset.

This part is the "Dry-Cleaning Solvent Cleanup Act of 1997" and may be cited by that name. Except as otherwise provided in this section, this part expires 1 January 2022.

(1) G.S. 143-215.104K is not repealed to the extent that it applies to liability arising from dry-cleaning solvent contamination described in a Dry-Cleaning Solvent Assessment Agreement or Dry-Cleaning Solvent Remediation Agreement entered into by the Environmental Management Commission pursuant to G.S. 143-215.104H and G.S. 143-215.104I.

(2) Any Dry-Cleaning Solvent Assessment Agreement or Dry-Cleaning Solvent Remediation Agreement in force as of 1 January 2012 shall continue to

be governed by the provisions of Part 6 of Article 21A of Chapter 143 of the General Statutes as though those provisions had not been repealed.

(3) G.S. 143-215.104D(b)(2) is not repealed; rules adopted by the Environmental Management Commission pursuant to G.S. 143-215.104D(b)(2) shall continue in effect; and those rules may be enforced pursuant to G.S. 143-215.104P, 143-215.104Q, and 143-215.104R, which shall remain in effect for that purpose. (1997-392, s. 1; 2009-483, ss. 5, 7.)

§ 143-215.104B. (Expires January 1, 2022 - see notes) Definitions.

(a) Unless a different meaning is required by the context or unless a different meaning is set out in subsection (b) of this section, the definitions in G.S. 143-215.77, 130A-2, and 130A-290 apply throughout this Part.

(b) Unless a different meaning is required by the context, the following definitions apply in this Part. The definitions set out in this subsection apply only to the implementation of this Part and do not define or limit the scope of any other remedial program:

(1) "Abandoned dry-cleaning facility site" or "abandoned site" means any real property or individual leasehold space on which a dry-cleaning facility or wholesale distribution facility formerly operated.

(2) "Affiliate" has the same meaning as in 17 Code of Federal Regulations § 240.12b-2 (1 April 1996 Edition).

(3) "Commission" means the Environmental Management Commission.

(4) "Contaminant" means a regulated substance released into the environment.

(5) Renumbered.

(6) "Disposal" shall have the meaning ascribed to it in G.S. 130A-290.

(7) "Dry-cleaning facility" means a place of business located in this State and engaged in on-site dry-cleaning operations, other than a commercial uniform service or commercial linen supply facility.

(8) "Dry-cleaning operations" means cleaning of apparel and household fabrics by using one or more dry-cleaning solvents instead of water.

(9) "Dry-cleaning solvent" means any hydrocarbon or halogenated hydrocarbon used as a solvent in a dry-cleaning operation or the degradation products from these solvents.

(10) "Dry-cleaning solvent assessment agreement" or "assessment agreement" means an agreement between the Commission and a potentially responsible party who desires an assessment of whether a release of dry-cleaning solvents at a dry-cleaning facility, an abandoned dry-cleaning facility site, or a wholesale distribution facility may be eligible for remediation under this Part and whether any other contaminants that are identified in the agreement may require remediation under other remedial programs operated or administered by the Department.

(11) "Dry-cleaning solvent contamination" means the presence of dry-cleaning solvent in the waters or surface or subsurface soils of the State, the bedrock or other rock formations, or buildings in a concentration above the level requiring remediation pursuant to the rules implementing Article 21A of Chapter 143.

(12) "Dry-cleaning solvent remediation agreement" or "remediation agreement" means an agreement between the Commission and a potentially responsible party who desires the cleanup of dry-cleaning solvent contamination resulting from a release at a dry-cleaning facility, an abandoned dry-cleaning facility site, or a wholesale distribution facility under this Part and any other contaminants that are identified in the agreement under other remedial programs operated or administered by the Department.

(13) "Facility" means a dry-cleaning facility or a wholesale distribution facility.

(14) "Fund" means the Dry-Cleaning Solvent Cleanup Fund.

(14a) "Halogenated hydrocarbon" means any hydrocarbon where at least one hydrogen atom is substituted by a halogen atom.

(15) "Hazardous waste" has the same meaning as in G.S. 130A-290.

(15a) "Hydrocarbon" means any linear, branched, saturated, or unsaturated compound whose molecules contain only carbon and hydrogen atoms.

(16) "Imminent hazard" means a situation that is likely to cause an immediate threat to human life, an immediate threat of serious physical injury, an immediate threat of serious adverse health effects, or a serious risk of irreparable damage to the environment if no immediate action is taken.

(17) "Local government" means a town, city, or county.

(18) "Operator" means any person operating a dry-cleaning facility or wholesale distribution facility, whether by lease, contract, or any other form of agreement.

(19) "Parent" has the same meaning as in 17 Code of Federal Regulations § 240.12b-2 (1 April 1996 Edition).

(20) Repealed by Session Laws 2000, ch. 19, s. 3, effective on and after April 1, 1998.

(21) "Potentially responsible party" means any person who may have liability for assessment, monitoring, treatment, mitigation, or remediation of dry-cleaning solvent contamination resulting from a release at a dry-cleaning facility, an abandoned dry-cleaning facility site, or a wholesale distribution facility.

(22) "Public health" means public health as the term is used in Article 9 of Chapter 130A of the General Statutes and "human health" as the term is used in Articles 21 and 21A of Chapter 143 of the General Statutes.

(23) "Regulated substance" means a hazardous waste, as defined in G.S. 130A-290; a hazardous substance, as defined in G.S. 143-215.77A; oil, as defined in G.S. 143-215.77; or other substance regulated under any remedial program implemented by the Department other than Part 2A of Article 21A of Chapter 143 of the General Statutes.

(24) "Release" means any spillage, leakage, pumping, placement, emptying, or dumping of dry-cleaning solvents resulting from a dry-cleaning operation or the operation of a wholesale distribution facility.

(25) "Remedial program" means a program implemented by the Department for the remediation of any contaminant, including the programs implemented under Article 9 of Chapter 130A of the General Statutes and the Oil Pollution and Hazardous Substances Control Act of 1978 under Part 2 of Article 21A of

Chapter 143 of the General Statutes but not the remedial program implemented under Part 2A of Article 21A of Chapter 143 of the General Statutes.

(26) "Remediation" means action to clean up, mitigate, correct, abate, minimize, eliminate, control, or prevent the spreading, migration, leaking, leaching, volatilization, spilling, transporting, or further release of a contaminant into the environment in order to protect public health or the environment.

(27) "Response costs" means costs incurred in connection with a certified facility or abandoned site that the Commission determines are reasonably necessary and consistent with the applicable requirements of the Commission and any applicable dry-cleaning solvent assessment agreement or dry-cleaning solvent remediation agreement.

(28) "Subsidiary" has the same meaning as in 17 Code of Federal Regulations § 240.12b-2 (1 April 1996 Edition).

(29) "Treatment" shall have the meaning ascribed to it in G.S. 130A-290.

(29a) "Unrestricted use standards" when used in connection with "cleanup," "remediated", or "remediation" means that cleanup or remediation of contamination complies with generally applicable standards, guidance, or established methods governing the contaminants that are established by statute or adopted, published, or implemented by the Commission, the Commission for Public Health, or the Department instead of the risk-based standards established by the Commission pursuant to this Part.

(30) "Waters" means any stream, river, creek, brook, run, canal, swamp, lake, sound, tidal estuary, bay, reservoir, waterway, wetlands, or any other body or accumulation of water, surface or underground, public or private, natural or artificial, that is contained within, flows through, or borders upon this State, or any portion thereof, including those portions of the Atlantic Ocean over which this State has jurisdiction.

(31) "Wholesale distribution facility" means a place of business located in this State and engaged in the storage, distribution, or sale of dry-cleaning solvents for use in dry-cleaning facilities.

(32) "Wholesale distributor" means a person who operates a wholesale distribution facility. (1997-392, s. 1; 2000-19, s. 3; 2001-384, s. 11; 2007-182, s. 2; 2007-530, s. 1.)

§ 143-215.104C. (Expires January 1, 2022 - see notes) Dry-Cleaning Solvent Cleanup Fund.

(a) Creation. - The Dry-Cleaning Solvent Cleanup Fund is established as a special revenue fund to be administered by the Commission. Accordingly, revenue in the Fund at the end of a fiscal year does not revert and interest and other investment income earned by the Fund must be credited to it. The Fund is created to provide revenue to implement this Part.

(b) Sources of Revenue. - The following revenue is credited to the Fund:

(1) Dry-cleaning solvent taxes collected under Article 5D of Chapter 105 of the General Statutes.

(2) Recoveries made pursuant to G.S. 143-215.104N and G.S. 143-215.104O.

(3) Gifts and grants made to the Fund.

(4) Revenues credited to the Fund under G.S. 105-164.44E.

(5) Application fees pursuant to G.S. 143-215.104F(a1).

(c) Disbursements. - A claim filed against the Fund may be paid only from monies in the Fund and only in accordance with the provisions of this Part. Any obligation to pay claims against the Fund shall be expressly contingent upon availability of monies in the Fund. Neither the State nor any of its agencies shall have any obligation to pay any costs for which monies are not available in the Fund. The provisions of this Part shall not constitute a contract, either express or implied, to pay costs in excess of the monies available in the Fund. In making disbursements from the Fund, the Commission shall obligate monies to facilities or sites with higher priority before facilities or sites of lower priority, and facilities or sites with equal priority in the order in which the facilities or sites were prioritized until the revenue is exhausted. Consistent with the provisions of this Part, the Commission may disburse monies from the Fund to abate imminent hazards by dry-cleaning solvent contamination at abandoned dry-cleaning facility sites that have not been certified. Up to twenty percent (20%) of the amount of revenue credited to the Fund in a year may be used to defray costs incurred by the Department and the Attorney General's Office in connection with administration of the program described in this Part, including oversight of response activities.

(d)   Up to one percent (1%) of the amount of the Fund balance may be used by the Department in each fiscal year for investigation of inactive hazardous substance disposal sites that the Department reasonably believes to be contaminated by dry-cleaning solvent. If the contamination is determined to originate from a dry-cleaning facility, a potentially responsible party may petition for certification of the facility or abandoned facility site. Acceptance of a petition shall be conditioned upon the written acceptance by the petitioner of responsibility for the costs of investigation incurred by the Department pursuant to this subsection. Costs of investigation that are recovered pursuant to this subsection shall not exceed, and shall be credited toward, the financial responsibility of the petitioner pursuant to G.S. 143-215.104F(f). If a potentially responsible party does not petition for certification of the facility or abandoned facility site, the Commission may request the Attorney General to commence a civil action to secure reimbursement of costs incurred under this subsection. (1997-392, s. 1; 2000-19, ss. 2, 5, 5.1-5.3; 2007-530, s. 2.)

§ 143-215.104D. (Expires January 1, 2022 - see notes) Powers of the Commission.

(a)   Administrative Functions. - The Commission may delegate any or all of the powers enumerated in this subsection to the Department. The Commission shall:

(1)   Accept petitions for certification and petitions to enter into dry-cleaning solvent assessment agreements or remediation agreements under this Part.

(2)   Prioritize certified dry-cleaning facilities, certified wholesale distribution facilities, or certified abandoned dry-cleaning facility sites for the initiation of assessment or remediation activities.

(3)   Repealed by Session Laws 2007-530, s. 3, effective August 31, 2007.

(4)   Schedule funding of assessment and remediation activities.

(5)   Determine whether assessment or remediation is necessary at a site at which dry-cleaning solvent contamination has occurred.

(5a) Enter into contracts with private contractors for assessment and remediation activities at certified dry-cleaning facilities, certified wholesale distribution facilities, and certified abandoned dry-cleaning facility sites.

(6) Determine that all necessary assessment and remediation has been completed at a contamination site.

(7) Make payments from the Fund for the costs of assessment and remediation.

(b) Rule making. - The Commission shall adopt rules as are necessary to implement the provisions of this Part. Rules adopted by the Commission shall be consistent with and shall not duplicate, but may incorporate by reference, the rules adopted by the Commission for Health Services pursuant to Article 9 of Chapter 130A of the General Statutes. The Commission shall not delegate the rule-making powers provided in this subsection.

(1) The Commission may adopt rules governing:

a. Repealed by Session Laws 2007-530, s. 3, effective August 31, 2007.

b. The certification and decertification of facilities or abandoned sites.

c. The prioritization of facilities or abandoned sites and scheduling of funding for assessment and remediation activities. These rules shall provide for:

1. Consideration of the degree of harm or risk to public health and the environment.

2. Consideration of the order in which certification is issued for the facility or abandoned site.

3. Consideration of the relative cost of assessment and remediation activities.

4. Use of the Fund so as to maximize the reduction of harm or risk posed by certified facilities, certified abandoned sites, uncertified facilities and uncertified sites.

d. The disbursement of revenue from the Fund for payment of approved assessment or remediation costs.

e.	The determination whether assessment or remediation is necessary at a contamination site.

f.	The determination that all necessary assessment and remediation has been completed at a contamination site.

g.	The terms and conditions of dry-cleaning solvent assessment agreements and remediation agreements.

h.	The determination whether additional assessment or remediation is necessary at a contamination site previously closed under this Part.

(2)	(See editor's note) The Commission may adopt rules establishing minimum management practices for handling of dry-cleaning solvent at dry-cleaning facilities and wholesale distribution facilities. The rules may:

a.	Require that all perchloroethylene dry-cleaning machines installed at a dry-cleaning facility after the effective date of the rule or temporary rule meet air emission standards that equal or exceed the standards that apply to comparable dry-to-dry perchloroethylene dry-cleaning machines with integral refrigerated condensation.

b.	Prohibit the discharge of dry-cleaning solvents or water that contains dry-cleaning solvents into sanitary sewers, septic systems, storm sewers, or waters of the State.

c.	Require spill containment structures around dry-cleaning machines, filters, stills, vapor adsorbers, solvent storage areas, and waste solvent storage areas.

d.	Require floor sealants for cleaning room areas if the Commission finds the sealants to be effective.

e.	Require, by 1 January 2002, the use of improved solvent transfer systems to prevent releases at the time of delivery of solvents to a dry-cleaning facility.

f.	Require any other solvent-handling practices the Commission may find necessary and appropriate to minimize the risk of releases at dry-cleaning facilities or wholesale distribution facilities.

(3) The Commission shall adopt rules establishing a risk-based approach applicable to the assessment, prioritization, and remediation of dry-cleaning solvent contamination resulting from releases at facilities or abandoned sites certified pursuant to G.S. 143-215.104G. The rules shall address, at a minimum:

a. Criteria and methods for determining remediation requirements, including the level of remediation necessary to assure adequate protection of public health and the environment.

b. The circumstances under which information specific to the dry-cleaning solvent contamination site should be considered and required.

c. The circumstances under which restrictions on the future use of any remediated dry-cleaning solvent contamination site should be considered and required as a means of achieving and maintaining an adequate level of protection for public health and the environment.

d. Strategies for the assessment and remediation of dry-cleaning solvent contamination, including presumptive remedial responses sufficient to provide an adequate level of protection as described under sub-subdivision a. of this subdivision.

(c) All rules adopted by the Commission shall be applicable to all dry-cleaning facilities, wholesale distribution facilities, and abandoned dry-cleaning facilities in the State and shall, to the maximum extent practicable, be cost-effective and technically feasible while protecting public health and the environment from the release of dry-cleaning solvents.

(d) Unless otherwise provided in this Part, the Commission may delegate any of its rights, duties, and responsibilities under this Part to the Department. (1997-392, s. 1; 2000-19, s. 6; 2007-182, s. 2; 2007-530, s. 3.)

§ 143-215.104E: Repealed by Session Laws 2000-19, s. 3.

§ 143-215.104F. (Expires January 1, 2022 - see notes) Requirements for certification, assessment agreements, and remediation agreements.

(a) General Requirements. - Any person petitioning for certification of a facility or an abandoned site pursuant to G.S. 143-215.104G, for a dry-cleaning solvent assessment agreement pursuant to G.S. 143-215.104H, or for a dry-cleaning solvent remediation agreement pursuant to G.S. 143-215.104I, shall meet the requirements set out in this section and any other applicable requirements of this Part.

(a1) Application Fees. - Each person petitioning or co-petitioning for certification of a facility or an abandoned site pursuant to G.S. 143-215.104G shall pay an application fee of one thousand dollars ($1,000) to the Commission.

(b) Requirements for Potentially Responsible Persons Generally. - Every petitioner shall provide the Commission with:

(1) Any information that the petitioner possesses relating to the contamination at the facility or abandoned site described in the petition.

(2) Information necessary to demonstrate the person's ability to incur the response costs specified in subsection (f) of this section.

(3) Repealed by Session Laws 2000, c. 19, s. 3, effective on and after April 1, 1998.

(4) Information necessary to demonstrate that the petitioner, and any parent, subsidiary, or other affiliate of the petitioner, has substantially complied with:

a. The terms of any dry-cleaning solvent assessment agreement, dry-cleaning solvent remediation agreement, brownfields agreement, or other similar agreement to which the petitioner or any parent, subsidiary, or other affiliate of the petitioner has been a party.

b. The requirements applicable to any remediation in which the petitioner has previously engaged.

c. Federal and State laws, regulations, and rules for the protection of the environment.

(5) Evidence demonstrating that a release of dry-cleaning solvent has occurred at the facility or abandoned site and that the release has resulted in dry-cleaning solvent contamination.

(c) Requirement for Property Owners. - In addition to the information required by subsection (b) of this section, a petitioner who is the owner of the property on which the dry-cleaning solvent contamination identified in the petition is located shall provide the Commission a written agreement authorizing the Commission, its agent, and its private contractor to have access to the property for purposes of conducting assessment or remediation activities or determining whether assessment or remediation activities are being conducted in compliance with this Part and any assessment agreement or remediation agreement.

(c1) Costs incurred by the petitioner for activities to obtain certification of a facility or abandoned site shall not be reimbursable from the Fund.

(d) The Commission may reject any petition made pursuant to this Part in any of the following circumstances:

(1) The petitioner is an owner or operator of the facility described in the petition and the facility was not being operated in compliance with minimum management practices adopted by the Commission pursuant to G.S. 143-215.104D(b)(2) at the time the contamination was discovered.

(2) The petitioner is an owner or operator of the facility described in the petition and the petitioner owed delinquent taxes under Article 5D of Chapter 105 of the General Statutes at the time the dry-cleaning solvent contamination was discovered.

(3) Repealed by Session Laws 2000, c. 19, s. 3, effective on and after April 1, 1998.

(4) The petitioner fails to provide the information required by subsection (b) of this section.

(5) The petitioner falsified any information in its petition that was material to the determination of the priority ranking, the nature, scope and extent of contamination to be assessed or remediated, or the appropriate means to contain and remediate the contaminants.

(e) Repealed by Session Laws 2007-530, s. 4, effective August 31, 2007.

(f) Financial Responsibility Requirements. - Each potentially responsible person who petitions the Commission to certify a facility or abandoned site shall accept written responsibility in the amount specified in this section for the assessment or remediation of the dry-cleaning solvent contamination identified in the petition. If two or more potentially responsible persons petition the Commission jointly, the requirements below shall be the aggregate requirements for the financial responsibility of all potentially responsible persons who are party to the petition. Unless an alternative arrangement is agreed to by co-petitioners, the financial responsibility requirements of this section shall be apportioned equally among the co-petitioners. The financial responsibility required shall be as follows:

(1) For dry-cleaning facilities owned by persons who employ fewer than five full-time employees, or the equivalent, in activities related to dry-cleaning operations during the calendar year preceding the date of the petition, one percent (1%) of the costs of assessment or remediation not exceeding one million dollars ($1,000,000).

(2) For abandoned dry-cleaning facility sites and for dry-cleaning facilities owned by persons who employ at least five but fewer than 10 full-time employees, or the equivalent, in activities related to dry-cleaning operations during the calendar year preceding the date of the petition, one and one-half percent (1.5%) of the costs of assessment or remediation not exceeding one million dollars ($1,000,000).

(3) For wholesale distribution facilities and for dry-cleaning facilities owned by persons who employ 10 or more full-time employees, or the equivalent, in activities related to dry-cleaning operations during the calendar year preceding the date of the petition, two percent (2%) of the costs of assessment or remediation not exceeding one million dollars ($1,000,000).

(4) Repealed by Session Laws 2007-530, s. 4, effective retroactively to August 1, 2001, and applicable to assessment agreements and remediation agreements entered into on or after that date.

(g) Repealed by Session Laws 2000, c. 19, s. 3, effective on and after April 1, 1998. (1997-392, s. 1; 2000-19, ss. 3, 4, 7; 2007-530, s. 4.)

§ 143-215.104G. (Expires January 1, 2022 - see notes) Certification of facilities and abandoned sites.

(a) A potentially responsible party may petition the Commission to certify a facility or abandoned site where a release of dry-cleaning solvent has occurred. The Commission shall certify the facility or abandoned site if the petitioner meets the applicable requirements of G.S. 143-215.104F. Upon its decision to certify a facility or abandoned site, the Commission shall inform the petitioner of its decision and of the initial priority ranking of the facility or site.

(b) Repealed by Session Laws 2000, c. 19, s. 8.

(c) A potentially responsible party who petitions for certification of a facility or abandoned site shall provide the Commission with either of the following:

(1) A written statement of the petitioner's intent to enter into an assessment agreement or remediation agreement.

(2) A written statement of the petitioner's intent to conduct assessment and remediation activities pursuant to subsection (d) of this section.

(d) A person who has access to property that is contaminated by dry-cleaning solvent and who has successfully petitioned for certification of the facility or abandoned site from which the contamination is believed to have resulted may undertake assessment or remediation of dry-cleaning solvent contamination located on the property consistent with the standards established by the Commission pursuant to G.S. 143-215.104D(b)(3) without first entering into a dry-cleaning solvent assessment agreement or a dry-cleaning solvent remediation agreement. No assessment or remediation activities undertaken pursuant to this subsection shall rely on standards that require the creation of land-use restrictions. A person who undertakes assessment or remediation activities pursuant to this subsection shall provide the Commission prior written notice of the activity. Costs associated with assessment or remediation activities undertaken pursuant to this subsection shall not be eligible for reimbursement from the Fund.

(e) The rejection of any petition filed pursuant to this section shall not affect the rights of any other petitioner, other than any parent, subsidiary, or other affiliate of the petitioner, under this Part. The rejection of a petition or the decertification of a facility or abandoned site may be the basis for rejection of a petition by any parent, subsidiary, or other affiliate of the petitioner for the facility or abandoned site. (1997-392, s. 1; 2000-19, s. 8.)

§ 143-215.104H. (Expires January 1, 2022 - see notes) Dry-Cleaning Solvent Assessment Agreements.

(a) Assessment Agreements. - One or more potentially responsible parties may petition the Commission to enter into a dry-cleaning solvent assessment agreement regarding a facility or abandoned site that has been certified pursuant to G.S. 143-215.104G. The Commission may, in its discretion, enter into an assessment agreement with any potentially responsible party who satisfies the requirements of this section and the applicable requirements of G.S. 143-215.104F. If more than one potentially responsible party petitions the Commission, the Commission may enter into a single assessment agreement with one or more of the petitioners. The Commission shall not unreasonably refuse to enter into an assessment agreement pursuant to this section. The Commission may require the petitioners to provide the Commission with any information necessary to demonstrate:

(1) The priority ranking assigned to the facility or site is consistent with the rules adopted by the Commission.

(2) through (4a) Repealed by Session Laws 2007-530, s. 5, effective August 31, 2007.

(5) The petitioner has and will continue to have available the financial resources necessary to pay the share of response costs imposed on the petitioner by G.S. 143-215.104F.

(6) The permits or other authorizations required to conduct the assessment activities and to lawfully dispose of any hazardous substances or wastes generated by the assessment activities have been or can be obtained.

(7) The assessment activities will not increase the existing level of public exposure to health or environmental hazards at the contamination site.

(8) Repealed by Session Laws 2007-530, s. 5, effective August 31, 2007.

(9) The petitioner has obtained the consent of other property owners to enter into their property for the purpose of conducting assessment activities specified in the assessment agreement.

(b) The terms and conditions of an assessment agreement regarding dry-cleaning solvent contamination shall be guided by and consistent with the rules adopted by the Commission pursuant to G.S. 143-215.104D and the disbursement authorities and limitations set out in this Part. An assessment agreement shall, subject to the availability of monies from the Fund:

(1) Repealed by Session Laws 2000, ch. 19, s. 9, effective June 26, 2000.

(1a) Require that the petitioner shall be liable to the Fund for an amount equal to the difference, if any, between the applicable amount for which the petitioner is responsible under G.S. 143-215.104F and the amount reasonably paid by the petitioner for assessment or remediation activities of the type specified in G.S. 143-215.104N(a)(1) through (7) and that are otherwise consistent with the requirements of this Part.

(2) Repealed by Session Laws 2007-530, s. 5, effective August 31, 2007.

(c) The Commission may refuse to enter into a dry-cleaning solvent assessment agreement with any petitioner if:

(1) The petitioner will not accept financial responsibility for the petitioner's share of the response costs required by G.S. 143-215.104F.

(2) Repealed by Session Laws 2007-530, s. 5, effective August 31, 2007.

(3) The petitioner fails to provide any information required by subsection (a) of this section.

(d) The refusal of the Commission to enter into a dry-cleaning solvent assessment agreement with any petitioner shall not affect the rights of any other petitioner under this Part, except that the refusal may be the basis for rejection of a petition by any parent, subsidiary or other affiliate of the petitioner for the facility or abandoned site.

(e) If the Commission determines from an assessment prepared pursuant to this Part that the degree of risk to public health or the environment resulting from dry-cleaning solvent contamination otherwise subject to assessment or remediation under this Part and Article 9 of Chapter 130A is acceptable in light of the criteria established pursuant to G.S. 143-215.104D(b)(3) and Article 9 of Chapter 130A, the Commission shall issue a written statement of its determination and notify the owner or operator of the facility or abandoned site responsible for the contamination that no cleanup, no further cleanup, or no further action is required in connection with the contamination.

(f) If the Commission determines that no remediation or further action is required in connection with dry-cleaning solvent contamination otherwise subject to assessment or remediation pursuant to this Part and Article 9 of Chapter 130A, the Commission shall not pay any costs otherwise payable under this Part from the Fund other than costs reasonable and necessary to conduct the risk assessment pursuant to this section and in compliance with a dry-cleaning solvent assessment agreement. (1997-392, s. 1; 2000-19, s. 9; 2007-530, s. 5.)

§ 143-215.104I. (Expires January 1, 2022 - see notes) Dry-Cleaning solvent remediation agreements.

(a) Upon the completion of assessment activities required by a dry-cleaning solvent assessment agreement, one or more potentially responsible parties may petition the Commission to enter into a dry-cleaning solvent remediation agreement for any contamination requiring remediation. The Commission may, in its discretion, enter into a remediation agreement with any petitioner who satisfies the requirements of this section and the applicable requirements of G.S. 143-215.104F. If more than one potentially responsible party petitions the Commission, the Commission may enter into a single remediation agreement with one or more of the petitioners. The Commission shall not unreasonably refuse to enter into a remediation agreement pursuant to this section. The Commission may, in its discretion, enter into a remediation agreement that includes the assessment described in G.S. 143-215.104H. Petitioners shall provide the Commission with any information necessary to demonstrate:

(1) Repealed by Session Laws 2000, c. 19, s. 10, effective June 26, 2000.

(2) As a result of the remediation agreement, the contamination site will be suitable for the uses specified in the remediation agreement while fully protecting public health and the environment from dry-cleaning solvent contamination and any other contaminants included in the remediation agreement.

(3) There is a public benefit commensurate with the liability protection provided under this Part.

(4)   Repealed by Session Laws 2007-530, s. 6, effective August 31, 2007.

(5)   The petitioner has complied with or will comply with all applicable procedural requirements.

(6)   The remediation agreement will not cause the Department to violate the terms and conditions under which the Department operates and administers remedial programs, including the programs established or operated pursuant to Article 9 of Chapter 130A of the General Statutes, by delegation or similar authorization from the United States or its departments or agencies, including the United States Environmental Protection Agency.

(7)   The priority ranking assigned to the facility or site is consistent with the rules adopted by the Commission or the priority ranking that the petitioner agrees to accept is consistent with the rules adopted by the Commission.

(8)   Repealed by Session Laws 2007-530, s. 6, effective August 31, 2007.

(9)   The petitioner will continue to have available the financial resources necessary to satisfy the share of response costs imposed on the petitioner by G.S. 143-215.104F.

(10)   Repealed by Session Laws 2007-530, s. 6, effective August 31, 2007.

(11)   The consent of other property owners to enter into their property for purposes of conducting remediation activities specified in the remediation agreement.

(b)   In negotiating a remediation agreement, parties may rely on land-use restrictions that will be included in a Notice of Dry-Cleaning Solvent Remediation required under G.S. 143-215.104M. A remediation agreement may provide for remediation in accordance with standards that are based on those land-use restrictions.

(b1)   For contaminated properties that are located in the area of a contamination site, in lieu of land-use restrictions authorized by subsection (b) of this section, parties may rely on other State or local land-use controls in negotiating a remediation agreement. Any land-use controls used shall adequately protect human health and the environment, both currently and in the future, from exposure to dry-cleaning solvent contamination. If controls are used in lieu of land-use restrictions, then a Notice of Dry-Cleaning Solvent

Remediation shall be prepared in accordance with the provisions set forth in subdivisions (1) through (4) of G.S. 143-215.104M(b) and filed in accordance with subsections (c) through (g) of G.S. 143-215.104M. In the event that the owner of the property fails to submit and file the required Notice within the time specified, the Commission may prepare and file the Notice. This subsection shall not apply to properties on which a dry-cleaning facility is or was located which is the source of the contamination.

(c)   A dry-cleaning solvent remediation agreement shall contain a description of the contamination site that would be sufficient as a description of the property in an instrument of conveyance and, as applicable, a statement of:

(1)   Any remediation, including remediation of contaminants other than dry-cleaning solvents, to be conducted on the property, including:

a.   A description of specific areas where remediation is to be conducted.

b.   The remediation method or methods to be employed.

c.   Repealed by Session Laws 2007-530, s. 6, effective August 31, 2007.

d.   A schedule of remediation activities.

e.   Applicable remediation standards. Applicable remediation standards for dry-cleaning solvent contamination shall not exceed the requirements adopted by the Commission pursuant to G.S. 143-104D(b)(3).

f.   A schedule and the method or methods for evaluating the remediation.

(2)   Any land-use restrictions and State and local land-use controls that will apply to the contamination site or other property.

(3)   The desired results of any remediation, land-use restrictions, or State or local land-use controls with respect to the contamination site.

(4)   The guidelines, including parameters, principles, and policies within which the desired results are to be accomplished.

(5)   The consequences of achieving or not achieving the desired results.

(6)   The priority ranking of the facility or abandoned site.

(7) Repealed by Session Laws 2007-530, s. 6, effective August 31, 2007.

(d) The Commission may refuse to enter into a dry-cleaning solvent assessment agreement or dry-cleaning solvent remediation agreement with any petitioner if the petitioner fails to provide any information that is necessary to demonstrate the facts required to be shown by subsection (a) of this section.

(e) In addition to the basis set forth in subsection (d) of this section, the Commission may refuse to enter into a dry-cleaning solvent remediation agreement with an owner of the property on which a contamination site is located if the owner refuses to accept limitations on the future use of the property and to give notice of these limitations pursuant to G.S. 143-215.104M.

(f) The refusal of the Commission to enter into a dry-cleaning remediation agreement with any petitioner shall not affect the rights of any other petitioner, other than any parent, subsidiary, or other affiliate of the petitioner, under this Part. The refusal of the Commission to enter into a remediation agreement may be the basis for rejection of a petition by any parent, subsidiary, or other affiliate of the petitioner for the facility or abandoned site.

(g) The terms and conditions of a dry-cleaning solvent remediation agreement concerned with dry-cleaning solvent contamination shall be guided by and consistent with the rules adopted by the Commission pursuant to G.S. 143-215.104D and the disbursement authorities and limitations set out in this Part. A remediation agreement shall provide that the Commission's private contractor conduct assessment and remediation activities at the facility or abandoned site.

(h) Any failure of a petitioner or the petitioner's agents or employees to comply with the dry-cleaning solvent remediation agreement constitutes a violation of this Part by the petitioner. (1997-392, s. 1; 2000-19, ss. 10, 11, 13; 2007-530, s. 6; 2009-483, s. 1.)

§ 143-215.104J. (Expires January 1, 2022 - see notes) Decertification; termination of assessment agreements and remediation agreements.

(a) The Commission may decertify a facility or abandoned site or renegotiate or terminate an assessment agreement or remediation agreement with respect to any party thereto in the following circumstances:

(1) The owner or operator of the facility, at any time subsequent to the certification of the facility, violates any of the minimum management requirements adopted by the Commission pursuant to G.S. 143-215.104D(b)(2).

(2) In the case of dry-cleaning contamination on property that is owned by a petitioner, the petitioner fails to file a Notice of Dry-Cleaning Solvent Remediation, if required, as provided in G.S. 143-215.104M.

(3) The potentially responsible persons who are parties to a dry-cleaning solvent assessment agreement are unable to reach an agreement with the Commission to enter into a dry-cleaning solvent remediation agreement within the time specified in the assessment agreement.

(4) The payment of taxes assessed to the facility under Article 5D of Chapter 105 of the General Statutes is delinquent.

(5) Repealed by Session Laws 2000, ch. 19, s. 3, effective on or after April 1, 1998.

(6) The owner or operator fails to comply with all applicable requirements of this Part or fails to comply with all applicable requirements of an assessment agreement or remediation agreement.

(7) The owner or operator of a facility for which an assessment or remediation activity is scheduled or in progress transfers the ownership or operation of the facility or abandoned site to another person without the prior consent of the Commission and the execution of a substitute assessment agreement or remediation agreement.

(8) The standards applied to the dry-cleaning solvent contamination remediation or containment under the provisions of this Part and the dry-cleaning solvent remediation agreement will, or are likely to, cause the Department to fail to comply with the terms and conditions under which it operates and administers a remediation program by delegation or similar authorization from the United States or one of its departments or agencies, including the Environmental Protection Agency.

(9) A petitioner fails to pay the Commission any amounts for which a petitioner is responsible pursuant to G.S. 143-215.104F.

(b) Prior to decertifying any facility or abandoned site or renegotiating or terminating any assessment agreement or remediation agreement, the Commission shall give the petitioners notice and opportunity for hearing. The Commission is not required to give the petitioners notice and opportunity for hearing when the Commission reasonably takes an emergency action to abate an imminent hazard caused by or arising from assessment or remediation activities at a contamination site whether the Commission issues a special order pursuant to G.S. 143-215.2 or takes other action.

(c) Decertification of any facility or abandoned site or renegotiation or termination of any assessment agreement or remediation agreement pursuant to this section shall not affect the rights of any petitioner, other than a petitioner whose violation of the provisions of subsection (a) of this section was the basis for the decertification, renegotiation, or termination and any parent, subsidiary, or other affiliate of that petitioner. If the Commission decertifies a facility or abandoned site or terminates an assessment agreement or remediation agreement with any party to the agreement pursuant to subsection (a) of this section, the Commission shall use its best efforts to negotiate a substitute agreement with any remaining parties to the agreement. (1997-392, s. 1; 2000-19, s. 3; 2007-530, s. 7.)

§ 143-215.104K. (Expires January 1, 2022 - see notes) Liability protection.

(a) A potentially responsible party who enters into an assessment agreement or remediation agreement with the Commission and who is complying with the agreement shall not be held liable for assessment or remediation of areas of contamination identified in the agreement except as specified in the assessment agreement or remediation agreement, so long as any activities conducted at the contamination site by or under the control or direction of the petitioner do not increase the risk of harm to public health or the environment and the petitioner is not required to undertake additional remediation to unrestricted use standards pursuant to subsection (c) of this section. The liability protection provided under this Part applies to all of the following persons to the same extent as the petitioner, so long as these persons are not otherwise potentially responsible parties or parents, subsidiaries, or affiliates of potentially responsible parties and the person is not required to undertake additional remediation to unrestricted use standards pursuant to subsection (c) of this section:

(1) Repealed by Session Laws 2007-503, s. 8, effective August 31, 2007.

(2) Any future owner of the contamination site.

(3) A person who occupies the contamination site.

(4) A successor or assign of any person to whom the liability protection provided under this Part applies.

(5) Any lender or fiduciary that provides financing to the petitioner to pay the petitioner's financial obligations under G.S. 143-215.104F.

(b) A person who conducts an environmental assessment or transaction screen on contamination resulting from a release at a certified facility or certified abandoned site consistent with a dry-cleaning solvent assessment agreement, if any was required under this Part, and who is not otherwise a potentially responsible party is not a potentially responsible party as a result of conducting the environmental assessment or transaction screen unless that person increases the risk of harm to public health or the environment by failing to exercise due diligence and reasonable care in performing the environmental assessment or transaction screen.

(c) If a land-use restriction set out in a Notice of Dry-Cleaning Solvent Remediation required under G.S. 143-215.104M is violated, the owner of the contamination site at the time the land-use restriction is violated, the owner's successors and assigns, and the owner's agents who direct or contract for alteration of the contamination site in violation of a land-use restriction shall be liable for remediation of all contaminants to unrestricted use standards. A petitioner who completes the remediation required under a dry-cleaning solvent remediation agreement or other person who receives liability protection under this Part shall not be required to undertake additional remediation unless:

(1) The petitioner knowingly or recklessly provides false information that forms a basis for the remediation agreement or that is offered to demonstrate compliance with the remediation agreement or fails to disclose relevant information about contamination related to a facility or abandoned site.

(2) New information indicates the existence of previously unreported dry-cleaning solvent contaminants or any other contaminants to be remediated under the remediation agreement, or an area of previously unreported contamination by contaminants addressed in the remediation agreement is

discovered to be associated with the facility or abandoned site and has not been remediated to unrestricted use standards, unless the remediation agreement is amended to include any previously unreported contaminants and any additional area of contamination. If the remediation agreement sets maximum concentrations for contaminants and new information indicates the existence of previously unreported areas of these contaminants, further remediation shall be required only if the areas of previously unreported contaminants raise the risk of the contamination to public health or the environment to a level less protective of public health and the environment than that required by the remediation agreement.

(3)   The level of risk to public health and the environment from contaminants is unacceptable at or in the vicinity of the contamination site due to changes in exposure conditions, including (i) a change in land use that increases the probability of exposure to contaminants at or in the vicinity of the contamination site; (ii) the failure of remediation to mitigate risks to the extent required to make the contamination site fully protective of public health and the environment as planned in the remediation agreement; or (iii) removal of a State or local land-use control.

(4)   The Commission obtains new information about a contaminant to be remediated under the remediation agreement and associated with the facility or abandoned site or exposures at or around the contamination site that raises the risk to public health or the environment associated with the contamination site beyond an acceptable range and in a manner or to a degree not anticipated in the remediation agreement. Any person whose use, including any change in use, of the contamination site causes an unacceptable risk to public health or the environment may be required by the Commission to undertake additional remediation measures under the provisions of this Part.

(5)   A petitioner fails to file a timely and proper Notice of Dry-Cleaning Solvent Remediation under this Part.

(6)   A facility or abandoned site loses its certification before the assessment and any remediation required under the provisions of this Part and the dry-cleaning solvent remediation agreement are completed to the satisfaction of the Department.

(7)   The remediation required in the remediation agreement has resulted in notification from the United States or its departments and agencies, including the Environmental Protection Agency, that the Department will violate the terms

and conditions under which it operates and administers remedial programs by delegation or similar authorization. (1997-392, s. 1; 2001-384, s. 11; 2007-530, s. 8; 2009-483, s. 2.)

§ 143-215.104L. (Expires January 1, 2022 - see notes) Public notice and community involvement.

(a)   If a petitioner desires to enter into a dry-cleaning solvent remediation agreement based on remediation standards that rely on the creation of land-use restrictions, or on the use of State or local land-use controls, the Commission or the Commission's private contractor on behalf of the petitioner shall notify the public and the community in which the facility or abandoned site is located of the planned remediation activities. On behalf of the petitioner, the Commission or the Commission's private contractor shall prepare a Notice of Intent to Remediate a Dry-Cleaning Solvent Facility or Abandoned Site and a summary of the Notice of Intent. The Notice of Intent shall provide, to the extent known, a legal description of the location of the contamination site, a map showing the location of the contamination site, a description of the contaminants involved and their concentrations in the media of the contamination site, a description of the future use of the contamination site, any proposed investigation and remediation, and a description of any land-use restrictions and State and local land-use controls that will be used. Both the Notice of Intent and the summary of the Notice of Intent shall state the time period and means for submitting written comment and for requesting a public meeting on the proposed dry-cleaning solvent remediation agreement. The summary of the Notice of Intent shall include a statement as to the public availability of the full Notice of Intent. After approval of the Notice of Intent and summary of the Notice of Intent by the Commission, the Commission or the Commission's private contractor shall provide a copy of the Notice of Intent to all local governments having jurisdiction over the contamination site. The Commission or Commission's private contractor shall publish the summary of the Notice of Intent in a newspaper of general circulation serving the area in which the contamination is located and shall mail a copy of the summary to each owner of property located within the contamination site and to each owner of property that is contiguous to the contamination site. The Commission or the Commission's private contractor shall also conspicuously post a copy of the summary of the Notice of Intent at the contamination site.

(b) Publication of the approved summary of the Notice of Intent in a newspaper of general circulation shall begin a public comment period of at least 30 days from the date of publication. During the public comment period, members of the public, residents of the community in which the contamination site is located, and local governments having jurisdiction over the contamination site may submit comment on the proposed dry-cleaning solvent remediation agreement, including methods and degree of remediation, future land uses, and impact on local employment.

(c) Any person who desires a public meeting on a proposed dry-cleaning solvent remediation agreement shall submit a written request for a public meeting to the Commission within 30 days after the public comment period begins. The Commission shall consider all requests for a public meeting and shall hold a public meeting if the Commission determines that there is significant public interest in the proposed remediation agreement. If the Commission decides to hold a public meeting, the Commission shall, at least 30 days prior to the public meeting, mail written notice of the public meeting to all persons who requested the public meeting and to any other person who had previously requested notice. The Commission shall also publish, at least 30 days prior to the date of the public meeting, a notice of the public meeting at least one time in a newspaper having general circulation in the county where the contamination site is located. In any county in which there is more than one newspaper having general circulation, the Commission shall publish a copy of the notice in as many newspapers having general circulation in the county as the Commission in its discretion determines to be necessary to assure that the notice is generally available throughout the county. The Commission shall prescribe the form and content of the notice to be published. The Commission shall prescribe the procedures to be followed in the public meeting. The Commission shall take detailed minutes of the meeting. The minutes shall include any written comments received during the public meeting. The Commission shall take into account the comment received during the comment period and at the public meeting if the Commission holds a public meeting. The Commission shall incorporate into the remediation agreement provisions that reflect comment received during the comment period and at the public meeting to the extent practical. The Commission shall give particular consideration to written comment that is supported by valid scientific and technical information and analysis. (1997-392, s. 1; 2007-530, s. 9; 2009-483, s. 3.)

§ 143-215.104M. (Expires January 1, 2022 - see notes) Notice of Dry-Cleaning Solvent Remediation; land-use restrictions in deeds.

(a) Land-Use Restriction. - In order to reduce or eliminate the danger to public health or the environment posed by a dry-cleaning solvent contamination site, the owner of property upon which dry-cleaning solvent contamination has been discovered may file a Notice of Dry-Cleaning Solvent Remediation approved by the Commission identifying the site on which the contamination has been discovered and providing for current or future restrictions on the use of the property. If a petitioner requests that a contamination site be remediated to standards that require land-use restrictions, the owner of the property must file a Notice of Dry-Cleaning Solvent Remediation for the remediation agreement to become effective.

(b) Notice of Restriction. - A Notice of Dry-Cleaning Solvent Remediation shall include:

(1) A survey plat of the contamination site that has been prepared and certified by a professional land surveyor and that meets the requirements of G.S. 47-30.

(2) A legal description of the property that would be sufficient as a description in an instrument of conveyance.

(3) A description of the location and dimensions of the areas of potential environmental concern with respect to permanently surveyed benchmarks.

(4) The type, location, and quantity of dry-cleaning solvent contamination known to exist on the property.

(5) Any restrictions on the current or future use of the property or other property that are necessary to assure adequate protection of public health and the environment as provided in rules adopted pursuant to G.S. 143-215.104D(b)(3). These land-use restrictions may apply to activities on, over, or under the land, including, but not limited to, use of groundwater, building, filling, grading, excavating, and mining. Where a contamination site encompasses more than one parcel or tract of land, a composite map or plat showing all parcels or tracts may be recorded.

(c) Recordation of Notice. - After the Commission approves and certifies the Notice of Dry-Cleaning Solvent Remediation under subsection (a) of this section, a certified copy of a Notice of Dry-Cleaning Solvent Remediation shall be filed in the office of the register of deeds of the county or counties in which the property described is located. The owner of the property shall file the Notice of Dry-Cleaning Solvent Remediation within 15 days of the property owner's receipt of the Commission's approval of the notice or the effective date of the dry-cleaning solvent remediation agreement, whichever is later.

(d) Notice of Transfer. - When property for which a Notice of Dry-Cleaning Solvent Remediation has been filed is sold, leased, conveyed, or transferred, the deed or other instrument of transfer shall contain in the description section, in no smaller type than that used in the body of the deed or instrument, a statement that the property has been contaminated with dry-cleaning solvent and, if appropriate, cleaned up under this Part.

(e) Cancellation of Notice. - A Notice of Dry-Cleaning Solvent Remediation filed pursuant to this Part may, at the request of the owner of the property subject to the Notice of Dry-Cleaning Solvent Remediation, be canceled by the Secretary after the risk to public health and the environment associated with the dry-cleaning solvent contamination and any other contaminants included in the dry-cleaning solvent remediation agreement has been eliminated as a result of remediation of the property. The Secretary shall forward notice of cancellation to the register of deeds of the county or counties where the Notice of Dry-Cleaning Solvent Remediation is recorded and request that the Notice of Dry-Cleaning Solvent Remediation be canceled. The notice of cancellation shall contain the names of the landowners as shown in the Notice of Dry-Cleaning Solvent Remediation.

(f) Enforcement. - Any restriction on the current or future use of property subject to a Notice of Dry-Cleaning Solvent Remediation filed pursuant to this section shall be enforced by any owner of the property or by any other potentially responsible party. Any land-use restriction may also be enforced by the Commission through the remedies provided in this Part or by means of a civil action in the superior court. The Commission may enforce any land-use restriction without first having exhausted any available administrative remedies. Restrictions also may be enforced by any unit of local government having jurisdiction over any part of the property by means of a civil action without the unit of local government having first exhausted any available administrative remedy. A land-use restriction may also be enforced by any person eligible for liability protection under this Part who will lose liability protection if the land-use restriction is violated. A restriction shall not be declared unenforceable due to lack of privity of estate or contract, due to lack of benefit to particular land, or due to lack of privity of any property interest in particular land. Any person who owns or leases a property subject to a land-use restriction under this section shall abide by the land-use restriction. Failure to submit an annual certification that land-use restrictions are properly recorded and followed shall result in a notice from the Commission to the property owner. The notice shall inform the person of the actions that need to be taken in order for the person to come into compliance and specify a date by which the person must comply, which shall not be less than 30 calendar days from the date the notice is mailed. Any person who fails to comply within the time specified shall then be subject to enforcement procedures as provided in this Part.

(g)   Relation to Brownfields Notice. - Unless the Commission decertifies a previously certified facility or a previously certified abandoned site, this section shall apply in lieu of the provisions of Article 9 of Chapter 130A of the General Statutes and Parts 1 and 2 of Article 21A of Chapter 143 of the General Statutes for properties remediated under this Part. (1997-392, s. 1; 1997-443, s. 11A.119(b); 2007-530, s. 10; 2011-186, s. 6; 2012-18, s. 1.21.)

§ 143-215.104N. (Expires January 1, 2022 - see notes) Disbursement of dry-cleaning solvent assessment and remediation costs; limitations; cost recovery.

(a)   Allowable Costs. - To the extent monies are available in the Fund, the Commission shall pay for reasonable and necessary assessment and remediation activities at a contamination site associated with a certified facility or a certified abandoned site pursuant to a dry-cleaning solvent assessment agreement or dry-cleaning solvent remediation agreement for the following assessment and remediation response costs, for which appropriate documentation is submitted:

(1)   Costs of assessment with respect to dry-cleaning solvent contamination.

(2)   Costs of treatment or replacement of potable water supplies affected by the contamination.

(3)   Costs of remediation of affected soil, groundwater, surface waters, bedrock or other rock formations, or buildings.

(4)   Monitoring of the contamination.

(5)   Inspection and supervision of activities described in this subsection.

(6)   Reasonable costs of restoring property as nearly as practicable to the conditions that existed prior to activities associated with assessment and remediation conducted pursuant to this Part.

(7)   Other activities reasonably required to protect public health and the environment.

(b)   Limitations. - Notwithstanding subsection (a) of this section, the Commission shall not make any disbursement from the Fund:

(1)   For costs incurred in connection with facilities or abandoned sites not certified pursuant to G.S. 143-215.104G.

(2)   For costs not incurred pursuant to a dry-cleaning solvent assessment agreement or a dry-cleaning solvent remediation agreement.

(3)   Repealed by Session Laws 2007-530, s. 11, effective August 31, 2007.

(4)   For costs at a contamination site that has been identified by the United States Environmental Protection Agency as a federal Superfund site pursuant to 40 Code of Federal Regulations, Part 300 (1 July 1996 Edition), except that the Commission may authorize distribution of the required State match in an amount not to exceed two hundred thousand dollars ($200,000) per year per site. The Commission shall not delegate its authority to disburse funds pursuant to this subdivision.

(5)   For remediation beyond the level required under the Commission's risk-based criteria for determining the appropriate level of remediation.

(6)   For assessment or remediation response costs incurred in connection with any individual dry-cleaning solvent assessment agreement or dry-cleaning solvent remediation agreement in excess of five hundred thousand dollars ($500,000) per year. However, that the Commission may disburse up to one million dollars ($1,000,000) per year for assessment and remediation costs incurred in connection with a facility or an abandoned site if the facility or abandoned site has been certified and poses an imminent hazard.

(7)   That would result in a diminution of the Fund balance below one hundred thousand dollars ($100,000), unless an emergency exists in connection

with a dry-cleaning solvent contamination abandoned site that constitutes an imminent hazard.

(8)   For any costs incurred in connection with dry-cleaning solvent contamination from a facility located on a United States military base or owned by the United States or a department or agency of the United States.

(9)   For any costs incurred in connection with dry-cleaning solvent contamination from a facility or abandoned site owned by the State or a department or agency of the State, unless the contamination at the State-owned site was not caused by the State, but was caused by another person.

(c)   Repealed by Session Laws 2007-530, s. 11, effective August 31, 2007.

(d)   If, at any time, the Commission determines that the cost of assessment and remediation activities incurred pursuant to existing dry-cleaning solvent assessment agreements and dry-cleaning solvent remediation agreements equals or exceeds the total revenues expected to be credited to the Fund over the life of the Fund, the Commission shall publish notice of the determination in the North Carolina Register. Following the publication of a notice pursuant to this section, the Commission may continue to enter into dry-cleaning solvent assessment agreements and dry-cleaning solvent remediation agreements until the day of adjournment of the first regular session of the General Assembly that begins after the date the notice is published, but shall have no authority to enter into additional dry-cleaning solvent assessment agreements and dry-cleaning solvent remediation agreements after that date unless the Commission first determines either (i) that revenues will be available from the Fund to pay the costs of assessment and remediation activities expected to be incurred pursuant to the agreements, or (ii) that assessment and remediation activities undertaken pursuant to the agreements will be paid entirely from sources other than the Fund. For the purposes of this subsection, the term "day of adjournment" shall mean: (i) in the case of a regular session held in an odd-numbered year, the day the General Assembly adjourns by joint resolution for more than 10 days, and (ii) in the case of a regular session held in an even-numbered year, the day the General Assembly adjourns sine die.

(e)   If the cleanup of the contamination site is not completed through fault of the petitioner as required by the remediation agreement, the petitioner shall reimburse the Fund for any response costs previously disbursed from the fund for the cleanup, with interest. The Commission shall request the Attorney General to commence a civil action to secure repayment of response costs and interest of the costs. (1997-392, s. 1; 2000-19, ss. 12, 14(a), (b); 2007-530, s. 11; 2009-483, s. 4.)

§ 143-215.104O. (Expires January 1, 2022 - see notes) Remediation of uncertified sites.

(a) In the event the owner or operator of a facility or the current owner of an abandoned site cannot be identified or located, unreasonably refuses to enter into either an assessment agreement or remediation agreement or cannot be made to comply with the provisions of an assessment agreement or remediation agreement between the petitioner and the Commission, the Commission may direct the Department or a private contractor engaged by the Commission to use staff, equipment, or materials under the control of the Department or contractor or provided by other cooperating federal, State, or local agencies to develop and implement a plan for abatement of an imminent hazard, or to provide interim alternative sources of drinking water to third parties affected by dry-cleaning solvent contamination resulting from a release at the facility or abandoned site. The cost of any of these actions shall be paid from the Fund. The Department or private contractor shall keep a record of all expenses incurred for personnel and for the use of equipment and materials and all other expenses of developing and implementing the remediation plan.

(b) The Commission shall request the Attorney General to commence a civil action to secure reimbursement of costs incurred under this section.

(c) In the event a civil action is commenced pursuant to this Part to recover monies paid from the Fund, the Commission may recover, in addition to any amount due, the costs of the action, including reasonable attorneys' fees and investigation expenses. Any monies received or recovered as reimbursement shall be paid into the Fund or other source from which the expenditures were made. (1997-392, s. 1; 2000-19, s. 15.)

§ 143-215.104P. (Expires January 1, 2022 - see notes) Enforcement procedures; civil penalties.

(a) The Secretary may assess a civil penalty of not more than ten thousand dollars ($10,000) or, if the violation involves a hazardous waste, as defined in

G.S. 130-290, of not more than twenty-five thousand dollars ($25,000) against any person who:

(1) Repealed by Session Laws 2000, ch. 19, s. 3, effective on and after April 1, 1998.

(2) Engages in dry-cleaning operations using dry-cleaning solvent for which the appropriate sales or use tax has not been paid.

(3) Fails to comply with rules adopted by the Commission pursuant to this Part.

(4) Fails to file, submit, or make available, as the case may be, any documents, data, or reports required by this Part.

(5) Violates or fails to act in accordance with the terms, conditions, or requirements of any special order or other appropriate document issued pursuant to G.S. 143-215.2.

(6) Falsifies or tampers with any recording or monitoring device or method required to be operated or maintained under this Part or rules implementing this Part.

(7) Knowingly renders inaccurate any recording or monitoring device or method required to be operated or maintained under this Part or rules implementing this Part.

(8) Knowingly makes any false statement, representation, or certification in any application, record, report, plan, or other document filed or required to be maintained under this Part or rule implementing this Part.

(9) Knowingly makes a false statement of material fact in a rule-making proceeding or contested case under this Part.

(10) Refuses access to the Commission or its duly designated representative to any premises for purposes of conducting a lawful inspection provided for in this Part or rule implementing this Part.

(b) If any action or failure to act for which a penalty may be assessed under subsection (a) of this section is continuous, the Secretary may assess a penalty not to exceed ten thousand dollars ($10,000) per day or, if the violation involves a hazardous waste, as defined in G.S. 130-290, not exceed twenty-five thousand dollars ($25,000) per day. A penalty for a continuous violation shall not exceed two hundred thousand dollars ($200,000) for each period of 30 days during which the violation continues.

(c)   In determining the amount of the penalty, the Secretary shall consider the factors set out in G.S. 143B-282.1(b). The procedures set out in G.S. 143B-282.1 shall apply to civil penalty assessments that are presented to the Commission for final agency decision.

(d)   The Secretary shall notify any person assessed a civil penalty for the assessment and the specific reasons therefor by registered or certified mail or by any means authorized by G.S. 1A-1, Rule 4. Contested case petitions shall be filed pursuant to G.S. 150B-23 within 30 days of receipt of the notice of assessment.

(e)   Requests for remission of civil penalties shall be filed with the Secretary. Remission requests shall not be considered unless made within 30 days of receipt of the notice of assessment. Remission requests must be accompanied by a waiver of the right to a contested case hearing pursuant to Chapter 150B of the General Statutes and a stipulation of the facts on which the assessment was based. Consistent with the limitations in G.S. 143B-282.1(c) and (d), remission requests may be resolved by the Secretary and the violator. If the Secretary and the violator are unable to resolve the request, the Secretary shall deliver the remission request and the recommended action to the Committee on Civil Penalty Remissions of the Environmental Management Commission appointed pursuant to G.S. 143B-282.1(c).

(f)   If any civil penalty has not been paid within 30 days after notice of assessment has been served on the violator, the Secretary shall request the Attorney General to institute a civil action in the superior court of any county in which the violator resides or the violator's principal place of business is located in order to recover the amount of the assessment, unless the violator contests the assessment as provided in subsection (d) of this section or requests remission of the assessment in whole or in part as provided in subsection (e) of this section. If any civil penalty has not been paid within 30 days after the final agency decision or order has been served on the violator, the Secretary shall request the Attorney General to institute a civil action in the superior court of any county in which the violator resides or the violator's principal place of business is located to recover the amount of the assessment. A civil action must be filed within three years of the date the final agency decision or court order was served on the violator. (1997-392, s. 1; 2000-19, s. 3; 2011-398, s. 53.)

§ 143-215.104Q. (Expires January 1, 2022 - see notes) Enforcement procedures; criminal penalties.

(a) Any person who negligently commits any of the offenses set out in subdivisions (1) through (10) of G.S. 143-215.104P(a) shall be guilty of a Class 2 misdemeanor, which may include a fine not to exceed fifteen thousand dollars ($15,000) per day of violation, provided that the fine shall not exceed a cumulative total of two hundred thousand dollars ($200,000) for each period of 30 days during which a violation continues.

(b) Any person who knowingly and willfully commits any of the offenses set out in subdivisions (1) through (10) of G.S. 143-215.104P(a) shall be guilty of a Class I felony, which may include a fine not to exceed one hundred thousand dollars ($100,000) per day of violation, provided that this fine shall not exceed a cumulative total of five hundred thousand dollars ($500,000) for each period of 30 days during which the violation continues. For the purposes of this subsection, the phrase "knowingly and willfully" shall mean "intentionally and consciously" as the courts of this State, according to the principles of common law, interpret the phrase in the light of reason and experience.

(c) (1) Any person who knowingly commits any of the offenses set out in subdivisions (3) through (10) of G.S. 143-215.104P(a) and who knows at that time that he thereby places another person in imminent danger of death or serious bodily injury shall be guilty of a Class C felony, which may include a fine not to exceed two hundred fifty thousand dollars ($250,000) per day of violation, provided that this fine shall not exceed a cumulative total of one million dollars ($1,000,000) for each period of 30 days during which the violation continues.

(2) For the purposes of this subsection, a person's state of mind is knowing with respect to:

a. His conduct, if he is aware of the nature of his conduct.

b. An existing circumstance, if he is aware or believes that the circumstance exists.

c. A result of his conduct, if he is aware or believes that his conduct is substantially certain to cause danger of death or serious bodily injury.

(3) Under this subsection, the following should be considered in determining whether a defendant who is a natural person knew that his conduct placed another person in imminent danger of death or serious bodily injury:

a. The person is responsible only for actual awareness or actual belief that he possessed, and

b. Knowledge possessed by a person other than the defendant but not by the defendant himself may not be attributed to the defendant.

(4) It is an affirmative defense to a prosecution under this subsection that the conduct charged was conduct consented to by the person endangered and that the danger and conduct charged were reasonably foreseeable hazards of an occupation, a business or profession, or of medical treatment or medical or scientific experimentation conducted by professionally approved methods, and the person had been made aware of the risks involved prior to giving consent. The defendant may establish an affirmative defense under this subdivision by a preponderance of the evidence.

(d) No proceeding shall be brought or continued under this section for or on account of a violation by any person who has previously been convicted of a federal violation based upon the same set of facts.

(e) In proving the defendant's possession of actual knowledge, circumstantial evidence may be used, including evidence that the defendant took affirmative steps to shield himself from relevant information. Consistent with the principles of common law, the subjective mental state of defendants may be inferred from their conduct.

(f) For the purposes of the felony provisions of this section, a person's state of mind shall not be found "knowingly and willfully" or "knowingly" if the conduct that is the subject of the prosecution is the result of any of the following occurrences or circumstances:

(1) A natural disaster or other act of God that could not have been prevented or avoided by the exercise of due care or foresight.

(2) An act of third parties other than agents, employees, contractors, or subcontractors of the defendant.

(3) An act done in reliance on the written advice or emergency on-site direction of an employee of the Department. In emergencies, oral advice may be relied upon if written confirmation is delivered to the employee as soon as practicable after receiving and relying on the advice.

(4) An act causing no significant harm to the environment or risk to public health, safety, or welfare and done in compliance with other conflicting environmental requirements or other constraints imposed in writing by environmental agencies or officials after written notice is delivered to all relevant agencies that the conflict exists and will cause a violation of the identified standard.

(5) Violations causing no significant harm to the environment or risk to public health, safety, or welfare for which no enforcement action or civil penalty could have been imposed under any written civil enforcement guidelines in use by the Department at the time. This subdivision shall not be construed to require the Department to develop or use written civil enforcement guidelines.

(6) Occasional, inadvertent, short-term violations causing no significant harm to the environment or risk to public health, safety, or welfare. If the violation occurs within 30 days of a prior violation or lasts for more than 24 hours, it is not an occasional, short-term violation.

(g) All general defenses, affirmative defenses, and bars to prosecution that may apply with respect to other criminal offenses under law may apply to prosecutions brought under this section or other criminal statutes that refer to this section and shall be determined by the courts of this State according to the principles of common law as they may be applied in light of reason and experience. Concepts of justification and excuse applicable under this section may be developed in light of reason and experience.

(h) All general defenses, affirmative defenses, and bars to prosecution that may apply with respect to other criminal offenses under law may apply to prosecutions brought under this section or other criminal statutes that refer to this section and shall be determined by the courts of this State according to the principles of common law as they may be applied in light of reason and experience. Concepts of justification and excuse applicable under this section may be developed in light of reason and experience.

(i) For purposes of this section, the term "person" means, in addition to the definition contained in G.S. 143-212, any responsible corporate or public office or employee. If a vote of the people is required to effectuate the intent and purpose of this Article by a county, city, town, or other political subdivision of the State and the vote on the referendum is against the means or machinery for carrying out the intent and purpose, then this section shall not apply to elected officials or to any responsible appointed officials or employees of the county, city, town, or other political subdivision. (1997-392, s. 1.)

§ 143-215.104R. (Expires January 1, 2022 - see notes) Enforcement procedures; injunctive relief.

Whenever the Commission has reasonable cause to believe that any person has violated or is threatening to violate any of the provisions of this Part or rule implementing this Part, the Commission may, either before or after the institution of any other action or proceeding authorized by this Part, request the Attorney General to institute a civil action in the name of the State upon the relation of the Commission for injunctive relief to restrain the violation or threatened violation and for other and further relief in the premises as the court shall deem proper. The Attorney General may institute an action in the superior court of the county in which the violation occurred or may occur or, in the Attorney General's discretion, in the superior court of the county in which the person responsible for the violation or threatened violation resides or has a principal place of business. Upon a determination by the court that the alleged violation of the provisions of this Part or the rules of the Commission has occurred or is threatened, the court shall grant the relief necessary to prevent or abate the violation or threatened violation. Neither the institution of the action nor any of the proceedings thereon shall relieve any party to the proceedings from any penalty prescribed for violation of this Part. In the event a civil action is commenced pursuant to this section, the Commission may recover the costs of the action, including attorneys' fees and investigation expenses. All monies received or recovered shall be paid into the Fund or other source from which the expenditures were made. (1997-392, s. 1.)

§ 143-215.104S. (Expires January 1, 2022 - see notes) Appeals.

Any person who is aggrieved by a decision of the Commission under G.S. 143-215.104F through G.S. 143-215.104O may commence a contested case by filing a petition under G.S. 150B-23 within 60 days after the Commission's decision. If no contested case is initiated within the allotted time period, the Commission's decision shall be final and not subject to review. Notwithstanding the provisions of G.S. 6-19.1, no party seeking to compel remediation of dry-cleaning solvent contamination in excess of that required by a dry-cleaning solvent remediation agreement approved by the Commission shall be eligible to recover attorneys' fees. (1997-392, s. 1; 2000-19, s. 16; 2002-165, s. 1.5; 2011-398, s. 54.)

§ 143-215.104T. (Expires January 1, 2022 - see notes) Construction of this Part.

(a) This Part is not intended to and shall not be construed to:

(1) Affect the ability of local governments to regulate land use under Article 19 of Chapter 160A of the General Statutes and Article 18 of Chapter 153A of the General Statutes. The use of the identified contamination site and any land-use restrictions in the dry-cleaning solvent remediation agreement shall be consistent with local land-use controls adopted under those statutes.

(2) Amend, modify, repeal, or otherwise alter any provision of any remedial program or other provision of law relating to civil and criminal penalties or enforcement actions and remedies available to the Department, except as may be provided in a dry-cleaning solvent remediation agreement.

(3) Prevent or impede the immediate response of the Department or responsible party to an emergency that involves an imminent or actual release of a regulated substance that threatens public health or the environment.

(4) Relieve a person receiving liability protection under this Part from any liability for contamination later caused by that person at a facility or abandoned site.

(5) Affect the right of any person to seek any relief available against any party to the dry-cleaning solvent remediation agreement who may have liability with respect to the facility or abandoned site, except that this Part does limit the relief available against any party to a remediation agreement with respect to

assessment or remediation of the contamination site to the assessment remediation required under the remediation agreement.

(6)   Affect the right of any person who may have liability with respect to the facility or abandoned site to seek contribution from any other person who may have liability with respect to the facility or abandoned site and who neither received nor has liability protection under this Part.

(7)   Prevent the State from enforcing specific numerical remediation standards, monitoring, or compliance requirements specifically required to be enforced by the federal government as condition to receive program authorization, delegation, primacy, or federal funds.

(8)   Create a defense against the imposition of criminal and civil fines or penalties or administrative penalties otherwise authorized by law and imposed as the result of the illegal disposal of waste or from the pollution of the land, air, or waters of this State on a facility or abandoned site.

(9)   Relieve a person of any liability for failure to exercise due diligence and reasonable care in performing an environmental assessment or transaction screen.

(b)   Notwithstanding the provision of the Tort Claims Act, G.S. 143-291 through G.S. 143-300.1 or any other provision of law waiving the sovereign immunity of the State of North Carolina, the State, its agencies, officers, employees, and agents shall be absolutely immune from any liability in any proceeding for any injury or claim arising from negotiating, entering into, implementing, monitoring, or enforcing a dry-cleaning solvent assessment agreement, a dry-cleaning solvent remediation agreement, or a Notice of Dry-Cleaning Solvent Remediation under this Part or any other action implementing this Part. (1997-392, s. 1; 2007-530, s. 12.)

§ 143-215.104U. (Expires January 1, 2022 - see notes) Reporting requirements.

(a)   The Secretary shall present an annual report to the Environmental Review Commission that shall include at least the following:

(1)   A list of all dry-cleaning solvent contamination reported to the Department.

(2)   A list of all facilities and abandoned sites certified by the Commission and the status of contamination associated with each facility or abandoned site.

(3)   An estimate of the cost of assessment and remediation required in connection with facilities or abandoned sites certified by the Commission and an estimate of assessment and remediation costs expected to be paid from the Fund.

(4)   A statement of receipts and disbursements for the Fund.

(5)   A statement of all claims against the Fund, including claims paid, claims denied, pending claims, anticipated claims, and any other obligations.

(6)   The adequacy of the Fund to carry out the purposes of this Part together with any recommendations as to measures that may be necessary to assure the continued solvency of the Fund.

(b)   The Secretary shall make the annual report required by this section on or before 1 October of each year. (1997-392, s. 1.)

Article 21B.

Air Pollution Control.

§ 143-215.105. Declaration of policy; definitions.

The declaration of public policy set forth in G.S. 143-211, the definitions in G.S. 143-212, and the definitions in G.S. 143-213, applicable to the control and abatement of air pollution, shall be applicable to this Article. (1973, c. 821, s. 6; 1987, c. 827, s. 203.)

§ 143-215.106. Administration of air quality program.

The Department shall administer the air quality program of the State. (1973, c. 821, s. 6; c. 1262, s. 23; 1977, c. 771, s. 4; 1987, c. 827, s. 204.)

§ 143-215.106A. Assessments to establish Title V program.

(a)   The holders of permits issued by the Commission for the control of sources of air pollution are assessed Title V program implementation fees on an annual basis in accordance with the schedule established in this section. The assessments are in addition to any other fees required to be paid by the permit holders in conjunction with the permits. The assessments shall be credited to the Title V Account. The Secretary shall issue annual notices of the assessments to permit holders on or before 1 July of each fiscal year. Each notice of assessment shall include a summary of the data on which the assessment is based. Assessments shall be payable 30 days after receipt of notice. Failure to make timely payment within 90 days shall be grounds to revoke the permit and to institute a collection action against the permit holder by the Attorney General.

(b)   Assessments are made in accordance with the following schedule:

(1)   Sources emitting at least 100 tons and less than 500 tons per year, two thousand dollars ($2,000) for fiscal year 1991-92 and two thousand five hundred dollars ($2,500) for each year thereafter;

(2)   Sources emitting at least 500 tons and less than 1,000 tons per year, four thousand dollars ($4,000) for fiscal year 1991-92 and twelve thousand five hundred dollars ($12,500) for each year thereafter;

(3)   Sources emitting at least 1,000 tons and less than 5,000 tons per year, six thousand dollars ($6,000) for fiscal year 1991-92, and twenty-five thousand dollars ($25,000) for each year thereafter; and

(4)   Sources emitting at least 5,000 tons per year, six thousand dollars ($6,000) for fiscal year 1991-92, and one hundred thousand dollars ($100,000) for each year thereafter.

(c)   Notices of assessment shall not be issued for any fiscal year in which the permit fees for the Title V program adopted by the Commission pursuant to G.S. 143-215.3(a)(1d) are in effect. Should a Title V program permit fee become due and payable during a fiscal year when the permit holder has paid an assessment, the Title V program permit fee shall be reduced in an amount equal to the pro rata share of the assessment for the months remaining in the fiscal year. The pro rata share is determined by dividing the assessment into 12 equal parts and multiplying that sum by the number of months remaining in the fiscal year. (1991, c. 552, s. 10; 1991 (Reg. Sess., 1992), c. 1039, s. 17.)

§ 143-215.107. Air quality standards and classifications.

(a)   Duty to Adopt Plans, Standards, etc. - The Commission is hereby directed and empowered, as rapidly as possible within the limits of funds and facilities available to it, and subject to the procedural requirements of this Article and Article 21:

(1)   To prepare and develop, after proper study, a comprehensive plan or plans for the prevention, abatement and control of air pollution in the State or in any designated area of the State.

(2)   To determine by means of field sampling and other studies, including the examination of available data collected by any local, State or federal agency or any person, the degree of air contamination and air pollution in the State and the several areas of the State.

(3)   To develop and adopt, after proper study, air quality standards applicable to the State as a whole or to any designated area of the State as the Commission deems proper in order to promote the policies and purposes of this Article and Article 21 most effectively.

(4)   To collect information or to require reporting from classes of sources which, in the judgment of the Environmental Management Commission, may cause or contribute to air pollution. Any person operating or responsible for the operation of air contaminant sources of any class for which the Commission requires reporting shall make reports containing such information as may be required by the Commission concerning location, size, and height of contaminant outlets, processes employed, fuels used, and the nature and time periods or duration of emissions, and such other information as is relevant to air pollution and available or reasonably capable of being assembled.

(5) To develop and adopt emission control standards as in the judgment of the Commission may be necessary to prohibit, abate, or control air pollution commensurate with established air quality standards. The Department shall implement rules adopted pursuant to this subsection as follows:

a. Except as provided in sub-subdivision b. of this subdivision, rules adopted pursuant to this subdivision that control emissions of toxic air pollutants shall not apply to an air emission source that is any of the following:

1. Subject to an applicable requirement under 40 C.F.R. Part 61, as amended.

2. An affected source under 40 C.F.R. Part 63, as amended.

3. Subject to a case-by-case maximum achievable control technology (MACT) permit requirement issued by the Department pursuant to 42 U.S.C. § 7412(j), as amended.

b. Upon receipt of a permit application for a new source or facility, or for the modification of an existing source or facility, that would result in an increase in the emission of toxic air pollutants, the Department shall review the application to determine if the emission of toxic air pollutants from the source or facility would present an unacceptable risk to human health. Upon making a written finding that a source or facility presents or would present an unacceptable risk to human health, the Department shall require the owner or operator of the source or facility to submit a permit application for any or all emissions of toxic air pollutants from the facility that eliminates the unacceptable risk to human health. The written finding may be based on modeling, epidemiological studies, actual monitoring data, or other information that indicates an unacceptable health risk. When the Department requires the owner or operator of a source or facility to submit a permit application pursuant to this sub-subdivision, the Department shall report to the Chairs of the Environmental Review Commission on the circumstances surrounding the permit requirement, including a copy of the written finding.

(6) To adopt motor vehicle emissions standards; to adopt, when necessary and practicable, a motor vehicle emissions inspection and maintenance program to improve ambient air quality; to require manufacturers of motor vehicles to furnish to the Equipment and Tool Institute and, upon request and at a reasonable charge, to any person who maintains or repairs a motor vehicle, all information necessary to fully make use of the on-board diagnostic equipment

and the data compiled by that equipment; to certify to the Commissioner of Motor Vehicles that ambient air quality will be improved by the implementation of a motor vehicle emissions inspection and maintenance program in a county. The Commission shall implement this subdivision as provided in G.S. 143-215.107A.

(7) To develop and adopt standards and plans necessary to implement programs for the prevention of significant deterioration and for the attainment of air quality standards in nonattainment areas.

(8) To develop and adopt standards and plans necessary to implement programs to control acid deposition and to regulate the use of sulfur dioxide (SO2) allowances and oxides of nitrogen (NOx) emissions in accordance with Title IV and implementing regulations adopted by the United States Environmental Protection Agency.

(9) To regulate the content of motor fuels, as defined in G.S. 105-449.60, to require use of reformulated gasoline as the Commission determines necessary, to implement the requirements of Title II and implementing regulations adopted by the United States Environmental Protection Agency, and to develop standards and plans to implement this subdivision. Rules may authorize the use of marketable oxygen credits for gasoline as provided in federal requirements.

(10) To develop and adopt standards and plans necessary to implement requirements of the federal Clean Air Act and implementing regulations adopted by the United States Environmental Protection Agency.

(11) To develop and adopt economically feasible standards and plans necessary to implement programs to control the emission of odors from animal operations, as defined in G.S. 143-215.10B.

(12) To develop and adopt a program of incentives to promote voluntary reductions of emissions of air contaminants, including, but not limited to, emissions banking and trading and credit for voluntary early reduction of emissions.

(13) To develop and adopt rules governing the certification of persons who inspect vehicle-mounted tanks used to transport motor fuel and to require that inspection of these tanks be performed only by certified personnel.

(14) To develop and adopt rules governing the sale and service of mobile source exhaust emissions analyzers and to require that vendors of these analyzers provide adequate surety to purchasers for the performance of the vendor's contractual or other obligations related to the sale and service of analyzers.

(b) Criteria for Standards. - In developing air quality and emission control standards, motor vehicle emissions standards, motor vehicle emissions inspection and maintenance requirements, rules governing the content of motor fuels or requiring the use of reformulated gasoline, and other standards and plans to improve ambient air quality, the Commission shall consider varying local conditions and requirements and may prescribe uniform standards and plans throughout the State or different standards and plans for different counties or areas as may be necessary and appropriate to improve ambient air quality in the State or within a particular county or area, achieve attainment or preclude violations of state or national ambient air quality standards, meet other federal requirements, or achieve the purposes of this Article and Article 21.

(c) Chapter 150B of the General Statutes governs the adoption and publication of rules under this Article.

(d), (e) Repealed by Session Laws 1987, c. 827, s. 205.

(f), (g) Repealed by Session Laws 1995, c. 507, s. 27. (1973, c. 821, s. 6; c. 1262, s. 23; 1975, c. 784; 1979, c. 545, s. 1; c. 931; 1987, c. 827, ss. 154, 205; 1989, c. 132; c. 168, s. 48; 1991, c. 403, s. 3; c. 552, s. 9; c. 761, s. 40; 1991 (Reg. Sess., 1992), c. 889, s. 3; 1993, c. 400, s. 7; 1993 (Reg. Sess., 1994), c. 686, s. 6; 1995, c. 123, s. 9; c. 507, s. 27.8(s); 1997-458, s. 3.1; 1999-328, s. 3.12; 2000-134, s. 1; 2002-4, s. 3; 2002-165, s. 1.7; 2012-91, s. 1.)

§ 143-215.107A. Motor vehicle emissions testing and maintenance program.

(a) General Provisions. -

(1) G.S. 143-215.107(a)(6) shall be implemented as provided in this section.

(2) Motor vehicle emissions inspections shall be performed by a person who holds an emissions inspection mechanic license issued as provided in G.S.

20-183.4A(c) at a station that holds an emissions inspection station license issued under G.S. 20-183.4A(a) or at a place of business that holds an emissions self-inspector license issued as provided in G.S. 20-183.4A(d). Motor vehicle emissions inspections may be performed by a decentralized network of test-and-repair stations as described in 40 Code of Federal Regulations § 51.353 (1 July 1998 Edition). The Commission may not require that motor vehicle emissions inspections be performed by a network of centralized or decentralized test-only stations.

(b) Repealed by Session Laws 2000-134, s. 2, effective July 14, 2000.

(c) Counties Covered. - Motor vehicle emissions inspections shall be performed in the following counties: Alamance, Buncombe, Burke, Cabarrus, Caldwell, Catawba, Chatham, Cleveland, Cumberland, Davidson, Durham, Edgecombe, Forsyth, Franklin, Gaston, Granville, Guilford, Harnett, Haywood, Henderson, Iredell, Johnston, Lee, Lenoir, Lincoln, Mecklenburg, Moore, Nash, Orange, Pitt, Randolph, Robeson, Rockingham, Rowan, Rutherford, Stanly, Stokes, Surry, Union, Wake, Wayne, Wilkes and Wilson.

(d) Repealed by Session Laws 2012-200, s. 12(a), effective August 1, 2012. (1999-328, ss. 3.1, 3.3, 3.4, 3.5, 3.6, 3.7; 2000-134, ss. 2, 3; 2004-203, s. 5(l); 2012-200, s. 12(a).)

§ 143-215.107B. Statewide goals for reduction in emissions of oxides of nitrogen; report.

It shall be the goal of the State to reduce emissions of oxides of nitrogen (NOx) from all sources by at least twenty-five percent (25%) by 1 July 2009. It shall be the goal of the State to reduce the growth of vehicle miles traveled in the State by at least twenty-five percent (25%) of that growth that would otherwise occur by 1 July 2009. The Department of Environment and Natural Resources and the Department of Transportation shall evaluate progress toward achieving these goals in each fiscal year and shall report their findings and recommendations as to any measures that may be needed to achieve these goals to the Environmental Review Commission on or before 1 October of each year. (1999-328, s. 1.1; 2003-340, s. 1.7.)

§ 143-215.107C. State agency goals, plans, duties, and reports.

(a) As used in this section, alternative-fueled vehicle means a motor vehicle capable of operating on electricity; natural gas; propane; hydrogen; reformulated gasoline; ethanol; other alcohol fuels, separately or in mixtures of eighty-five percent (85%) or more of alcohol by volume; or fuels, other than alcohol, derived from biological materials. For purposes of this section, a vehicle that has been converted to operate on a fuel other than the fuel for which it was originally designed is not a new or replacement vehicle.

(b) It shall be the goal of the State that on and after 1 January 2004 at least seventy-five percent (75%) of the new or replacement light duty cars and trucks purchased by the State will be alternative-fueled vehicles or low emission vehicles. The Department of Administration, the Department of Transportation, and the Department of Environment and Natural Resources shall jointly develop a plan to achieve this goal and to fuel and maintain these vehicles. For purposes of this section, a light duty car or truck is one that is rated at 8,500 pounds or less Gross Vehicle Weight Rating (GVWR).

(c) Repealed by Session Laws 2006-79, s. 13, effective July 10, 2006.

(d) The Department of Administration, the Office of State Human Resources, the Department of Transportation, and the Department of Environment and Natural Resources shall jointly develop and periodically update a plan to reduce vehicle miles traveled by State employees and vehicle emissions resulting from job-related travel, including commuting to and from work. The plan shall consider the use of carpooling, vanpooling, public transportation, incentives, and other appropriate strategies. The Department of Transportation shall report on the development and implementation of the plan to the Joint Legislative Transportation Oversight Committee and the Environmental Review Commission on or before 1 October of each year beginning 1 October 2000.

(e) The Department of Transportation, the Department of Commerce, and the Department of Environment and Natural Resources shall jointly develop and periodically update a plan to reduce vehicle miles traveled by private sector employees and vehicle emissions resulting from job-related travel, including commuting to and from work. The plan shall consider the use of incentives for both private sector employees and employers to promote carpooling, vanpooling, use of public transportation, and other appropriate strategies. The Department of Transportation shall report on the development and implementation of the plan to the Joint Legislative Transportation Oversight

Committee and the Environmental Review Commission on or before 1 October of each year beginning 1 October 2000.

(f) The Office of State Human Resources shall implement a policy that promotes teleworkelecommuting for State employees as recommended by the report of the State Auditor entitled "Establishing a Formal Teleworkelecommuting Program for State Employees" and dated October 1997. It shall be the goal of the State to reduce State employee vehicle miles traveled in commuting by twenty percent (20%) without reducing total work hours or productivity. (1999-328, ss. 4.1, 4.2, 4.5, 4.6, 4.7, 4.8; 2004-195, s. 2.4; 2005-386, s. 2.2; 2006-79, s. 13; 2013-382, s. 9.1(c).)

§ 143-215.107D. Emissions of oxides of nitrogen (NOx) and sulfur dioxide (SO2) from certain coal-fired generating units.

(a) As used in this section:

(1) "Coal-fired generating unit" means a coal-fired generating unit, as defined by 40 Code of Federal Regulations § 96.2 (1 July 2001 Edition), that is located in this State and has the capacity to generate 25 or more megawatts of electricity.

(2) "Investor-owned public utility" means an investor-owned public utility, as defined in G.S. 62-3.

(b) An investor-owned public utility that owns or operates coal-fired generating units that collectively emitted more than 75,000 tons of oxides of nitrogen (NOx) in calendar year 2000:

(1) Shall not collectively emit from the coal-fired generating units that it owns or operates more than 35,000 tons of oxides of nitrogen (NOx) in any calendar year beginning 1 January 2007.

(2) Shall not collectively emit from the coal-fired generating units that it owns or operates more than 31,000 tons of oxides of nitrogen (NOx) in any calendar year beginning 1 January 2009.

(c) An investor-owned public utility that owns or operates coal-fired generating units that collectively emitted 75,000 tons or less of oxides of nitrogen (NOx) in calendar year 2000 shall not collectively emit from the coal-fired generating units that it owns or operates more than 25,000 tons of oxides of nitrogen (NOx) in any calendar year beginning 1 January 2007.

(d)   An investor-owned public utility that owns or operates coal-fired generating units that collectively emitted more than 225,000 tons of sulfur dioxide (SO2) in calendar year 2000:

(1)   Shall not collectively emit from the coal-fired generating units that it owns or operates more than 150,000 tons of sulfur dioxide (SO2) in any calendar year beginning 1 January 2009.

(2)   Shall not collectively emit from the coal-fired generating units that it owns or operates more than 80,000 tons of sulfur dioxide (SO2) in any calendar year beginning 1 January 2013.

(e)   An investor-owned public utility that owns or operates coal-fired generating units that collectively emitted 225,000 tons or less of sulfur dioxide (SO2) in calendar year 2000:

(1)   Shall not collectively emit from the coal-fired generating units that it owns or operates more than 100,000 tons of sulfur dioxide (SO2) in any calendar year beginning 1 January 2009.

(2)   Shall not collectively emit from the coal-fired generating units that it owns or operates more than 50,000 tons of sulfur dioxide (SO2) in any calendar year beginning 1 January 2013.

(f)   Each investor-owned public utility to which this section applies may determine how it will achieve the collective emissions limitations imposed by this section. Compliance with the emissions limitations set out in this section does not alter the obligation of any person to comply with any other federal or State law, regulation, or rule related to air quality or visibility. This subsection shall not be construed to limit the authority of the Commission to impose specific limitations on the emission of oxides of nitrogen (NOx) and sulfur dioxide (SO2) from an individual coal-fired generating unit owned or operated by an investor-owned public utility.

(g)   A coal-fired generating unit that is subject to the collective emissions limitations set out in this section on 1 July 2002 shall remain subject to the collective emissions limitations whether or not it thereafter continues to be owned or operated by an investor-owned public utility.

(h) The Commission shall require that any permit or modified permit issued for a coal-fired generating unit that is subject to this section include conditions that provide for testing, monitoring, record keeping, and reporting adequate to assure compliance with the requirements of this section.

(i) The Governor may enter into an agreement with an investor-owned public utility under which the investor-owned public utility voluntarily agrees to transfer to the State any emissions allowances acquired or that may be acquired by the investor-owned public utility pursuant to 42 U.S.C. §§ 7651-7651o, as implemented by 40 Code of Federal Regulations §§ 73.1 through 73.90 (1 July 2001 Edition); 42 U.S.C. 7410(a)(2)(D)(i)(I), as implemented by 40 Code of Federal Regulations § 51.121 (1 July 2001 Edition), related federal regulations, and the associated State Implementation Plan; 42 U.S.C. § 7426, as implemented by 40 Code of Federal Regulations § 52.34 (1 July 2001 Edition) and related federal regulations; or any similar program established under federal law that result from compliance with the emissions limitations set out in this section. An agreement entered into pursuant to this subsection shall be binding and shall be enforceable by specific performance. If the Governor enters into an agreement that provides for the transfer of emissions allowances to the State, the Governor shall file verified copies of the agreement with the Attorney General, the Secretary of State, the State Treasurer, the Secretary of Environment and Natural Resources, and the Utilities Commission. The State Treasurer shall hold all emissions allowances that are transferred to the State as provided in this subsection in trust for the people of this State and shall sell, trade, transfer, or otherwise dispose of the emissions allowances only as the General Assembly shall provide by law.

(j) An investor-owned public utility that is subject to the emissions limitations set out in this section shall submit to the Utilities Commission and to the Department on or before 1 April of each year a verified statement pursuant to subsection (i) of G.S. 62-133.6. (2002-4, s. 1.)

§ 143-215.108. Control of sources of air pollution; permits required.

(a) Except as provided in subsections (a1) and (a2) of this section, no person shall do any of the following things or carry out any of the following activities that contravene or will be likely to contravene standards established pursuant to G.S. 143-215.107 or set out in G.S. 143-215.107D unless that person has obtained a permit for the activity from the Commission and has complied with any conditions of the permit:

(1)   Establish or operate any air contaminant source, except as provided in G.S. 143-215.108A.

(2)   Build, erect, use, or operate any equipment that may result in the emission of an air contaminant or that is likely to cause air pollution, except as provided in G.S. 143-215.108A.

(3)   Alter or change the construction or method of operation of any equipment or process from which air contaminants are or may be emitted.

(4)   Repealed by Session Laws 2003-428, s. 1, effective August 19, 2003.

(a1)   The Commission may by rule establish procedures that meet the requirements of section 502(b)(10) of Title V (42 U.S.C. § 7661a(b)(10)) and 40 Code of Federal Regulations § 70.4(b) (12) (1 July 1993 Edition) to allow a permittee to make changes within a permitted facility without requiring a revision of the permit.

(a2)   The Commission may adopt rules that provide for a minor modification of a permit. At a minimum, rules that provide for a minor modification of a permit shall meet the requirements of 40 Code of Federal Regulations § 70.7(e)(2) (1 July 1993 Edition). If the Commission adopts rules that provide for a minor modification of a permit, a permittee shall not make a change in the permitted facility while the application for the minor modification is under review unless the change is authorized under the rules adopted by the Commission.

(b)   The Commission shall act upon all applications for permits so as to effectuate the purposes of this Article by reducing existing air pollution and preventing, so far as reasonably possible, any increased pollution of the air from any additional or enlarged sources.

(c)   The Commission shall have the power:

(1)   To grant and renew a permit with any conditions attached that the Commission believes necessary to achieve the purposes of this Article or the

requirements of the Clean Air Act and implementing regulations adopted by the United States Environmental Protection Agency;

(2) To grant and renew any temporary permit for such period of time as the Commission shall specify even though the action allowed by such permit may result in pollution or increase pollution where conditions make such temporary permit essential;

(3) To terminate, modify, or revoke and reissue any permit upon not less than 60 days' written notice to any person affected;

(3a) To suspend any permit pursuant to the provisions of G.S. 150B-3(c);

(4) To require all applications for permits and renewals to be in writing and to prescribe the form of such applications;

(5) To request such information from an applicant and to conduct such inquiry or investigation as it may deem necessary and to require the submission of plans and specifications prior to acting on any application for a permit;

(5a) To require that an applicant satisfy the Department that the applicant, or any parent, subsidiary, or other affiliate of the applicant or parent:

a. Is financially qualified to carry out the activity for which a permit is required under subsection (a); and

b. Has substantially complied with the air quality and emission control standards applicable to any activity in which the applicant has previously engaged, and has been in substantial compliance with federal and state laws, regulations, and rules for the protection of the environment.

As used in this subdivision, the words "affiliate," "parent," and "subsidiary" have the same meaning as in 17 Code of Federal Regulations 240.12b-2 (1 April 1990 Edition);

(6) To adopt rules, as it deems necessary, establishing the form of applications and permits and procedures for the granting or denial of permits and renewals pursuant to this section; and all permits, renewals and denials shall be in writing;

(7) To prohibit any stationary source within the State from emitting any air pollutant in amounts that will prevent attainment or maintenance by any other state of any national ambient air quality standard or that will interfere with measures required to be included in the applicable implementation plan for any other state to prevent deterioration of air quality or protect visibility; and

(8) To designate certain classes of activities for which a general permit may be issued, after considering the environmental impact of an activity, the frequency of the activity, the need for individual permit oversight, and the need for public review and comment on individual permits.

(d) (1) The Commission may conduct any inquiry or investigation it considers necessary before acting on an application and may require an applicant to submit plans, specifications, and other information the Commission considers necessary to evaluate the application. A permit application may not be deemed complete unless it is accompanied by a copy of the request for determination as provided in subsection (f) of this section that bears a date of receipt entered by the clerk of the local government and until the 15-day period for issuance of a determination has elapsed.

(2) The Commission shall adopt rules specifying the times within which it must act upon applications for permits required by Title V and other permits required by this section. The times specified shall be extended for the period during which the Commission is prohibited from issuing a permit under subdivisions (3) and (4) of this subsection. The Commission shall inform a permit applicant as to whether or not the application is complete within the time specified in the rules for action on the application. If the Commission fails to act on an application for a permit required by Title V or this section within the time period specified, the failure to act on the application constitutes a final agency decision to deny the permit. A permit applicant, permittee, or other person aggrieved, as defined in G.S. 150B-2, may seek judicial review of a failure to act on the application as provided in G.S. 143-215.5 and Article 4 of Chapter 150B of the General Statutes. Notwithstanding the provisions of G.S. 150B-51, upon review of a failure to act on an application for a permit required by Title V or this section, a court may either: (i) affirm the denial of the permit or (ii) remand the application to the Commission for action upon the application within a specified time.

(3) If the Administrator of the United States Environmental Protection Agency validly objects to the issuance of a permit required by Title V within 45 days after the Administrator receives the proposed permit and the required

portions of the permit application, the Commission shall not issue the permit until the Commission revises the proposed permit to meet all objections noted by the Administrator or otherwise satisfies all objections consistent with Title V and implementing regulations adopted by the United States Environmental Protection Agency.

(4)   If the Administrator of the United States Environmental Protection Agency validly objects to the issuance of a permit required by Title V after the expiration of the 45-day review period specified in subdivision (3) of this subsection as a result of a petition filed pursuant to section 505(b)(2) of Title V (42 U.S.C. § 7661d(b)(2)) and prior to the issuance of the permit by the Commission, the Commission shall not issue the permit until the Commission revises the proposed permit to meet all objections noted by the Administrator or otherwise satisfies all objections consistent with Title V and implementing regulations adopted by the United States Environmental Protection Agency.

(d1)   No Title V permit issued pursuant to this section shall be issued or renewed for a term exceeding five years. All other permits issued pursuant to this section shall be issued for a term of eight years.

(e)   A permit applicant, permittee, or third party who is dissatisfied with a decision of the Commission may commence a contested case by filing a petition under G.S. 150B-23 within 30 days after the Commission notifies the applicant or permittee of its decision. If the permit applicant, permittee, or third party does not file a petition within the required time, the Commission's decision on the application is final and is not subject to review.

(f)   An applicant for a permit under this section for a new facility or for the expansion of a facility permitted under this section shall request each local government having jurisdiction over any part of the land on which the facility and its appurtenances are to be located to issue a determination as to whether the local government has in effect a zoning or subdivision ordinance applicable to the facility and whether the proposed facility or expansion would be consistent with the ordinance. The request to the local government shall be accompanied by a copy of the draft permit application and shall be delivered to the clerk of the local government personally or by certified mail. The determination shall be verified or supported by affidavit signed by the official designated by the local government to make the determination and, if the local government states that the facility is inconsistent with a zoning or subdivision ordinance, shall include a copy of the ordinance and the specific reasons for the determination of inconsistency. A copy of any such determination shall be provided to the applicant when it is submitted to the Commission. The Commission shall not act upon an application for a permit under this section until it has received a determination from each local government requested to make a determination by the applicant. If a local government determines that the new facility or the expansion of an existing facility is inconsistent with a zoning or subdivision ordinance, and unless the local government makes a subsequent determination of consistency with all ordinances cited in the determination or the proposed facility is determined by a court of competent jurisdiction to be consistent with the cited ordinances, the Commission shall attach as a condition of the permit a requirement that the applicant, prior to construction or operation of the facility under the permit, comply with all lawfully adopted local ordinances, including those cited in the determination, that apply to the facility at the time of construction or operation of the facility. If a local government fails to submit a determination to the Commission as provided by this subsection within 15 days after receipt of the request, the Commission may proceed to consider the permit application without regard to local zoning and subdivision ordinances. This subsection shall not be construed to affect the validity of any lawfully adopted franchise, local zoning, subdivision, or land-use planning ordinance or to affect the responsibility of any person to comply with any lawfully adopted franchise, local zoning, subdivision, or land-use planning ordinance. This subsection shall not be construed to limit any opportunity a local government may have to comment on a permit application under any other law or rule. This subsection shall not apply to any facility with respect to which local ordinances are subject to review under either G.S. 104E-6.2 or G.S. 130A-293.

(g)   Any person who is required to hold a permit under this section shall submit to the Department a written description of his current and projected plans to reduce the emission of air contaminants under such permit by source reduction or recycling. The written description shall accompany the payment of the annual permit fee. The written description shall also accompany any application for a new permit, or for modification of an existing permit, under this section. The written description required by this subsection shall not be considered part of a permit application and shall not serve as the basis for the denial of a permit or permit modification.

(h)   Expedited Review of Applications Certified by a Professional Engineer. - The Commission shall adopt rules governing the submittal of permit applications certified by a professional engineer, including draft permits, that can be sent to public notice and hearing upon receipt and subjected to technical review by personnel within the Department. These rules shall specify, at a minimum, any forms to be used; a checklist for applicants that lists all items of information required to prepare a complete permit application; the form of the certification required on the application by a professional engineer; and the information that must be included in the draft permit. The Department shall process an application that is certified by a professional engineer as provided in subdivisions (1) through (7) of this subsection.

(1)   Initiation of Review. Upon receipt of an application certified by a professional engineer in accordance with this subsection and the rules adopted pursuant to this subsection, the Department shall determine whether the application is complete as provided in subdivision (2) of this subsection. Within 30 days after the date on which an application is determined to be complete, the Department shall:

a.   Publish any required notices, using the draft permit included with the application;

b.   Schedule any required public meetings or hearings on the application and permit; and

c.   Initiate any and all technical review of the application in a manner to ensure substantial completion of the technical review by the time of any public hearing on the application, or if there is no hearing, by the close of the notice period.

(2)   Completeness Review. Within 10 working days of receipt of the permit application certified by a professional engineer under this subsection, the Department shall determine whether the application is complete for purposes of this subsection. The Department shall determine whether the permit application certified by a professional engineer is complete by comparing the information provided in the application with the checklist contained in the rules adopted by the Commission pursuant to this subsection.

a.   If the application is not complete, the Department shall promptly notify the applicant in writing of all deficiencies of the application, specifying the items that need to be included, modified, or supplemented in order to make the application complete, and the 10-day time period is suspended after this request for further information. If the applicant submits the requested information within the time specified, the 10-day time period shall begin again on the day the additional information was submitted. If the additional information is not submitted within the time periods specified, the Department shall return the application to the applicant, and the applicant may treat the return of the application as a denial of the application or may resubmit the application at a later time.

b. If the Department fails to notify the applicant that an application is not complete within the time period set forth in this subsection, the application shall be deemed to be complete.

(3) Time for Permit Decision. For any application found to be complete under subdivision (2) of this subsection, the Department shall issue a permit decision within 30 days of the last day of any public hearing on the application, or if there is no hearing, within 30 days of the close of the notice period.

(4) Rights if Permit Decision Not Made in Timely Fashion. If the Department fails to issue a permit decision within the time periods specified in subdivision (3) of this subsection, the applicant may:

a. Take no action, thereby consenting to the continued review of the application; or

b. Treat the failure to issue a permit decision as a denial of the application and appeal the denial as provided in subdivision (2) of subsection (d) of this section.

(5) Power to Halt Review. At any time after the permit application certified by a professional engineer has been determined to be complete under subdivision (2) of this subsection, the Department may immediately terminate review of that application, including technical review and any hearings or meetings scheduled on the application, upon a determination of one of the following:

a. The permit application is not in substantial compliance with the applicable rules; or

b. The applicant failed to pay all permit application fees.

(6) Rights if Review Halted. If the Department terminates review of an application under subdivision (5) of this subsection, the applicant may take any of the following actions:

a. Revise and resubmit the application; or

b. Treat the action as a denial of the application and appeal the denial under Article 3 of Chapter 150B of the General Statutes.

(7) Option; No Additional Fee. The submittal of a permit application certified by a professional engineer to be considered under this subsection shall be an option and shall not be required of any applicant. The Department shall not impose any additional fees for the receipt or processing of a permit application certified by a professional engineer.

(i) Rules for Review of Applications Other Than Those Certified by a Professional Engineer. - The Commission shall adopt rules governing the times of review for all permit applications submitted pursuant to this section other than those certified by a professional engineer pursuant to subsection (h) of this section. Those rules shall specify maximum times for, among other things, the following actions in reviewing the permit applications covered by this subsection:

(1) Determining that the permit application is complete;

(2) Requesting additional information to determine completeness;

(3) Determining that additional information is needed to conduct a technical review of the application;

(4) Completing all technical review of the permit application;

(5) Holding and completing all public meetings and hearings required for the application;

(6) Completing the record from reviewing and acting on the application; and

(7) Taking final action on the permit, including granting or denying the application. (1973, c. 821, s. 6; c. 1262, s. 23; 1979, c. 545, ss. 2, 3; 1987, c. 461, s. 2; c. 827, ss. 154, 206; 1989, c. 168, s. 30; c. 492; 1989 (Reg. Sess., 1990), c. 1037, s. 2; 1991, c. 552, s. 5; c. 629, s. 1; c. 761, s. 27(a)-(c); 1993, c. 400, s. 8; 1995, c. 484, s. 2; 1995 (Reg. Sess., 1996), c. 728, s. 1; 2002-4, s. 2; 2003-340, s. 1.8(b); 2003-428, ss. 1, 2; 2011-398, s. 60(a); 2013-413, s. 29.)

§ 143-215.108A. Control of sources of air pollution; construction of new facilities; alteration or expansion of existing facilities.

(a) New Facilities. - A person may not, without obtaining a permit under G.S. 143-215.108, construct or operate an air contaminant source, equipment, or associated air cleaning device at a site or facility where, at the time of the construction, there is no other air contaminant source, equipment, or associated air cleaning device for which a permit is required under G.S. 143-215.108. A person may, however, undertake the following activities prior to obtaining a permit if the person complies with the requirements of this section:

(1) Clearing and grading.

(2) Construction of access roads, driveways, and parking lots.

(3) Construction and installation of underground pipe work, including water, sewer, electric, and telecommunications utilities.

(4) Construction of ancillary structures, including fences and office buildings, that are not a necessary component of an air contaminant source, equipment, or associated air cleaning device for which a permit is required under G.S. 143-215.108.

(b) Permitted Facilities. - A person who holds a permit under G.S. 143-215.108 may apply to the Commission for a modification of the permit to allow the person to alter or expand the physical arrangement or operation of an air contaminant source, equipment, or associated air cleaning device in a manner that alters the emission of air contaminants. The permittee may not operate the altered, expanded, or additional air contaminant source, equipment, or associated air cleaning device in a manner that alters the emission of any air contaminant without obtaining a permit modification under G.S. 143-215.108. A permittee may, however, alter or expand the physical arrangement or operation of an air contaminant source, equipment, or associated air cleaning device at a facility permitted under G.S. 143-215.108 if the permittee complies with the requirements of this section. At least 15 days prior to commencing alteration or expansion under this subsection, the permittee shall give notice by publication and shall submit to the Commission a notice of the permittee's intent to alter or expand the physical arrangement or operation of an air contaminant source, equipment, or associated air cleaning device. Notice by publication shall be in a newspaper having general circulation in the county or counties where the facility is to be located; shall be at the permittee's own expense; shall include a statement that written comment may be submitted to the Commission, that the Commission will consider any comment that it receives, and the Commission's address for submission of written comment; and shall include all the information required by subdivisions (1) through (6) of this subsection. The permittee shall submit a proof of publication of the notice to the Commission within 15 days of the date of publication. The notice of intent to the Commission shall include all of the following:

(1)   The name and location of the facility and the name and address of the permittee.

(2)   The permit number of each permit issued under G.S. 143-215.108 for the facility.

(3)   The nature of the air contaminant sources and equipment associated with the proposed modification of the permit.

(4)   An estimate of total regulated air contaminant emissions associated with the proposed modification of the permit.

(5)   The air cleaning devices that are to be employed to address each of the air contaminant sources associated with the modification of the permit.

(6)   The schedule for alteration or expansion of the facility associated with the proposed modification of the permit.

(7)   An acknowledgment by the permittee that the air contaminant sources, equipment, and associated air cleaning devices may not be operated in a manner that alters the emission of any air contaminant until the permittee has obtained a modified permit under G.S. 143-215.108.

(8)   An acknowledgment by the permittee that any alteration or expansion of the physical arrangement or operation of an air contaminant source, equipment, or associated air cleaning device prior to the modification of a permit under G.S. 143-215.108 is undertaken at the permittee's own risk and with the knowledge that the permittee may be denied a modification of the permit under G.S. 143-215.108 without regard to the permittee's financial investment or alteration or expansion of the facility.

(9)   A certification under oath that all of the information contained in the notice of intent is complete and accurate to the best of the permittee's knowledge and ability, executed by the permittee or, if the permittee is a corporation, by the appropriate officers of the corporation.

(c) Review and Determination by the Commission. -

(1) Upon receipt of a complete notice of intent required under subsection (b) of this section, the Commission shall determine whether:

a. The permittee is and has been in substantial compliance with other permits issued the permittee.

b. The facility will be altered or expanded so that it will be used for either the same or a similar use as the use already permitted.

c. The alteration or expansion will not result in a disproportionate increase in the size of the facility already permitted.

d. The alteration or expansion will result in the same or substantially similar emissions as that of the facility already permitted.

e. The alteration or expansion will not have a significant effect on air quality.

f. The Commission is likely to issue the permit modification.

(2) Within 15 days after the Commission receives a complete notice of intent required under subsection (b) of this section, the Commission shall notify the permittee of its determination as to whether each of the conditions set out in subdivision (1) of this subsection has or has not been met. If the Commission finds that all of the conditions have been met, the notice shall state that the alteration or expansion of the physical arrangement or operation of an air contaminant source, equipment, or associated air cleaning device may begin. If the Commission finds that one or more of the conditions has not been met, the notice shall state that the alteration or expansion of the physical arrangement or operation of an air contaminant source, equipment, or associated air cleaning device may not begin.

(d) Order to Cease Construction, Alteration, or Expansion. - If at any time during the construction, alteration, or expansion of the physical arrangement or operation of an air contaminant source, equipment, or associated air cleaning device, the Commission determines that the permittee will not qualify for a permit or permit modification under G.S. 143-215.108, the Commission may order that the construction, alteration, or expansion cease until the Commission makes a decision on the application for a permit or permit modification. If the

Commission orders that construction, alteration, or expansion cease, then construction, alteration, or expansion may resume only if the Commission either makes a subsequent determination that the circumstances that resulted in the order to cease construction, alteration, or expansion have been adequately addressed or if the Commission issues a permit or permit modification under G.S. 143-215.108 that authorizes construction, alteration, or expansion to resume.

(e) Evaluation of Permit Applications; Administrative and Judicial Review of Permit Decisions. - The Commission shall evaluate an application for a permit or permit modification under G.S. 143-215.108 and make its decision on the same basis as if the construction, alteration, or expansion allowed under this section had not occurred. The Commission shall consider any written comment that it receives in response to a notice by publication given pursuant to subsection (b) of this section. No evidence regarding any contract entered into, financial investment made, construction, alteration, or expansion undertaken, or economic loss incurred by any person or permittee who proceeds under this section without first obtaining a permit under G.S. 143-215.108 is admissible in any contested case or judicial proceeding involving any permit required under G.S. 143-215.108. No evidence as to any determination or order by the Commission pursuant to subsection (c) or (d) of this section shall be admissible in any contested case or judicial proceeding related to any permit required under G.S. 143-215.108.

(f) State, Commission, and Employees Not Liable. - Every person, permittee, and owner of a facility who proceeds under this section shall hold the State, the Commission, and the officials, agents, and employees of the State and the Commission harmless and not liable for any loss resulting from any contract entered into, financial investment made, construction, alteration, or expansion undertaken, or economic loss incurred by any person, permittee, or owner of any facility pursuant to this section.

(g) Local Zoning Ordinances Not Affected. - This section shall not be construed to affect the validity of any lawfully adopted franchise, local zoning, subdivision, or land-use planning ordinance or to affect the responsibility of any person to comply with any lawfully adopted franchise, local zoning, subdivision, or land-use planning ordinance.

(h) Compliance With Other State Laws Not Affected. - This section does not relieve any person of the obligation to comply with any other requirement of State law, including any requirement to obtain any other permit or approval prior to undertaking any activity associated with preparation of the site or the alteration or expansion of the physical arrangement or operation of an air contaminant source, equipment, or associated air cleaning device at a facility for which a permit is required under G.S. 143-215.108.

(i)   Federal Air Quality Programs Not Affected. - This section does not relieve any person from any preconstruction or construction prohibition imposed by any federal requirement, federal delegation, federally approved requirement in any State Implementation Plan, or federally approved requirement under the Title V permitting program, as determined solely by the Commission or by a local air pollution control program certified by the Commission as provided in G.S. 143-215.112. This section does not apply to any construction, alteration, or expansion that is subject to requirements for prevention of significant deterioration or federal nonattainment new source review, as determined solely by the Commission or by a local air pollution control program certified by the Commission as provided in G.S. 143-215.112. This section does not apply if it is inconsistent with any federal requirement, federal delegation, federally approved requirement in any State Implementation Plan, or federally approved requirement under the Title V permitting program, as determined solely by the Commission or by a local air pollution control program certified by the Commission as provided in G.S. 143-215.112.

(j)   Fee. - A permittee who submits a notice of intent under subsection (b) of this section shall pay a fee of two hundred dollars ($200.00) for each notice of intent submitted to cover a portion of the administrative costs of implementing this section. (2003-428, s. 3.)

§ 143-215.109. Control of complex sources.

(a)   The Commission may by rule establish criteria for controlling the effects of complex sources on air quality. The rules shall set forth such basic minimum criteria or standards under which the Commission shall approve or disapprove any such construction or modification. The rules shall further provide for the submission of plans, specifications and such other information as may be necessary for the review and evaluation of proposed or modified complex sources.

(b)   If the Commission shall determine that the construction or modification of any complex sources will result in a violation of ambient air quality standards or interfere with the attainment of such standards in any area where an air pollution abatement control program has been established, the Commission shall have authority to disapprove such construction or modification or to approve such construction or modification under such conditions as the Commission shall deem necessary or appropriate.

(c)   Repealed by Session Laws 1987, c. 827, s. 207. (1973, c. 821, s. 6; c. 1262, s. 23; 1987, c. 827, ss. 154, 207; 2013-413, s. 27.)

§ 143-215.110. Special orders.

(a)   Issuance. - The Commission is hereby empowered, after the effective date of standards and classifications adopted pursuant to G.S. 143-215.107, to issue (and from time to time to modify or revoke) a special order or other appropriate instrument, to any person whom it finds responsible for causing or contributing to any pollution of the air within the area for which standards have been established. Such an order or instrument may direct such person to take or refrain from taking such action, or to achieve such results, within a period of time specified by such special order, as the Commission deems necessary and feasible in order to alleviate or eliminate such pollution. The Commission is authorized to enter into consent special orders, assurances of voluntary compliance or other similar documents by agreement with the person responsible for pollution of the air, subject to the provisions of subsection (a1) of this section regarding proposed orders, and such consent order, when entered into by the Commission after public review, shall have the same force and effect as a special order of the Commission issued pursuant to hearing.

(a1)   Public Notice and Review of Consent Orders.

(1)   The Commission shall give notice of a proposed consent order to the proper State, interstate, and federal agencies, to interested persons, and to the public. The Commission may also provide any other data it considers appropriate to those notified. The Commission shall prescribe the form and content of the notice. The notice shall be given at least 45 days prior to any final action regarding the consent order. Public notice shall be given by publication of the notice one time in a newspaper having general circulation within the county in which the pollution originates.

(2) Any person who desires a public meeting on any proposed consent order may request one in writing to the Commission within 30 days following date of the notice of the proposed consent order. The Commission shall consider all such requests for meetings. If the Commission determines that there is significant public interest in holding a meeting, the Commission shall schedule a meeting and shall give notice of such meeting at least 30 days in advance to all persons to whom notice of the proposed consent order was given and to any other person requesting notice. At least 30 days prior to the date of meeting, the Commission shall also have a copy of the notice of the meeting published at least one time in a newspaper having general circulation within the county in which the pollution originates. The Commission shall prescribe the form and content of notices under this subsection.

(3) The Commission shall prescribe the procedures to be followed in such meetings. If the meeting is not conducted by the Commission, detailed minutes of the meeting shall be kept and shall be submitted, along with any other written comment, exhibits or other documents presented at the meeting, to the Commission for its consideration prior to final action granting or denying the consent order.

(4) The Commission shall take final action on a proposed consent not later than 60 days following notice of the proposed consent order or, if a public meeting is held, within 90 days following such meeting.

(b) Procedure to Contest Certain Orders. - A special order that is issued without the consent of the person affected may be contested by that person by filing a petition for a contested case under G.S. 150B-23 within 30 days after the order is issued. If the person affected does not file a petition within the required time, the order is final and is not subject to review.

(c) Repealed by Session Laws 1987, c. 827, s. 208.

(d) Effect of Compliance. - Any person who installs an air-cleaning device for purpose of alleviating or eliminating air pollution in compliance with the terms of, or as result of the conditions specified in, a permit issued pursuant to G.S. 143-215.108, or a special order, consent special order, assurance of voluntary compliance or similar document issued pursuant to this section, or a final decision of the Commission or a court, rendered pursuant to either of said sections, shall not be required to take or refrain from any further action nor be required to achieve any further results under the terms of this or any other State law relating to the control of air pollution, for a period to be fixed by the

Commission or court as it shall deem fair and reasonable in the light of all the circumstances after the date such special order, consent special order, assurance of voluntary compliance, other document or decision, or the conditions of such permit become finally effective, if:

(1)   The air-cleaning devices result in the elimination or alleviation of air pollution to the extent required by such permit, special order, consent special order, assurance of voluntary compliance, or other document or decision and complies with any other terms thereof; and

(2)   Such person complies with the terms and conditions of such permit, special order, consent special order, assurance of voluntary compliance, other document or decision within the time limit, if any, specified therein or as the same may be extended, and thereafter remains in compliance.

(e)   Compliance Bonds. - A special order or other instrument authorized by this section may provide that a bond or other surety be posted to ensure compliance. In determining the amount of such bond the Commission shall consider the degree and extent of harm which may result if the person to whom the special order is directed fails to comply with the terms of the order, the cost of rectifying such harm, the economic consequences to the person to whom the special order is directed if the special order is issued as compared to the consequences of a denial, suspension, or revocation of the special order or permit, and the person's history of compliance with pollution control requirements, other special orders, history of payment of any penalties which may have been previously assessed by the Commission. In the event of noncompliance with the special order or other instrument, the bond shall be forfeited and the clear proceeds of the bond shall be remitted to the Civil Penalty and Forfeiture Fund in accordance with G.S. 115C-457.2. (1973, c. 821, s. 6; c. 1262, s. 23; 1987, c. 827, ss. 154, 208; 1989, c. 133; c. 766, s. 2; 1998-215, s. 72.)

§ 143-215.111. General powers of Commission; auxiliary powers.

In addition to the specific powers prescribed elsewhere in this Article and the applicable general powers prescribed in G.S. 143-215.3, and for the purpose of carrying out its duties, the Commission shall have the power:

(1) To make a continuing study of the effects of the emission of air contaminants from motor vehicles on the quality of the outdoor atmosphere of the State and the several areas thereof, and make recommendations to the General Assembly and other appropriate public and private bodies for the control of such air contaminants.

(2) To consult, upon request, with any person proposing to construct, install, or otherwise acquire an air pollution source or air-cleaning device for the control of air contaminants concerning the efficacy of such device, or the air problem which may be related to such source, or device; provided, however, that nothing in any such consultation shall be construed to relieve any person from compliance with this Article and Article 21, rules adopted pursuant thereto, or any other provision of law.

(3) To encourage local units of government to handle air pollution problems within their respective jurisdictions and on a cooperative basis, and to provide such local units technical and consultative assistance to the maximum extent possible.

(4) To establish procedures providing for public notice, public comment, and public hearings on applications for permits required by Title V to meet the requirements of Title V and implementing regulations adopted by the United States Environmental Protection Agency.

(5) To establish procedures providing for notice to the Administrator of the United States Environmental Protection Agency and affected states of proposals to issue permits required by Title V and allowing affected states the opportunity to submit written comment as required by section 505(a) of Title V (42 U.S.C. § 7661d) and implementing regulations adopted by the United States Environmental Protection Agency. (1973, c. 821, s. 6; c. 1262, s. 23; 1987, c. 827, ss. 154, 209; 1993, c. 400, s. 9.)

§ 143-215.112. Local air pollution control programs.

(a) The Commission is authorized and directed to review and have general oversight and supervision over all local air pollution control programs and to this end shall review and certify such programs as being adequate to meet the requirements of this Article and Article 21 of this Chapter and any applicable standards and rules adopted pursuant thereto. The Commission shall certify any local program which:

(1) Provides by ordinance or local law for requirements compatible with those imposed by the provisions of this Article and Article 21 of this Chapter, and the standards and rules issued pursuant thereto; provided, however, the Commission upon request of a municipality or other local unit may grant special permission for the governing body of such unit to adopt a particular class of air contaminant regulations which would result in more effective air pollution control than applicable standards or rules promulgated by the Commission;

(2) Provides for the adequate enforcement of such requirements by appropriate administrative and judicial process;

(3) Provides for an adequate administrative organization, staff, financial and other resources necessary to effectively and efficiently carry out its programs; and

(4) Is approved by the Commission as adequate to meet the requirements of this Article and any applicable rules pursuant thereto.

(b) No municipality, county, local board or commission or group of municipalities and counties may establish and administer an air pollution control program unless such program meets the requirements of this section and is so certified by the Commission.

(c) (1) The governing body of any county, municipality, or group of counties and municipalities within a designated area of the State, as defined in this Article and Article 21, subject to the approval of the Commission, is hereby authorized to establish, administer, and enforce a local air pollution control program for the county, municipality, or designated area of the State which includes but is not limited to:

a. Development of a comprehensive plan for the control and abatement of new and existing sources of air pollution;

b. Air quality monitoring to determine existing air quality and to define problem areas, as well as to provide background data to show the effectiveness of a pollution abatement program;

c. An emissions inventory to identify specific sources of air contamination and the contaminants emitted, together with the quantity of material discharged into the outdoor atmosphere;

d. Adoption, after notice and public hearing, of air quality and emission control standards, or adoption by reference, without public hearing, of any applicable rules and standards duly adopted by the Commission; and administration of such rules and standards in accordance with provisions of this section.

e. Provisions for the establishment or approval of time schedules for the control or abatement of existing sources of air pollution and for the review of plans and specifications and issuance of approval documents covering the construction and operation of pollution abatement facilities at existing or new sources;

f. Provision for adequate administrative staff, including an air pollution control officer and technical personnel, and provision for laboratory and other necessary facilities.

(2) Subject to the approval of the Commission as provided in this Article and Article 21, the governing body of any county or municipality may establish, administer, and enforce an air pollution control program by any of the following methods:

a. Establishing a program under the administration of the duly elected governing body of the county or municipality.

b. Appointing an air pollution control board consisting of not less than five nor more than seven members who shall serve for terms of six years each and until their successors are appointed and qualified. Two members shall be appointed for two-year terms, two shall be appointed for four-year terms, and the remaining member or members shall be appointed for six-year terms. Where the term "governing body" is referred to in this section, it shall include the air pollution control board. Such board shall have all the powers and authorities granted to any local air pollution control program. The board shall elect a chairman and shall meet at least quarterly or upon the call of the chairman or any two members of the board.

c. Appointing an air pollution control board as provided in this subdivision, and by appropriate written agreement designating the local health department or other department of county or municipal government as the administrative agent for the air pollution control board.

d. Designating, by appropriate written agreement, the local board of health and the local health department as the air pollution control board and agency.

(2a) Any board or body which approves permits or enforcement orders shall have at least a majority of members who represent the public interest and do not derive any significant portion of their income from persons subject to permits or enforcement orders under the Clean Air Act and any potential conflicts of interest by members of such board or body or the head of an executive agency with similar powers shall be adequately disclosed.

(3) If the Commission finds that the location, character or extent of particular concentrations of population, air contaminant sources, the geographic, topographic or meteorological considerations, or any combinations thereof, are such as to make impracticable the maintenance of appropriate levels of air quality without an area-wide air pollution control program, the Commission may determine the boundaries within which such program is necessary and require such area-wide program as the only acceptable alternative to direct State administration. Subject to the provisions of this section, each governing body of a county or municipality is hereby authorized and empowered to establish by contract, joint resolution, or other agreement with any other governing body of a county or municipality, upon approval by the Commission, an air pollution control region containing any part or all of the geographical area within the jurisdiction of those boards or governing bodies which are parties to such agreement, provided the counties involved in the region are contiguous or lie in a continuous boundary and comprise the total area contained in any region designated by the Commission for an area-wide program. The participating parties are authorized to appoint a regional air pollution control board which shall consist of at least five members who shall serve for terms of six years and until their successors are appointed and qualified. Two members shall be appointed for two-year terms, two shall be appointed for four-year terms and the remaining member or members shall be appointed for six-year terms. A participant's representation on the board shall be in relation to its population to the total population of the region based on the latest official United States census with each participant in the region having at least one representative; provided, that where the region is comprised of less than five counties, each participant will be entitled to appoint members in relation to its population to that of the region so as to provide a board of at least five members. Where the term "governing body" is used, it shall include the governing board of a region. The

regional board is hereby authorized to exercise any and all of the powers provided in this section. The regional air pollution control board shall elect a chairman and shall meet at least quarterly or upon the call of the chairman or any two members of the board. In lieu of employing its own staff, the regional air pollution control board is authorized, through appropriate written agreement, to designate a local health department as its administrative agent.

(4) Each governing body is authorized to adopt any ordinances, resolutions, rules or regulations which are necessary to establish and maintain an air pollution control program and to prescribe and enforce air quality and emission control standards, a copy of which must be filed with the Commission and with the clerk of court of any county affected. Provisions may be made therein for the registration of air contaminant sources; for the requirement of a permit to do or carry out specified activities relating to the control of air pollution, including procedures for application, issuance, denial and revocation; for notification of violators or potential violators about requirements or conditions for compliance; for procedures to grant temporary permits or variances from requirements or standards; for the declaration of an emergency when it is found that a generalized condition of air pollution is causing imminent danger to the health or safety of the public and the issuance of an order to the responsible person or persons to reduce or discontinue immediately the emission of air contaminants; for notice and hearing procedures for persons aggrieved by any action or order of any authorized agent; for the establishment of an advisory council and for other administrative arrangements; and for other matters necessary to establish and maintain an air pollution control program.

(5) No permit required by section 305(e) of Title III (42 U.S.C. § 7429(e)) for a solid waste incineration unit combusting municipal waste shall be issued by a local air pollution control program that is administered by the governing body of a unit of local government that is responsible, in whole or in part, for the design, construction, or operation of the unit.

(d) (1) Violation of any ordinances, resolutions, rules or regulations duly adopted by a governing body are punishable as provided in G.S. 143-215.114B.

(1a) Each governing body, or its authorized agent, shall have the power to assess civil penalties under G.S. 143-215.114A. Any person assessed shall be notified of the assessment by registered or certified mail, and the notice shall specify the reasons for the assessment. If the person assessed fails to pay the amount of the assessment to the governing body or its authorized agent within 30 days after receipt of notice, or such longer period not to exceed 180 days as the governing body or its authorized agent may specify, the governing body may institute a civil action in the superior court of the county in which the violation occurred, to recover the amount of the assessment. If any action or failure to act for which a penalty may be assessed under this section is continuous, the governing body or its authorized agent may assess a penalty not to exceed twenty-five thousand dollars ($25,000) per day for so long as the violation continues. In determining the amount of the penalty, the governing body or its authorized agent shall consider the degree and extent of harm caused by the violation, the cost of rectifying the damage, and the amount of money the violator saved by not having made the necessary expenditures to comply with the appropriate pollution control requirements.

(2) Each governing body, or its duly authorized agent, may institute a civil action in the superior court, brought in the name of the agency having jurisdiction, for injunctive relief to restrain any violation or immediately threatened violation of such ordinances, orders, rules, or regulations and for such other relief as the court shall deem proper. Neither the institution of the action nor any of the proceedings thereon shall relieve any party to such proceedings from the penalty prescribed by this Article and Article 21 for any violation of same.

(d1) (1) The governing body responsible for each local air pollution control program shall require that the owner or operator of all air contaminant sources subject to the requirement to obtain a permit under Title V pay an annual fee, or the equivalent over some other period, sufficient to cover costs as provided in section 502(b)(3)(A) of Title V (42 U.S.C. § 7661a(b)(3)(A)) and G.S. 143-215.3(a)(1d). Fees collected pursuant to this subdivision shall be used solely to cover all reasonable direct and indirect costs required to develop and administer the Title V permit program.

(2) Each governing body is authorized to expend tax funds, nontax funds, or any other funds available to it to finance an air pollution control program and such expenditures are hereby declared to be for a public purpose and a necessary expense.

(d2) (1) Any final administrative decision rendered in an air pollution control program of such governing body shall be subject to judicial review as provided by Article 4 of Chapter 150B of the General Statutes, and "administrative agency" or "agency" as used therein shall mean and include for this purpose the governing body of any county or municipality, regional air pollution control governing board, and any agency created by them in connection with an air pollution control program.

(2) A local air pollution control program shall inform a permit applicant as to whether or not the application is complete within the time specified in the rules for action on the application. If a local air pollution program fails to act on an application for a permit required by Title V or this Article within the time periods specified by the Commission under G.S 143-215.108(d)(2), the failure to act on the application constitutes a final agency decision to deny the permit. A permit applicant, permittee, or other person aggrieved, as defined in G.S. 150B-2, may seek judicial review of a failure to act on the application as provided in G.S. 143-215.5 and Article 4 of Chapter 150B of the General Statutes. Notwithstanding the provisions of G.S. 150B-51, upon review of a failure to act on an application for a permit required by Title V or this Article, a court may either: (i) affirm the denial of the permit or (ii) remand the application to the local air pollution control program for action upon the application within a specified time.

(e) (1) If the Commission has reason to believe that a local air pollution control program certified and in force pursuant to the provisions of this section is inadequate to abate or control air pollution in the jurisdiction to which such program relates, or that such program is being administered in a manner inconsistent with the requirement of this Article, the Commission shall, upon due notice, conduct a hearing on the matter.

(2) If, after such hearing, the Commission determines that an existing local air pollution control program or one which has been certified by the Commission is inadequate to abate or control air pollution in the municipality, county, or municipalities or counties to which such program relates, or that such program is not accomplishing the purposes of this Article, it shall set forth in its findings the corrective measures necessary for continued certification and shall specify a reasonable period of time, not to exceed one year, in which such measures must be taken if certification is not to be rescinded.

(3) If the municipality, county, local board or commission or municipalities or counties fail to take such necessary corrective action within the time specified, the Commission shall rescind any certification as may have been issued for such program and shall administer within such municipality, county, or municipalities or counties all of the regulatory provisions of this Article and Article 21. Such air pollution control program shall supersede all municipal, county or local laws, regulations, ordinances and requirements in the affected jurisdiction.

(4)   If the Commission finds that the control of a particular class of air contaminant source because of its complexity or magnitude is beyond the reasonable capability of the local air pollution control authorities or may be more efficiently and economically performed at the State level, it may assume and retain jurisdiction over that class of air contaminant source. Classification pursuant to this subdivision may be either on the basis of the nature of the sources involved or on the basis of their relationship to the size of the communities in which they are located.

(5)   Any municipality or county in which the Commission administers its air pollution control program pursuant to subdivision (3) of this subsection may, with the approval of the Commission, establish or resume a municipal, county, or local air pollution control program which meets the requirements for certification by the Commission.

(6)   Repealed by Session Laws 1993, c. 400, s. 10.

(7)   Any municipality, county, local board or commission or municipalities or counties or designated area of this State for which a local air pollution control program is established or proposed for establishment may make application for, receive, administer and expend federal grant funds for the control of air pollution or the development and administration of programs related to air pollution control; provided that any such application is first submitted to and approved by the Commission. The Commission shall approve any such application if it is consistent with this Article, Article 21 and other applicable requirements of law.

(8)   Notwithstanding any other provision of this section, if the Commission determines that an air pollution source or combination of sources is operating in violation of the provisions of this Article and that the appropriate local authorities have not acted to abate such violation, the Commission, upon written notice to the appropriate local governing body, may act on behalf of the State to require any person causing or contributing to the pollution to cease immediately the emission of air pollutants causing or contributing to the violation or may require such other action as it shall deem necessary. (1973, c. 821, s. 6; c. 1262, s. 23; c. 1331, s. 3; 1979, c. 545, s. 7; 1987, c. 748, s. 1; c. 827, ss. 1, 154, 210; 1989, c. 135, s. 7; 1993, c. 400, s. 10; 1997-496, s. 6; 2010-180, s. 6.)

§ 143-215.113: Repealed by Session Laws 1987, c. 827, s. 211.

§ 143-215.114: Recodified as §§ 143-215.114A through 143-215.114C.

(a) Recodified as G.S. 143-215.114A by Session Laws 1989 (Reg. Sess., 1990), c. 1045, s. 4.

(b) Recodified as G.S. 143-215.114B by Session Laws 1989 (Reg. Sess., 1990), c. 1045, s. 5.

(c) Recodified as G.S. 143-215.114C by Session Laws 1989 (Reg. Sess., 1990), c. 1045, s. 6.

§ 143-215.114A. Enforcement procedures: civil penalties.

(a) A civil penalty of not more than twenty-five thousand dollars ($25,000) may be assessed by the Secretary against any person who:

(1) Violates any classification, standard or limitation established pursuant to G.S. 143-215.107.

(2) Is required but fails to apply for or to secure a permit required by G.S. 143-215.108 or who violates or fails to act in accordance with the terms, conditions, or requirements of such permit.

(3) Violates or fails to act in accordance with the terms, conditions, or requirements of any special order or other appropriate document issued pursuant to G.S. 143-215.110.

(4) Fails to file, submit, or make available, as the case may be, any documents, data or reports required by this Article or Parts 1 or 7 of Article 21 of this Chapter.

(5) Violates a rule of the Commission or a local governing body implementing this Article or Parts 1 or 7 of Article 21.

(6) Violates the offenses set out in G.S. 143-215.114B.

(7) Violates the emissions limitations set out in G.S. 143-215.107D.

(b)   If any action or failure to act for which a penalty may be assessed under this section is continuous, the Secretary may assess a penalty not to exceed twenty-five thousand dollars ($25,000) per day for so long as the violation continues.

(b1)   The Secretary may assess a civil penalty of not more than twenty-five thousand dollars ($25,000) per day for a violation of the emissions limitations set out in G.S. 143-215.107D as provided in this subsection. If at the end of any calendar year, an investor-owned public utility has violated an emissions limitation set out in G.S. 143-215.107D, the violation shall be considered to be continuous from the day that the collective emissions first exceeded the emissions limitation set out in G.S. 143-215.107D through the end of the calendar year and the Secretary may assess a separate civil penalty for each day.

(c)   In determining the amount of the penalty the Secretary shall consider the factors set out in G.S. 143B-282.1(b). The procedures set out in G.S. 143B-282.1 shall apply to civil penalty assessments that are presented to the Commission for final agency decision.

(d)   The Secretary shall notify any person assessed a civil penalty of the assessment and the specific reasons therefor by registered or certified mail, or by any means authorized by G.S. 1A-1, Rule 4. Contested case petitions shall be filed within 30 days of receipt of the notice of assessment.

(e)   Requests for remission of civil penalties shall be filed with the Secretary. Remission requests shall not be considered unless made within 30 days of receipt of the notice of assessment. Remission requests must be accompanied by a waiver of the right to a contested case hearing pursuant to Chapter 150B and a stipulation of the facts on which the assessment was based. Consistent with the limitations in G.S. 143B-282.1(c) and (d), remission requests may be resolved by the Secretary and the violator. If the Secretary and the violator are unable to resolve the request, the Secretary shall deliver remission requests and his recommended action to the Committee on Civil Penalty Remissions of the Environmental Management Commission appointed pursuant to G.S. 143B-282.1(c).

(f)   If any civil penalty has not been paid within 30 days after notice of assessment has been served on the violator, the Secretary shall request the Attorney General to institute a civil action in the Superior Court of any county in which the violator resides or has his or its principal place of business to recover the amount of the assessment, unless the violator contests the assessment as provided in subdivision (4) of this subsection, or requests remission of the assessment in whole or in part as provided in subdivision (5) of this subsection. If any civil penalty has not been paid within 30 days after the final agency decision or court order has been served on the violator, the Secretary shall request the Attorney General to institute a civil action in the Superior Court of any county in which the violator resides or has his or its principal place of business to recover the amount of the assessment. Such civil actions must be filed within three years of the date the final agency decision or court order was served on the violator.

(g)   Repealed by Session Laws 1996, Second Extra Session c. 18, s. 27.34(f).

(h)   The clear proceeds of penalties provided for in this section shall be remitted to the Civil Penalty and Forfeiture Fund in accordance with G.S. 115C-457.2. (1973, c. 821, s. 6; c. 1262, s. 23; c. 1331, s. 3; 1975, c. 19, s. 53; c. 842, ss. 6, 7; 1977, c. 771, s. 4; 1979, c. 545, ss. 4-6; 1987, c. 748, s. 2; c. 827, ss. 154, 212; 1989, c. 135, s. 8; 1989 (Reg. Sess., 1990), c. 1036, s. 8; c. 1045, s. 4; 1991, c. 552, s. 4; c. 725, s. 7; 1991 (Reg. Sess., 1992), c. 890, s. 18; 1996, 2nd Ex. Sess., c. 18, s. 27.34(f); 1997-496, s. 7; 1998-215, s. 73; 2002-4, ss. 4, 5; 2002-165, s. 1.12; 2007-296, s. 1.)

§ 143-215.114B. Enforcement procedures: criminal penalties.

(a)   For purposes of this section, the term "person" shall mean, in addition to the definition contained in G.S. 143-212, any responsible corporate or public officer or employee; provided, however, that where a vote of the people is required to effectuate the intent and purpose of this Article by a county, city, town, or other political subdivision of the State, and the vote on the referendum is against the means or machinery for carrying said intent and purpose into effect, then, and only then, this section shall not apply to elected officials or to any responsible appointed officials or employees of such county, city, town, or political subdivision.

(b)   No proceeding shall be brought or continued under this section for or on account of a violation by any person who has previously been convicted of a federal violation based upon the same set of facts.

(c) In proving the defendant's possession of actual knowledge, circumstantial evidence may be used, including evidence that the defendant took affirmative steps to shield himself from relevant information. Consistent with the principles of common law, the subjective mental state of defendants may be inferred from their conduct.

(d) For the purposes of the felony provisions of this section, a person's state of mind shall not be found "knowingly and willfully" or "knowingly" if the conduct that is the subject of the prosecution is the result of any of the following occurrences or circumstances:

(1) A natural disaster or other act of God which could not have been prevented or avoided by the exercise of due care or foresight.

(2) An act of third parties other than agents, employees, contractors, or subcontractors of the defendant.

(3) An act done in reliance on the written advice or emergency on-site direction of an employee of the Department. In emergencies, oral advice may be relied upon if written confirmation is delivered to the employee as soon as practicable after receiving and relying on the advice.

(4) An act causing no significant harm to the environment or risk to the public health, safety, or welfare and done in compliance with other conflicting environmental requirements or other constraints imposed in writing by environmental agencies or officials after written notice is delivered to all relevant agencies that the conflict exists and will cause a violation of the identified standard.

(5) Violations of permit limitations causing no significant harm to the environment or risk to the public health, safety, or welfare for which no enforcement action or civil penalty could have been imposed under any written civil enforcement guidelines in use by the Department at the time, including but not limited to, guidelines for the pretreatment permit civil penalties. This subdivision shall not be construed to require the Department to develop or use written civil enforcement guidelines.

(6) Occasional, inadvertent, short-term violations of permit limitations causing no significant harm to the environment or risk to the public health, safety, or welfare. If the violation occurs within 30 days of a prior violation or lasts for more than 24 hours, it is not an occasional, short-term violation.

(e) All general defenses, affirmative defenses, and bars to prosecution that may apply with respect to other criminal offenses under State criminal offenses may apply to prosecutions brought under this section or other criminal statutes that refer to this section and shall be determined by the courts of this State according to the principles of common law as they may be applied in the light of reason and experience. Concepts of justification and excuse applicable under this section may be developed in the light of reason and experience.

(f) Any person who negligently violates any classification, standard or limitation established pursuant to G.S. 143-215.107 or by G.S. 143-215.107D any term, condition, or requirement of a permit issued pursuant to G.S. 143-215.108 or of a special order or other appropriate document issued pursuant to G.S. 143-215.110 or any rule of the Commission implementing any of the said section, shall be guilty of a Class 2 misdemeanor which may include a fine not to exceed fifteen thousand dollars ($15,000) per day of violation, provided that such fine shall not exceed a cumulative total of two hundred thousand dollars ($200,000) for each period of 30 days during which a violation continues.

(g) Any person who knowingly and willfully violates any classification, standard, or limitation established in the rules of the Commission pursuant to G.S. 143-215.107; the emissions limitations set out in G.S. 143-215.107D; any term, condition, or requirement of a permit issued pursuant to G.S. 143-215.108; or of a special order or other appropriate document issued pursuant to G.S. 143-215.110, shall be guilty of a Class H felony, which may include a fine not to exceed one hundred thousand dollars ($100,000) per day of violation, provided that this fine shall not exceed a cumulative total of five hundred thousand dollars ($500,000) for each period of 30 days during which a violation continues. For the purposes of this subsection, the phrase "knowingly and willfully" shall mean intentionally and consciously as the courts of this State, according to the principles of common law, interpret the phrase in the light of reason and experience.

(h) (1) Any person who knowingly violates any classification, standard, or limitation established in the rules of the Commission pursuant to G.S. 143-215.107; the emissions limitations set out in G.S. 143-215.107D; any term, condition, or requirement of a permit issued pursuant to G.S. 143-215.108; or of a special order or other appropriate document issued pursuant to G.S. 143-215.110 and who knows at that time that he thereby places another person in imminent danger of death or serious bodily injury shall be guilty of a Class C felony, which may include a fine not to exceed two hundred fifty thousand dollars ($250,000) per day of violation, provided that this fine shall not exceed a cumulative total of one million dollars ($1,000,000) for each period of 30 days during which a violation continues.

(2)   For the purposes of this subsection, a person's state of mind is knowing with respect to:

a.   His conduct, if he is aware of the nature of his conduct;

b.   An existing circumstance, if he is aware or believes that the circumstance exists; or

c.   A result of his conduct, if he is aware or believes that his conduct is substantially certain to cause danger of death or serious bodily injury.

(3)   Under this subsection, in determining whether a defendant who is a natural person knew that his conduct placed another person in imminent danger of death or serious bodily injury:

a.   The person is responsible only for actual awareness or actual belief that he possessed; and

b.   Knowledge possessed by a person other than the defendant but not by the defendant himself may not be attributed to the defendant.

(4)   It is an affirmative defense to a prosecution under this subsection that the conduct charged was conduct consented to by the person endangered and that the danger and conduct charged were reasonably foreseeable hazards of an occupation, a business, or a profession; or of medical treatment or medical or scientific experimentation conducted by professionally approved methods and such other person had been made aware of the risks involved prior to giving consent. The defendant may establish an affirmative defense under this subdivision by a preponderance of the evidence.

(i)   Any person who knowingly makes any false statement, representation, or certification in any application, record, report, plan, or other document filed or required to be maintained under this Article or Article 21, or a rule implementing this Article or Article 21; or who knowingly makes a false statement of a material fact in a rulemaking or contested case under this Article or Article 21; or who falsifies, tampers with, or knowingly renders inaccurate any recording or monitoring device or method required to be operated or maintained under this Article or Article 21 or rules of the Commission implementing this Article or

Article 21, shall be guilty of a Class 2 misdemeanor which may include a fine not to exceed ten thousand dollars ($10,000).

(j) Repealed by Session Laws 1993, c. 539, s. 1320. (1973, c. 821, s. 6; c. 1262, s. 23; c. 1331, s. 3; 1975, c. 19, s. 53; c. 842, ss. 6, 7; 1977, c. 771, s. 4; 1979, c. 545, ss. 4-6; 1987, c. 748, s. 2; c. 827, ss. 154, 212; 1989, c. 135, s. 8; 1989 (Reg. Sess., 1990), c. 1004, s. 49; c. 1045, s. 5; 1993, c. 539, ss. 1026, 1027, 1318, 1319, 1320; 1994, Ex. Sess., c. 24, s. 14(c); 2002-4, ss. 6-8.)

§ 143-215.114C. Enforcement procedures: injunctive relief.

Whenever the Department has reasonable cause to believe that any person has violated or is threatening to violate any of the provisions of this Article or Article 21 of this Chapter or a rule implementing this Article or Article 21 of this Chapter, the Department, either before or after the institution of any other action or proceeding authorized by this Article or Article 21 of this Chapter, may request the Attorney General to institute a civil action in the name of the State upon the relation of the Department for injunctive relief to restrain the violation or threatened violation and for such other and further relief in the premises as the court shall deem proper. The Attorney General may institute such action in the Superior Court of Wake County, or, in his discretion, in the superior court of the county in which the violation occurred or may occur. Upon a determination by the court that the alleged violation of the provisions of this Article or Article 21 of this Chapter or the regulation of the Commission has occurred or is threatened, the court shall grant the relief necessary to prevent or abate the violation or threatened violation. Neither the institution of the action nor any of the proceedings thereon shall relieve any party to such proceedings from any penalty prescribed for violation of this Article or Article 21 of this Chapter. (1973, c. 821, s. 6; c. 1262, s. 23; c. 1331, s. 3; 1975, c. 19, s. 53; c. 842, ss. 6, 7; 1977, c. 771, s. 4; 1979, c. 545, ss. 4-6; 1987, c. 748, s. 2; c. 827, ss. 154, 212; 1989, c. 135, s. 8; 1989 (Reg. Sess., 1990), c. 1045, s. 6.)

Article 21C.

Permitting of Wind Energy Facilities.

§ 143-215.115. Definitions.

In addition to the definitions set forth in G.S. 143-212, the following definitions apply to this Article:

(1) "Major military installation" means Fort Bragg, Pope Army Airfield, Marine Corps Base Camp Lejeune, New River Marine Corps Air Station, Cherry Point Marine Corps Air Station, Military Ocean Terminal at Sunny Point, the United States Coast Guard Air Station at Elizabeth City, Naval Support Activity Northwest, Air Route Surveillance Radar (ARSR-4) at Fort Fisher, and Seymour Johnson Air Force Base, in its own right and as the responsible entity for the Dare County Bombing Range, and any facility located within the State that is subject to the installations' oversight and control.

(2) "Wind energy facility" means the turbines, accessory buildings, transmission facilities, and any other equipment necessary for the operation of the facility that cumulatively, with any other wind energy facility whose turbines are located within one-half mile of one another, have a rated capacity of one megawatt or more of energy.

(3) "Wind energy facility expansion" means any activity that (i) adds or substantially modifies turbines or transmission facilities, including increasing the height of such equipment, over that which was initially permitted or (ii) increases the footprint of the wind energy facility over that which was initially permitted. (2013-51, s. 1.)

§ 143-215.116. Permit to site wind energy facilities.

No person shall undertake construction, operation, or expansion activities associated with a wind energy facility in this State without first obtaining a permit from the Department. (2013-51, s. 1.)

§ 143-215.117. Permit preapplication site evaluation meeting; notice; preapplication package requirements.

(a) Permit Preapplication Site Evaluation Meeting. - No less than 180 days prior to filing an application for a permit to construct, operate, or expand a wind energy facility, a person shall request a preapplication site evaluation meeting to be held between the applicant and the Department. The preapplication site evaluation meeting shall be held no less than 120 days prior to filing an application for a permit to construct, operate, or expand a wind energy facility and may be used by the participants to:

(1)   Conduct a preliminary evaluation of the site or sites for the proposed wind energy facility or wind energy facility expansion. The preliminary evaluation of the proposed wind energy facility or proposed wind energy facility expansion shall determine if the site or sites:

a.   Pose serious risk to civil air navigation or military air navigation routes, air traffic control areas, military training routes, special-use air space, radar, or other potentially affected military operations.

b.   Pose serious risk to natural resources and uses, including to species of concern or their habitats.

(2)   Identify areas where proposed construction or expansion activities pose minimal risk of interference with civil air navigation or military air navigation routes, air traffic control areas, military training routes, special-use air space, radar, or other potentially affected military operations.

(3)   Identify areas where proposed construction or expansion activities pose minimal risk to natural resources and uses, including avian, bat, and endangered and threatened species.

(b)   Permit Preapplication Package. - No less than 45 days prior to the date of the permit preapplication site evaluation meeting scheduled in accordance with subsection (a) of this section, the applicant for a wind energy facility or wind energy facility expansion shall submit a preapplication package to the Department. To the extent that any documents contain trade secrets or confidential business information, those portions of the documents shall not be subject to disclosure under the North Carolina Public Records Act. The preapplication package shall include all of the following:

(1)   A narrative description of the proposed wind energy facility or proposed wind energy facility expansion, including (i) the approximate number, type, and height of wind turbines to be constructed; (ii) the total planned capacity of the facility; and (iii) a description of any ancillary facilities.

(2) A map showing the approximate location of the proposed wind energy facility or proposed wind energy facility expansion.

(3) A description of any known potential impacts of the proposed wind energy project location on civil air navigation or military air navigation routes, air traffic control areas, military training routes, special-use air space, radar, or other potentially affected military operations. The applicant may use data made available by the Department pursuant to G.S. 143-215.123 to satisfy this requirement.

(4) A description of species of concern, habitats that support species of concern, critical areas of wildlife congregation, and protected lands, as those species, habitats, and critical areas are referenced in the March 23, 2012, United States Fish and Wildlife Service Land-Based Wind Energy Guidelines (OMB Control No. 1018-0148) that are or believed to be present at the site of the proposed wind energy facility or proposed wind energy facility expansion. The applicant may use data made available by the North Carolina Wildlife Resources Commission, the Department, or other governmental agency to satisfy this requirement.

(5) A list of the federal, State, and local agencies from which approvals will be obtained and the name of those approvals required in order to authorize the construction, operation, or expansion of the proposed wind energy facility.

(6) A schedule showing the anticipated dates for commencement of construction, testing, and commercial operation of the proposed wind energy facility or proposed wind energy facility expansion.

(c) Notice to Interested Parties. - No less than 21 days prior to the date of the permit preapplication site evaluation meeting scheduled in accordance with subsection (a) of this section, the Department shall provide written notice of the meeting to the United States Army Corps of Engineers, the United States Fish and Wildlife Service, the North Carolina Wildlife Resources Commission, the commanding military officer or the commanding military officer's designee of any potentially affected major military installation, and any other party that the Department deems relevant. The notice shall include an invitation to participate in the permit preapplication site evaluation meeting. (2013-51, s. 1.)

§ 143-215.118. Permit application scoping meeting and notice.

(a) Scoping Meeting. - No less than 60 days prior to filing an application for a permit for a proposed wind energy facility or proposed wind energy facility expansion, the applicant shall request the scheduling of a scoping meeting between the applicant and the Department. The scoping meeting shall be held no less than 30 days prior to filing an application for a permit for a proposed wind energy facility or proposed wind energy facility expansion. The applicant and the Department shall review the permit for the proposed wind energy facility or proposed facility expansion at the scoping meeting.

(b) Notice of Scoping Meeting. - No less than 21 days prior to the scheduled permit application scoping meeting with an applicant, the Department shall provide written notice of the meeting to the commanding military officer of each major military installation, or the commanding military officer's designee, the Federal Aviation Administration, the North Carolina Wildlife Resources Commission, the United States Fish and Wildlife Service, the board of commissioners for each county and the governing body of each municipality in which the wind energy facility or proposed wind energy facility expansion is proposed to be located, and those local governments with jurisdictions over areas in which a major military installation is located. The notice shall include an invitation to participate in the scoping meeting. (2013-51, s. 1.)

§ 143-215.119. Permit application requirements; fees; notice of receipt of completed permit; public hearing; public comment.

(a) Permit Requirements. - A person applying for a permit for a proposed wind energy facility or proposed wind energy facility expansion shall include all of the following in an application for the permit:

(1) A narrative description of the proposed wind energy facility or proposed wind energy facility expansion.

(2) A map showing the location of the proposed wind energy facility or proposed wind energy facility expansion that identifies the specific location of each turbine.

(3) A copy of a deed, purchase agreement, lease agreement, or other legal instrument demonstrating the right to construct, expand, or otherwise develop a wind energy facility on the property.

(4)   Identification by name and address of property owners adjacent to the proposed wind energy facility or proposed wind energy facility expansion. The applicant shall notify every property owner identified pursuant to this subdivision by registered or certified mail or by any means authorized by G.S. 1A-1, Rule 4, in a form approved by the Department. The notice shall include all of the following:

a.   The location of the proposed wind energy facility or proposed wind energy facility expansion and the specific location of each turbine proposed to be located within one-half mile of the boundary of the adjacent property owner.

b.   A description of the proposed wind energy facility or proposed wind energy facility expansion.

(5)   A description of civil air navigation or military air navigation routes, air traffic control areas, military training routes, special-use air space, radar, or other military operations that may be affected by the construction or operation of the proposed wind energy facility or proposed wind energy facility expansion.

(6)   Documentation that addresses any potential adverse impact on military operations and readiness as identified by the Department of Defense Clearinghouse pursuant to Part 211 of Title 32 Code of Federal Regulations (July 1, 2012 edition) and any mitigation actions agreed to by the applicant.

(7)   Documentation that the applicant has either (i) submitted Federal Aviation Administration Form 7460-1 for the turbines associated with the proposed wind energy facility or proposed wind energy facility expansion or (ii) initiated an informal review by the Department of Defense Siting Clearinghouse of the proposed wind energy facility or proposed wind energy facility expansion. If the applicant has submitted Federal Aviation Administration Form 7460-1 in order to fulfill the requirements of this subdivision, the applicant shall provide any determination reached by the Federal Aviation Administration at the time the application is submitted to the Department. If the Federal Aviation Administration has not made a determination at the time the application is submitted to the Department, the application shall include a description of the status of the applicant's engagement with the Federal Aviation Administration and the Department of Defense Siting Clearinghouse.

(8)   A study of the noise impacts of the turbines to be associated with the proposed wind energy facility or proposed wind energy facility expansion.

(9) A study on shadow flicker impacts of the turbines to be associated with the proposed wind energy facility or proposed wind energy facility expansion, unless the turbines will be located in a sound or in offshore waters.

(10) A study of the impact of the proposed wind energy facility or proposed wind energy facility expansion on natural resources and uses, including avian, bat, and endangered and threatened species.

(11) An explanation of how the proposed wind energy facility or proposed wind energy facility expansion would be consistent with the criteria in subsection (a) of G.S. 143-215.120.

(12) The application fee required by subsection (c) of this section.

(13) A plan regarding the action to be taken upon the decommissioning and removal of the wind energy facility. The plan shall include an estimate of the cost to decommission and remove the wind energy facility. The plan shall also include the anticipated life of the project, an estimate of the cost to decommission and remove the wind energy facility, a description of the manner in which the facility will be decommissioned, and a description of the expected condition of the site once the wind energy facility has been decommissioned and removed.

(14) Other data or information the Department may reasonably require.

(b) Confidentiality of Trade Secrets and Business Information. - To the extent that any documents included in the permit application contain trade secrets or confidential business information, those portions of the documents shall not be subject to disclosure under the North Carolina Public Records Act.

(c) Fees. - An applicant for a permit for a proposed wind energy facility or proposed wind energy facility expansion under this section shall submit with the application required pursuant to subsection (a) of this section, an application fee of three thousand five hundred dollars ($3,500).

(d) Notice of Receipt of Complete Permit Application. - Within 10 days of receipt of a complete permit application for a proposed wind energy facility or proposed wind energy facility expansion submitted pursuant to subsection (a) of this section, the Department shall provide notice of the permit application to (i) the commanding military officer of all major military installations, (ii) the commanding military officer of any military installation located outside the State that is located within 50 nautical miles of the location of the proposed wind energy facility or proposed wind energy facility expansion, and (iii) the board of commissioners for each county and the governing body of each municipality in which the wind energy facility or wind energy facility expansion is proposed to be located. The notice shall include:

(1) A copy of the map showing the location of the proposed wind energy facility or proposed wind energy facility expansion that includes the specific locations of wind turbines.

(2) A written request to the commanding military officer of a major military installation or the commanding military officer's designee, for technical information related to any adverse impact on the installation's operations, training, or mission, including military air navigation routes, air traffic control areas, military training routes, special-use air space, radar or other military operations that may be affected.

(3) A written request for information related to potential adverse impacts of the proposed wind energy facility or proposed wind energy facility expansion on local governments from the board of commissioners for each county and the governing body of each municipality.

(e) Provision of Permit Application to Affected Entities. - Except as provided by G.S. 143-215.124, within 10 days of receipt of a written request from the commanding military officer of any major military installation or the commanding military officer's designee, the board of commissioners for any county in which the site is proposed to be located or the governing body of any municipality in which the site is proposed to be located, the Department shall provide a copy of a permit application filed pursuant to subsection (a) of this section, in addition to any supplements, changes, or amendments to the permit application to the requesting commanding military officer or local government.

(f) Public Hearing and Comment. - The Department shall hold a public hearing in each county in which the wind energy facility or wind energy facility expansion is proposed to be located within 75 days of receipt of a completed permit application. The Department shall provide notice including the time and location of the public hearing in a newspaper of general circulation in each applicable county. The notice of public hearing shall be published for at least two consecutive weeks beginning no less than 45 days prior to the scheduled date of the hearing. The notice shall provide that any comments on the proposed wind energy facility or proposed wind energy facility expansion should be submitted to the Department by a specified date, not less than 15 days from the date of the newspaper publication of the notice or 15 days after distribution of the mailed notice, whichever is later. No less than 30 days prior to the scheduled public hearing, the Department shall provide written

notice of the hearing to:

(1)   The North Carolina Utilities Commission.

(2)   The Office of the Attorney General of North Carolina.

(3)   The commanding military officer of any potentially affected major military installation or the commanding military officer's designee.

(4)   The board of commissioners for each county and the governing body of each municipality with jurisdictions over areas in which a potentially affected major military installation is located. (2013-51, s. 1.)

§ 143-215.120. Criteria for permit approval; time frame; permit conditions; other approvals required.

(a)   Permit Approval. - The Department shall approve an application for a permit for a proposed wind energy facility or proposed wind energy facility expansion unless the Department finds any one or more of the following:

(1)   Construction or operation of the proposed wind energy facility or proposed wind energy facility expansion would be inconsistent with or violate rules adopted by the Department or any other provision of law.

(2)   Construction or operation of the proposed wind energy facility or proposed wind energy facility expansion would encroach upon or would otherwise have a significant adverse impact on the mission, training, or operations of any major military installation or branch of military in North Carolina and result in a detriment to continued military presence in the State. In its evaluation, the Department may consider whether the proposed wind energy facility or proposed wind energy facility expansion would cause interference with air navigation routes, air traffic control areas, military training routes, or radar based on information submitted by the applicant pursuant to subdivisions (5) and (6) of subsection (a) of G.S. 143-215.119, and any information received by

the Department pursuant to subdivision (2) of subsection (d) of G.S. 143-215.119.

(3) Construction or operation of the proposed wind energy facility or proposed wind energy facility expansion would result in significant adverse impacts to ecological systems, natural resources, cultural sites, recreation areas, or historic sites of more than local significance; including national or State parks or forests, wilderness areas, historic sites, recreation areas, segments of the natural and scenic rivers system, wildlife refuges, preserves and management areas, areas that provide habitat for threatened or endangered species, primary nursery areas designated by the Marine Fisheries Commission and the Wildlife Resources Commission, and critical fisheries habitat identified pursuant to the Coastal Habitat Protection Plan.

(4) Construction or operation of the proposed wind energy facility or proposed wind energy facility expansion would have a significant adverse impact on fish or wildlife.

(5) Construction or operation of the proposed wind energy facility or proposed wind energy facility expansion would have a significant adverse impact on views from any State or national park, wilderness area, significant natural heritage area as compiled by the North Carolina Natural Heritage Program, or other public lands or private conservation lands designated or dedicated due to their high recreational values.

(6) Construction or operation of the proposed wind energy facility or proposed wind energy facility expansion would obstruct major navigation channels or create a significant obstacle to navigation in coastal waters, as determined by the United States Army Corps of Engineers and the United States Coast Guard.

(7) A permit for a proposed wind energy facility or proposed wind energy facility expansion would be denied under any other criteria set out in G.S. 113A-120.

(8) Construction of the proposed wind energy facility or proposed wind energy facility expansion would be prohibited under Article 14 of Chapter 113A of the General Statutes, the Mountain Ridge Protection Act of 1983.

(9)   The applicant is not in compliance with all applicable federal, State, or local permit requirements, licenses, or approvals, including local zoning requirements.

(b)   Permit Decision. - The Department shall make a final decision on a permit application within 90 days following receipt of a completed application, except that the Department shall not be required to make a final decision until the Department has received a written "Determination of No Hazard to Air Navigation" issued by the Federal Aviation Administration pursuant to Subpart D of Part 77 of Title 14 of the Code of Federal Regulations (January 1, 2012 edition). If the Department requests additional information following the receipt of a completed application, the Department shall make a final decision on a permit application within 30 days of receipt of the requested information. If the Department determines that an application for a wind energy facility or a wind energy facility expansion fails to meet the requirements for a permit under this section, the Department shall deny the application, and the application shall be returned to the applicant accompanied by a written statement of the reasons for the denial and any modifications to the permit application that would make the application acceptable. If the Department fails to act within the time period set forth in this subsection, the applicant may treat the failure to act as a denial of the permit and may challenge the denial as provided under Chapter 150B of the General Statutes.

(c)   Permit Conditions. - The Department (i) may include as a condition of a permit for a proposed wind energy facility or proposed wind energy facility expansion a requirement that the permit holder mitigate any adverse impacts and (ii) shall include as a condition of a permit for a proposed wind energy facility or proposed wind energy facility expansion a requirement that the permit holder obtain a written "Determination of No Hazard to Air Navigation" issued by the Federal Aviation Administration pursuant to Subpart D of Part 77 of Title 14 of the Code of Federal Regulations (January 1, 2012 edition) for the facility. No permit for a wind energy facility or wind energy facility expansion shall become effective until the Department has received and reviewed the "Determination of No Hazard to Air Navigation" issued by the Federal Aviation Administration for the facility. If the specific location of a turbine authorized to be constructed pursuant to a "Determination of No Hazard to Air Navigation" or the configuration of the wind energy facility varies from the information submitted by the applicant upon which the Department has made its permit decision, the Department may reevaluate the permit application and require the applicant to submit any additional information the Department deems necessary to approve or deny a permit for the facility as reconfigured.

(d) Other Approvals Required. - The issuance of a permit under this section shall not obviate the need for the applicant to obtain any and all other applicable local, State, or federal permits, licenses, or approvals. Furthermore, nothing in this Article shall be interpreted to limit, as applicable, (i) the application of Article 7 of Chapter 113A of the General Statutes to facilities permitted under this section, including the permitting requirements of G.S. 113A-118, (ii) the ability of a city or county to plan for and regulate the siting of a wind energy facility in accordance with land-use regulations authorized under Chapter 160A and Chapter 153A of the General Statutes, or (iii) the applicable requirements of Chapter 62 of the General Statutes. (2013-51, s. 1.)

§ 143-215.121. Financial assurance requirements.

The applicant for a permit or a permit holder for a wind energy facility shall establish financial assurance that will ensure that sufficient funds are available for decommissioning of the facility and reclamation of the property to its condition prior to commencement of activities on the site, even if the applicant or permit holder becomes insolvent or ceases to reside in, be incorporated, do business, or maintain assets in the State. To establish sufficient availability of funds under this section, the applicant for a permit or a permit holder for a wind energy facility may use insurance, financial tests, third-party guarantees by persons who can pass the financial test, guarantees by corporate parents who can pass the financial test, irrevocable letters of credit, trusts, surety bonds, or any other financial device, or any combination of the foregoing, shown to provide protection equivalent to the financial protection that would be provided by insurance if insurance were the only mechanism used. (2013-51, s. 1.)

§ 143-215.122. Monitoring and reporting.

The applicant shall annually submit copies to the Department of any post-construction monitoring, such as reports on the impacts on wildlife in the location of and in the area proximate to the wind energy facility or wind energy facility expansion and any impacts on military operations that are required by the United States Fish and Wildlife Service, the North Carolina Wildlife Resources Commission, the North Carolina Utilities Commission, or any other government agency. (2013-51, s. 1.)

§ 143-215.123. Annual review of military presence.

The Department shall consult with representatives of the major military installations to review information regarding military air navigation routes, air traffic control areas, military training routes, special-use air space, radar, or other potentially affected military operations at least once per year. The Department shall provide relevant information on civil air navigation or military air navigation routes, air traffic control areas, military training routes, special-use air space, radar, or other potentially affected military operations to permit applicants as requested. (2013-51, s. 1.)

§ 143-215.124. Record keeping.

The Department shall serve as the custodian of all data, information, and records received from a permit applicant or a major military installation pursuant to this Article and shall ensure that information provided to the Department that constitutes trade secrets, as that term is defined in G.S. 66-152, and that is designated as confidential or as a trade secret under G.S. 132-1.2, is limited only to the Department, State employees, and other persons who have executed a confidentiality agreement with the owner of such information. Information designated as confidential or as a trade secret under G.S. 132-1.2 shall not be subject to disclosure pursuant to G.S. 132-6. (2013-51, s. 1.)

§ 143-215.125. Rule making.

The Environmental Management Commission shall adopt any rules necessary for the implementation of this Article. In adopting rules, the Commission shall consult with the Coastal Resources Commission to ensure that the development of statewide permitting requirements is consistent with and in consideration of the characteristics unique to the coastal area of the State to the maximum extent practicable. (2013-51, s. 1.)

§ 143-215.126. Civil penalties.

(a) The Secretary of Environment and Natural Resources may impose an administrative penalty on a person who constructs a wind energy facility or wind energy facility expansion without obtaining a permit under this Article or who constructs or operates a wind energy facility in violation of its permit terms and conditions. Each day of a continuing violation shall constitute a separate violation. The penalty shall not exceed ten thousand dollars ($10,000) per day.

(b) The Secretary of Environment and Natural Resources, irrespective of all other remedies at law, may institute an action for injunctive relief against a person who constructs a wind energy facility without first obtaining a permit under this Article or who constructs or operates a wind energy facility or wind energy facility expansion in violation of its permit terms and conditions. (2013-51, s. 1.)

Article 22.

State Ports Authority.

§§ 143-216 through 143-228.1: Recodified as §§ 143B-452 to 143B-467 by Session Laws 1977, c. 198, s. 9.

Article 23.

Armories.

§ 143-229. Repealed by Session Laws 1975, c. 604, s. 1.

§§ 143-230 through 143-231. Repealed by Session Laws 1973, c. 620, s. 9.

§§ 143-232 through 143-236.1. Repealed by Session Laws 1975, c. 604, s. 1.

Article 23A.

Stadium Authority.

§§ 143-236.2 through 143-236.28. Repealed by Session Laws 1971, c. 882, s. 2.

Article 24.

Wildlife Resources Commission.

§ 143-237. Title.

This Article shall be known and may be cited as the North Carolina Wildlife Resources Law. (1947, c. 263, s. 1.)

§ 143-238. Definitions.

As used in this Article unless the context clearly requires otherwise:

(1)   The word "Commission" shall mean the North Carolina Wildlife Resources Commission.

(2)   The word "Director" shall mean the Executive Director of the North Carolina Wildlife Resources Commission.

(3)   The terms "wildlife resources" and "wildlife" shall be defined in accordance with the definitions in G.S. 113-129. (1947, c. 263, s. 2; 1965, c. 957, s. 12.)

§ 143-239. Statement of purpose.

The purpose of this Article is to create a separate State agency to be known as the North Carolina Wildlife Resources Commission, the function, purpose, and duty of which shall be to manage, restore, develop, cultivate, conserve, protect, and regulate the wildlife resources of the State of North Carolina, and to administer the laws relating to game, game and freshwater fishes, and other wildlife resources enacted by the General Assembly to the end that there may be provided a sound, constructive, comprehensive, continuing, and economical game, game fish, and wildlife program directed by qualified, competent, and representative citizens, who shall have knowledge of or training in the protection, restoration, proper use and management of wildlife resources. (1947, c. 263, s. 3; 1965, c. 957, s. 13.)

§ 143-240. Creation of Wildlife Resources Commission; districts; qualifications of members.

(a)   There is hereby created the Wildlife Resources Commission of the Department of Environment and Natural Resources which shall consist of 19 citizens of North Carolina who shall be appointed as is provided in G.S. 143-241.

Each member of the Commission shall be an experienced hunter, fisherman, farmer, or biologist, who shall be generally informed on wildlife conservation and restoration problems.

Members of the Commission shall receive per diem and necessary travel and subsistence expenses in accordance with the provisions of G.S. 138-5 or G.S. 138-6 as the case may be, which shall be paid from fees collected by the Wildlife Resources Commission.

(b)   There are established the following geographical wildlife districts:

First district to be composed of the following counties: Bertie, Camden, Chowan, Currituck, Dare, Gates, Hertford, Hyde, Martin, Pasquotank, Perquimans, Tyrrell, Washington.

Second district to be composed of the following counties: Beaufort, Carteret, Craven, Duplin, Greene, Jones, Lenoir, New Hanover, Onslow, Pamlico, Pender, Pitt.

Third district to be composed of the following counties: Edgecombe, Franklin, Halifax, Johnston, Nash, Northampton, Vance, Wake, Warren, Wayne, Wilson.

Fourth district to be composed of the following counties: Bladen, Brunswick, Columbus, Cumberland, Harnett, Hoke, Robeson, Sampson, Scotland.

Fifth district to be composed of the following counties: Alamance, Caswell, Chatham, Durham, Granville, Guilford, Lee, Orange, Person, Randolph, Rockingham.

Sixth district to be composed of the following counties: Anson, Cabarrus, Davidson, Mecklenburg, Montgomery, Moore, Richmond, Rowan, Stanly, Union.

Seventh district to be composed of the following counties: Alexander, Alleghany, Ashe, Davie, Forsyth, Iredell, Stokes, Surry, Watauga, Wilkes, Yadkin.

Eighth district to be composed of the following counties: Avery, Burke, Caldwell, Catawba, Cleveland, Gaston, Lincoln, McDowell, Mitchell, Rutherford, Yancey.

Ninth district to be composed of the following counties: Buncombe, Cherokee, Clay, Graham, Haywood, Henderson, Jackson, Macon, Madison, Polk, Swain, Transylvania. (1947, c. 263, s. 4; 1961, c. 737, s. 11/2; 1965, c. 859, s. 2; 1971, c. 285; 1977, c. 771, s. 4; c. 906, s. 1; 1981 (Reg. Sess., 1982), c. 1191, s. 79; 1989, c. 68, s. 1; c. 727, s. 218(112); 1993 (Reg. Sess., 1994), c. 684, s. 13; 1997-443, s. 11A.119(a); 2001-486, s. 2.11(a).)

§ 143-241. Appointment and terms of office of Commission members; filling of vacancies.

The members of the North Carolina Wildlife Resources Commission shall be appointed as follows:

The Governor shall appoint one member each from the first, fourth, and seventh wildlife districts to serve six-year terms;

The Governor shall appoint one member each from the second, fifth, and eighth wildlife districts to serve two-year terms;

The Governor shall appoint one member each from the third, sixth, and ninth wildlife districts to serve four-year terms;

The Governor shall also appoint two at-large members to serve four-year terms.

The General Assembly shall appoint eight members of the Commission to serve two-year terms, four upon the recommendation of the Speaker of the House, four upon the recommendation of the President Pro Tempore of the Senate, in accordance with G.S. 120-121. Of the members appointed upon the recommendation of the Speaker of the House and upon the recommendation of the President Pro Tempore of the Senate, at least one of each shall be a member of the political party to which the largest minority of the members of the General Assembly belongs.

Thereafter as the terms of office of the members of the Commission appointed by the Governor from the several wildlife districts expire, their successors shall be appointed for terms of six years each. As the terms of office of the members of the Commission appointed by the General Assembly expire, their successors shall be appointed for terms of two years each. All members appointed by the Governor serve at the pleasure of the Governor that appointed them and they may be removed by that Governor at any time. A successor to the appointing Governor may remove a Commission member only for cause as provided in G.S. 143B-13. Members appointed by the General Assembly serve at the pleasure of that body and may be removed by law at any time. In the event that a Commission member is removed, the member appointed to replace the removed member shall serve only for the unexpired term of the removed member. (1947, c. 263, s. 5; 1961, c. 737, s. 1; 1965, c. 859, s. 3; 1973, c. 825, s. 2; 1977, c. 906, s. 2; 1981 (Reg. Sess., 1982), c. 1191, s. 80; 1989, c. 68, s. 3; 1993 (Reg. Sess., 1994), c. 684, s. 14; 1995, c. 490, s. 64; 2001-486, s. 2.11(b).)

§ 143-242. Vacancies by death, resignation or otherwise.

Appointments to fill vacancies of gubernatorial appointees on the Commission occurring by reason of death, disability, resignation or otherwise shall be made by the Governor for the balance of the unexpired terms by appointment of a member from the State at large, or from the appropriate district in accordance with the procedure set out in G.S. 143-241. Appointments to fill vacancies of those members of the Commission appointed by the General Assembly shall be made under G.S. 120-122. The Governor shall have the power to remove any member of the Commission from office for misfeasance, malfeasance or nonfeasance. (1947, c. 263, s. 6; 1973, c. 825, s. 3; 1977, c. 906, s. 3; 1981 (Reg. Sess., 1982), c. 1191, s. 81.)

§ 143-243. Organization of the Commission; election of officers; Robert's Rules of Order.

The Commission shall hold at least two meetings annually, one in January and one in July, and seven members of the Commission shall constitute a quorum for the transaction of business. Additional meetings may be held at such other times within the State as may be deemed necessary for the efficient transaction of the business of the Commission. The Commission may hold additional or special meetings at any time at the call of the chairman or on call of any five members of the Commission. The Commission shall determine its own organization and methods of procedure in accordance with the provisions of this Article, and shall have an official seal, which shall be judicially noticed.

At the first scheduled meeting of the Commission after July 1, 1977, and on July 1 of each odd-numbered year thereafter, the Commission shall select from among its membership a chairman and a vice-chairman who shall serve for terms of two years or until their successors are elected and qualified. The Secretary of Environment and Natural Resources or his designee shall serve as secretary of the Commission.

The chairman shall guide and coordinate the official actions and official activities of the Commission in fulfilling its program responsibility for (i) the appointment and separation of the executive director of the Commission, (ii) organizing the personnel of the Commission, (iii) setting the statewide policy of the Commission, (iv) budgeting and planning the use of the Wildlife and Motorboat Funds, subject to the approval of the General Assembly, (v) holding public hearings, and (vi) adopting rules as authorized by law. The chairman shall report to and advise the Governor on the official actions and work of the Commission and on all wildlife conservation and boating safety matters that affect the interest of the people of the State.

Meetings of the Commission shall be conducted pursuant to Robert's Rules of Order. (1947, c. 263, s. 7; 1973, c. 825, s. 4; 1977, c. 771, s. 4; c. 906, s. 4; 1983, c. 717, ss. 71, 72; 1987, c. 827, s. 213; 1989, c. 727, s. 218(113); 1997-443, s. 11A.119(a).)

§ 143-244. Location of offices.

The Board of Public Buildings and Grounds shall provide the Commission with offices in the city of Raleigh, North Carolina. (1947, c. 263, s. 8.)

§ 143-245. Repealed by Session Laws 1977, c. 906, s. 5.

§ 143-246. Executive Director; appointment, qualifications and duties.

The North Carolina Wildlife Resources Commission as soon as practicable after its organization shall select and appoint a competent person qualified as hereinafter set forth as Executive Director of the North Carolina Wildlife Resources Commission. The Executive Director shall be charged with the supervision of all activities under the jurisdiction of the Commission and shall serve as the chief administrative officer of the said Commission. Subject to the approval of the Commission and the Director of the Budget, he is hereby authorized to employ such clerical and other assistants as may be deemed necessary. The person selected as Executive Director shall have had training and experience in conservation, protection and management of wildlife resources. The salary of such Director shall be fixed by the Wildlife Resources Commission, in an amount at least equal to the salary of the Director of the Division of Marine Fisheries. The Director shall be allowed actual expenses incurred while on official duties away from resident headquarters. The salary and expenses of the Director shall be paid from the Wildlife Resources Fund subject to the provisions of the Executive Budget Act. The term of office of the Executive Director shall be at the pleasure of the Commission. Such bond shall be made as part of the blanket bond of State officers and employees provided for in G.S. 128-8. (1947, c. 263, s. 10; 1957, c. 541, s. 17; 1969, c. 844, s. 5; 1979, c. 830, s. 7; 1981, c. 884, s. 11; 1983, c. 717, s. 73; 1985, c. 479, s. 221; 1998-212, s. 28.19(a).)

§ 143-247. Transfer of powers, duties, jurisdiction, and responsibilities.

All duties, powers, jurisdiction, and responsibilities now vested by statute in and heretofore exercised by the Department of Conservation and Development, the Board of Conservation and Development, the Director of Conservation and Development, the Division of Game and Inland Fisheries, the Commissioner of Game and Inland Fisheries, or any predecessor organization, board, commission, commissioner or official relating to or pertaining to the wildlife resources of North Carolina, subject to the provisions of Subchapter IV of Chapter 113 of the General Statutes, are hereby transferred to and vested by law in the North Carolina Wildlife Resources Commission hereby created, subject to the provisions of this Article. The powers, duties, jurisdiction, and responsibilities hereby transferred shall be vested in the Commission immediately upon its organization under the provisions of this Article. Provided however, that no provision of this Article shall be construed as transferring to or conferring upon the North Carolina Wildlife Resources Commission, herein created, jurisdiction over the administration of any laws regulating the pollution of streams or public waters in North Carolina. (1947, c. 263, s. 11; 1965, c. 957, s. 14.)

§ 143-247.1. Commission may accept gifts.

The Wildlife Resources Commission is hereby authorized and empowered to accept gifts, donations or contributions from any source, which funds shall be held in a separate account and used solely for the purposes of wildlife conservation and management. Such funds shall be administered by the Wildlife Resources Commission and shall be used for wildlife conservation and management in a manner consistent with wildlife conservation management principles. (1971, c. 388.)

§ 143-247.2. Wildlife Conservation Account; emblems for those who donate to the Account.

(a)   Account. - The Wildlife Conservation Account is established within the Wildlife Resources Fund and is subject to the oversight of the State Auditor pursuant to Article 5A of Chapter 147 of the General Statutes. Revenue is credited to the Account from donations of income tax refunds, from other donations, from revenue derived from the sale of wildlife resources license plates, and from interest earned on the Account balance. The Commission may use revenue in the Account only for the following purposes:

(1)   To manage, preserve, or protect wildlife species that are endangered, threatened, or of special concern and are included on the State's protected animal lists.

(2)   To manage, preserve, or protect nongame wildlife species that are not on the State's protected animal lists.

(3)   To administer and enforce nongame wildlife programs under the jurisdiction of the Commission.

(b) Emblems. - The Commission may issue and sell appropriate emblems by which to identify recipients of the emblems as contributors to the Wildlife Conservation Account. Emblems of different size, shape, type, or design may be used to recognize contributions in different amounts. The Commission may not issue an emblem for a contribution of less than five dollars ($5.00). (1975, c. 77; 1993, c. 257, s. 14; c. 543, s. 7; 1995, c. 509, s. 81; 2007-448, s. 1.)

§ 143-248. Transfer of lands, buildings, records, equipment, and other properties.

There is hereby transferred to the North Carolina Wildlife Resources Commission all lands, buildings, structures, records, reports, equipment, vehicles, supplies, materials, and other properties, and the possession and use thereof, which have heretofore been acquired or obtained and now remain in the possession of, or which are now and heretofore have been used or intended for use by the Department of Conservation and Development, the Director of Conservation and Development, the Division of Game and Inland Fisheries, and the Commission of Game and Inland Fisheries, and any predecessor organization or division or official of either, for the purpose of protecting, propagating, and developing game, fur-bearing animals, game fish, inland fisheries, and all other wildlife resources which heretofore have been used or held by them in connection with any program conducted for said purposes, whether said lands or properties were acquired, purchased, or obtained by deed, gift, grant, contract, or otherwise; the said lands and other properties hereby transferred, subject to the limitations hereinafter set forth to the said Wildlife Resources Commission shall be held and used by it subject to the provisions of this Article and other provisions of law in furtherance of the intents, purposes, and provisions of this Article and other provisions of law in such manner and for such purposes as may be determined by the Commission. In the event that there shall arise any conflict in the transfer of any properties or functions as herein provided, the Governor of the State is hereby authorized and empowered to issue such executive order, or orders, as may be necessary clarifying and making certain the issue, or issues, thus arising: Provided, further, nothing herein contained shall be construed to transfer any of the State parks or State forests to the North Carolina Wildlife Resources Commission: Provided, further, title to the property transferred by virtue of the provisions of this Article shall be held by the State of North Carolina for the use and benefit of the North Carolina Wildlife Resources Commission and the use, control and sale of any of such property shall be governed by the general law of the State affecting such matters. (1947, c. 263, s. 12; 1965, c. 957, s. 15.)

§ 143-249. Transfer of personnel.

Upon July 1, 1947, the Division of Game and Inland Fisheries of the North Carolina Department of Conservation and Development shall cease to exist and all employees of said Division shall continue as employees of the Commission at their option or until further action by the Commission. (1947, c. 263, s. 13.)

§ 143-249.1. Operating budget.

No more than twenty-five percent (25%) of the certified operating budget of the Wildlife Resources Commission shall be allowed to accumulate in a cash balance. It is the intent of the General Assembly to implement in any subsequent fiscal year a nonrecurring reduction in an amount equal to the cash balance that exceeds twenty-five percent (25%) of the authorized operating budget in the prior fiscal year. (2013-283, s. 18.)

§ 143-250. Wildlife Resources Fund.

All moneys in the game and fish fund or any similar State fund when this Article becomes effective shall be credited forthwith to a special fund in the office of the State Treasurer, and the State Treasurer shall deposit all such moneys in said special fund, which shall be known as the Wildlife Resources Fund.

All unexpended appropriations made to the Department of Conservation and Development, the Board of Conservation and Development, the Division of Game and Inland Fisheries or to any other State agency for any purpose pertaining to wildlife and wildlife resources shall also be transferred to the Wildlife Resources Fund.

Except as otherwise specifically provided by law, all moneys derived from hunting, fishing, trapping, and related license fees, exclusive of commercial fishing license fees, including the income received and accruing from the investment of license revenues, and all funds thereafter received from whatever sources shall be deposited to the credit of the Wildlife Resources Fund and made available to the Commission until expended subject to the provisions of this Article. License revenues include the proceeds from the sale of hunting, fishing, trapping, and related licenses, from the sale, lease, rental, or other granting of rights to real or personal property acquired or produced with license revenues, and from federal aid project reimbursements to the extent that license revenues originally funded the project for which the reimbursement is being made. For purposes of this section, real property includes lands, buildings, minerals, energy resources, timber, grazing rights, and animal products. Personal property includes equipment, vehicles, machines, tools, and annual crops. The Wildlife Resources Fund herein created shall be subject to the provisions of the State Budget Act, Chapter 143C of the General Statutes of North Carolina as amended, and the provisions of the General Statutes of North Carolina as amended, and the provisions of the Personnel Act, Chapter 143, Article 2 of the General Statutes of North Carolina as amended.

All moneys credited to the Wildlife Resources Fund shall be made available to carry out the intent and purposes of this Article in accordance with plans approved by the North Carolina Wildlife Resources Commission, and all such funds are hereby appropriated, reserved, set aside and made available until expended, for the enforcement and administration of this Article, Chapter 75A, Article 1, and Chapter 113, Subchapter IV of the General Statutes of North Carolina. No later than October 1 of each year, the Wildlife Resources Commission shall report to the Joint Legislative Commission on Governmental Operations on the expenditures from the Wildlife Resources Fund during the fiscal year that ended the previous July 1 of that year and on the planned expenditures for the current fiscal year.

In the event any uncertainty should arise as to the funds to be turned over to the North Carolina Wildlife Resources Commission the Governor shall have full power and authority to determine the matter and his recommendation shall be final and binding to all parties concerned. (1947, c. 263, s. 14; 1965, c. 957, s. 16; 1981, c. 482, s. 2; 1982 (Reg. Sess., 1982), c. 1182, s. 1; 1987, c. 816; 1991, c. 689, s. 167(a); 2006-203, s. 92; 2011-145, s. 13.28(a).)

§ 143-250.1. Wildlife Endowment Fund.

(a) Recognizing the inestimable importance to the State and its people of conserving the wildlife resources of North Carolina, and for the purpose of providing the opportunity for citizens and residents of the State to invest in the future of its wildlife resources, there is created the North Carolina Wildlife Endowment Fund, the income and principal of which shall be used only for the purpose of supporting wildlife conservation programs of the State in accordance with this section. This fund shall also be known as the Eddie Bridges Fund.

(b) There is created the Board of Trustees of the Wildlife Endowment Fund of the Wildlife Resources Commission, with full authority over the administration of the Wildlife Endowment Fund, whose ex officio chairman, vice-chairman, and members shall be the chairman, vice-chairman, and members of the Wildlife Resources Commission. The State Treasurer shall be the custodian of the Wildlife Endowment Fund and shall invest its assets in accordance with the provisions of G.S. 147-69.2 and 147-69.3.

(c) The assets of the Wildlife Endowment Fund shall be derived from the following:

(1) The proceeds of any gifts, grants and contributions to the State which are specifically designated for inclusion in the fund;

(2) The proceeds from the sale of lifetime sportsman combination licenses issued pursuant to G.S. 113-270.1D;

(3) The proceeds from the sale of lifetime hunting and lifetime fishing licenses pursuant to G.S. 113-270.2(c)(2) and G.S. 113-271(d)(3);

(4) The proceeds of lifetime subscriptions to the magazine Wildlife in North Carolina at such rates as may be established from time to time by the Wildlife Resources Commission;

(5) Any amount in excess of the statutory fee for a particular lifetime license or lifetime subscription shall become an asset of the fund and shall qualify as a tax exempt donation to the State;

(5a) The proceeds from the sale of lifetime combination hunting and fishing licenses for disabled residents pursuant to G.S. 113-270.1C(b)(4);

(6) Such other sources as may be specified by law.

(d) The Wildlife Endowment Fund is declared to constitute a special trust derived from a contractual relationship between the State and the members of the public whose investments contribute to the fund. In recognition of such special trust, the following limitations and restrictions are placed on expenditures from the funds:

(1) Any limitations or restrictions specified by the donors on the uses of the income derived from gifts, grants and voluntary contributions shall be respected but shall not be binding.

(2) No expenditures or disbursements from the income from the proceeds derived from the sale of Infant Lifetime Sportsman or Youth Lifetime Sportsman Licenses pursuant to G.S. 113-270.1D(b)(1) or (2) shall be made for any purpose until the respective holders of such licenses attain the age of 16 years. The State Treasurer, as custodian of the fund, shall determine actuarially from time to time the amount of income within the fund which remains encumbered by and which is free of this restriction. For such purpose, the executive director shall cause deposits of proceeds from Infant Lifetime Sportsman Licenses to be distinguished and deposits of proceeds from Youth Lifetime Sportsman Licenses to be accompanied by information as to the ages of the license recipients.

(3) No expenditure or disbursement shall be made from the principal of the Wildlife Endowment Fund except as otherwise provided by law.

(4) The income received and accruing from the investments of the Wildlife Endowment Fund must be spent only in furthering the conservation of wildlife resources and the efficient operation of the North Carolina Wildlife Resources Commission in accomplishing the purposes of the agency as set forth in G.S. 143-239.

(e) The Board of Trustees of the Wildlife Endowment Fund may accumulate the investment income of the fund until the income, in the sole judgment of the trustees, can provide a significant supplement to the budget of the Wildlife Resources Commission. After that time the trustees, in their sole discretion and authority, may direct expenditures from the income of the fund for the purposes set out in division (4) of subsection (d).

(f) Expenditure of the income derived from the Wildlife Endowment Fund shall be made through the State budget accounts of the Wildlife Resources Commission in accordance with the provisions of the Executive Budget Act. The

Wildlife Endowment Fund is subject to the oversight of the State Auditor pursuant to Article 5A of Chapter 147 of the General Statutes.

(f1) At all times during which the cash balance in the Wildlife Endowment Fund is equal to or greater than the sum of one hundred million dollars ($100,000,000), the Wildlife Resources Commission shall budget at least fifty percent (50%) of the annual expendable interest from the Fund, as determined by the Board of Trustees of the Fund, to implement the conservation goals set forth in the Wildlife Resource Commission's strategic plan.

(g) The Wildlife Endowment Fund and the income therefrom shall not take the place of State appropriations or agency receipts placed in the Wildlife Resources Fund, or any part thereof, but any portion of the income of the Wildlife Endowment Fund available for the purpose set out in division (4) of subsection (d) shall be used to supplement other income of and appropriations to the Wildlife Resources Commission to the end that the Commission may improve and increase its services and become more useful to a greater number of people.

(h) In the event of a future dissolution of the Wildlife Resources Commission, such State agency as shall succeed to its budgetary authority shall, ex officio, assume the trusteeship of the Wildlife Endowment Fund and shall be bound by all the limitations and restrictions placed by this section on expenditures from the fund. No repeal or modification of this section or of G.S. 143-239 shall alter the fundamental purposes to which the Wildlife Endowment Fund may be applied. No future dissolution of the Wildlife Resources Commission or substitution of any agency in its stead shall invalidate any lifetime license issued in accordance with G.S. 113-270.1D(b), 113-270.2(c)(2), or 113-271(d)(3). (1981, c. 482, s. 1; 1993, c. 257, s. 15; 1993 (Reg. Sess., 1994), c. 684, ss. 10-12; 1997-326, s. 4; 2013-283, s. 19.)

§ 143-251. Cooperative agreements.

In furtherance of the purposes of this Article the Commission is hereby authorized and empowered to enter into cooperative agreements pertaining to the management and development of the wildlife resources with federal, State, and other agencies, or governmental subdivisions. (1947, c. 263, s. 15.)

§ 143-252. Article subject to Chapter 113.

Nothing in this Article shall be construed to affect the jurisdictional division between the North Carolina Wildlife Resources Commission and the Department of Environment and Natural Resources contained in Subchapter IV of Chapter 113 of the General Statutes, or in any way to alter or abridge the powers and duties of the two agencies conferred in that Subchapter. (1947, c. 263, s. 16; 1965, c. 957, s. 17; 1973, c. 1262, s. 86; 1977, c. 771, s. 4; 1989, c. 727, s. 166; 1997-443, s. 11A.119(a).)

§ 143-253. Jurisdictional questions.

In the event of any questions arising between the Department of Environment and Natural Resources and the North Carolina Wildlife Resources Commission as to any duty or responsibility or authority imposed upon either of said bodies by law, or in case of any conflicting rules or administrative practices adopted by said bodies, such questions or matters shall be determined by the Governor and his determination shall be binding on each of said bodies. (1947, c. 263, s. 17; 1973, c. 1262, s. 86; 1977, c. 771, s. 4; 1989, c. 727, s. 167; 1997-443, s. 11A.119(a).)

§ 143-254: Repealed by Session Laws, 1987, c. 827, s. 214.

§ 143-254.1. Repealed by Session Laws 1979, c. 830, s. 8.

§ 143-254.2. Enforcement of local laws.

(a)   It shall be the duty and responsibility of the North Carolina Wildlife Resources Commission to enforce all local acts heretofore or hereinafter enacted respecting game animals, fur-bearing animals and birds, including local acts which prohibit or restrict hunting from, to or across public roads and highways and including local acts which prohibit or restrict the taking of specified animals or birds.

Provided, however, that the provisions of this section shall not apply on the lands of the Eastern Band of Cherokee Indians.

(b) The provisions of this section shall not be construed to require the hiring of additional personnel by the North Carolina Wildlife Resources Commission. (1977, c. 120, ss. 1-3.)

§ 143-254.5. Disclosure of personal identifying information.

Social security numbers and identifying information obtained by the Commission shall be treated as provided in G.S. 132-1.10. For purposes of this section, "identifying information" also includes a person's mailing address, residence address, date of birth, and telephone number. (2005-455, s. 1.17; 2006-255, s. 11.1.)

Article 25.

National Park, Parkway and Forests Development Commission.

§§ 143-255 through 143-257. Repealed by Session Laws 1973, c. 1262, s. 86.

§ 143-258: Repealed by Session Laws 2002-165, s. 1.8, effective October 23, 2002.

§§ 143-259 through 143-260. Repealed by Session Laws 1973, c. 1262, s. 86.

Article 25A.

Historic Sites Commission; Historic and Archeological Sites.

§§ 143-260.1 through 143-260.5. Repealed by Session Laws 1955, c. 543, s. 5.

Article 25B.

State Nature and Historic Preserve Dedication Act.

§ 143-260.6. Short title.

This Article shall be known and may be cited as the State Nature and Historic Preserve Dedication Act. (1973, c. 443, s. 1.)

§ 143-260.7. Purpose.

It is the purpose of this Article to prescribe the conditions and procedures under which properties may be specially dedicated for the purposes enumerated by Article XIV, Sec. 5 of the North Carolina Constitution ("Conservation of Natural Resources"), accepted by the General Assembly for said purposes, and thereby constituted part of the State Nature and Historic Preserve. (1973, c. 443, s. 2.)

§ 143-260.8. Procedures.

(a)   Within the meaning of this section:

(1)   "Local governing body" means, as the case may be, the board of commissioners of a county, the city council (or equivalent legislative body) of a city, or the board of aldermen or board of commissioners (or equivalent legislative body) of a town.

(2)   "Local government" means a county, city or town.

(3)   "Properties" include any properties or interest in properties acquired by purchase or gift.

(b)   The Council of State may petition the General Assembly to enact a law pursuant to Article XIV, Sec. 5 of the North Carolina Constitution, accepting any properties owned by the State of North Carolina (or proposed for gift to or purchase by the State) and designated in the petition for inclusion in the State Nature and Historic Preserve.

(c)   The governing body of any local government, or any combination of two or more such bodies may petition the General Assembly to enact a law pursuant to Article XIV, Sec. 5 of the North Carolina Constitution, accepting any properties owned by the local government (or proposed for gift to or purchase by the local government) and designated in the petition for inclusion in the State Nature and Historic Preserve.

(d) The petition referred to in subsections (a) and (b) of this section shall identify the properties sought to be included in the Preserve. The General Assembly may then enact a law to accept the designated properties in the Preserve and enactment of the law by the General Assembly shall constitute the special dedication and acceptance of the designated properties in the State Nature and Historic Preserve contemplated by Article XIV, Sec. 5 of the North Carolina Constitution.

(e) In order to provide accessible information to the public concerning the State Nature and Historic Preserve, every law accepting or removing properties in the Preserve shall be codified in the General Statutes. A certified copy of every law accepting or removing properties in the Preserve shall be transmitted by the Secretary of State to the register of deeds in each county wherein these properties, or any part of them, are located, for filing and indexing in the grantor index.

(f) This Article shall constitute an exclusive procedure only for placing properties in the State Nature and Historic Preserve, and shall not preclude the dedication of properties by other means for purposes identical or similar to those enumerated by Article XIV, Sec. 5 of the North Carolina Constitution.

(g) It is the intent of this Article to complement any applicable provisions of federal and State law and regulations relating to dedication or acceptance of properties for purposes similar to those enumerated by Article XIV, Sec. 5 of the North Carolina Constitution. The Council of State is hereby authorized to adopt rules and regulations to implement the provisions of this Article, including rules and regulations consistent with this Article to comport with applicable federal and State law and regulations. A copy of this Article, and of any rules affecting properties owned by local governments shall be filed by the Council of State with the chairman of the local governing body of every county, city and town within 30 days after ratification. (1973, c. 443, s. 3; 1999-268, s. 6; 2003-234, s. 3.)

§ 143-260.9. Dedication shall not affect maintenance and improvement of existing structures or facilities.

The dedication of property to the State Nature and Historic Preserve shall not prevent the administering State agency or local governing body from carrying out normal maintenance and improvement of existing structures or facilities that are appropriate to, and consistent with, the purpose for which the property in question was obtained by the State agency or local governing body. (1973, c. 443, s. 4.)

§ 143-260.10. Components of State Nature and Historic Preserve.

The following are components of the State Nature and Historic Preserve accepted by the North Carolina General Assembly pursuant to G.S. 143-260.8:

(1) All lands and waters within the boundaries of the following units of the State Parks System as of May 5, 2009: Baldhead Island State Natural Area, Bay Tree Lake State Park, Bear Paw State Natural Area, Beech Creek Bog State Natural Area, Bullhead Mountain State Natural Area, Bushy Lake State Natural Area, Carolina Beach State Park, Carvers Creek State Park, Cliffs of the Neuse State Park, Chowan Swamp State Natural Area, Deep River State Trail, Dismal Swamp State Park, Elk Knob State Park, Fort Fisher State Recreation Area, Fort Macon State Park, Goose Creek State Park, Gorges State Park, Haw River State Park, Hammocks Beach State Park, Jones Lake State Park, Lake Norman State Park, Lea Island State Natural Area, Lower Haw River State Natural Area, Lumber River State Park, Mayo River State Park, Medoc Mountain State Park, Merchants Millpond State Park, Mitchells Millpond State Natural Area, Mount Mitchell State Park, Occoneechee Mountain State Natural Area, Pettigrew State Park, Pilot Mountain State Park, Pineola Bog State Natural Area, Raven Rock State Park, Run Hill State Natural Area, Sandy Run Savannas State Natural Area, Singletary Lake State Park, Sugar Mountain State Natural Area, Theodore Roosevelt State Natural Area, and Weymouth Woods-Sandhills Nature Preserve.

(2) All lands and waters within the boundaries of William B. Umstead State Park as of May 5, 2009, with the exception of Tract Number 65, containing 22.93140 acres as shown on a survey prepared by John S. Lawrence (RLS) and Bennie R. Smith (RLS), entitled "Property of The State of North Carolina William B. Umstead State Park", dated January 14, 1977 and filed in the State Property Office, which was removed from the State Nature and Historic Preserve by Chapter 450, Section 1 of the 1985 Session Laws. The tract excluded from the State Nature and Historic Preserve under this subdivision is deleted from the State Parks System in accordance with G.S. 113-44.14. The State of North Carolina may only exchange this land for other land for the expansion of William B. Umstead State Park or sell and use the proceeds for

that purpose. The State of North Carolina may not otherwise sell or exchange this land.

(3)   Repealed by Session Laws 1999-268, s. 2.

(4)   All lands within the boundaries of Morrow Mountain State Park as of May 5, 2009, with the exception of the following tract: That certain tract or parcel of land at Morrow Mountain State Park in Stanly County, North Albemarle Township, containing 0.303 acres, more or less, as surveyed and platted by Thomas W. Harris R.L.S., on a map dated August 27, 1988, and filed in the State Property Office, reference to which is hereby made for a more complete description.

(5)   Repealed by Session Laws 1999-268, s. 2.

(6)   All land within the boundaries of Crowders Mountain State Park as of May 5, 2009, with the exception of the following tracts. The tracts excluded from the State Nature and Historic Preserve under this subdivision are deleted from the State Parks System in accordance with G.S. 113-44.14. The State of North Carolina may only exchange this land for other land for the expansion of Crowders Mountain State Park or sell this land and use the proceeds for that purpose. The State may not otherwise sell or exchange this land.

a.   The portion of that certain tract or parcel of land at Crowders Mountain State Park in Gaston County, Crowders Mountain Township, described in Deed Book 1939, page 800, and containing 757.28 square feet and as shown in a survey by Tanner and McConnaughey, P.A. dated July 22, 1988 and filed in the State Property Office.

b.   The portion of that certain tract or parcel of land at Crowders Mountain State Park in Gaston County, east of and including the right-of-way along and across Old Peach Orchard Road, as shown in a survey by the City of Gastonia, File No. 400-194, dated November 23, 1998, and filed in the State Property Office.

c.   The portion of that certain tract or parcel of land at Crowders Mountain State Park in Cleveland County, described in Deed Book 1286, Page No. 85, located on the north side of SR 2245 (Bethlehem Road) and containing 14,964 square feet as shown on the survey entitled "Survey for Crowders Mountain State Park, Deed Book 1103-107, Township 4 Kings Mountain, Cleveland County, N.C." by David W. Dickson, P.A. dated February 28, 2008.

(7)   All lands owned in fee simple by the State within the boundaries of New River State Park as of May 5, 2009.

(8)   All lands and waters within the boundaries of Stone Mountain State Park as of May 5, 2009, with the exception of the following tracts: The portion of that certain tract or parcel of land at Stone Mountain State Park in Wilkes County, Traphill Township, described as parcel 33-02 in Deed Book 633-193, and more particularly described as all of the land in this parcel lying to the west of the eastern edge of the Air Bellows Road, as shown on the National Park Service Land Status Map 33 dated March 24, 1981 and filed in the State Property Office, containing approximately 72 acres. The tract excluded from the State Nature and Historic Preserve under this subdivision is deleted from the State Parks System in accordance with G.S. 113-44.14.

(9)   All lands and waters located within the boundaries of the following State Historic Sites as of May 5, 2009: Alamance Battleground, Charles B. Aycock Birthplace, Historic Bath, Bennett Place, Bentonville Battleground, Brunswick Town/Fort Anderson, C.S.S. Neuse and Governor Caswell Memorial, Charlotte Hawkins Brown Memorial, Duke Homestead, Historic Edenton, Fort Dobbs, Fort Fisher, Historic Halifax, Horne Creek Living Historical Farm, House in the Horseshoe, North Carolina Transportation Museum, James K. Polk Memorial, Reed Gold Mine, Somerset Place, Stagville, State Capitol, Town Creek Indian Mound, Tryon Palace Historic Sites & Gardens, Zebulon B. Vance Birthplace, and Thomas Wolfe Memorial.

(10), (11)   Repealed by Session Laws 2001-217, s. 2, effective June 15, 2001.

(12)   All lands and waters located within the boundaries of Hanging Rock State Park as of May 5, 2009, with the exception of the following tract: The portion of that tract or property at Hanging Rock State Park in Stokes County, Danbury Township, described in Deed Book 360, Page 160, for a 30-foot wide right-of-way beginning approximately 183 feet south of SR 1001 and extending in a southerly direction approximately 1,479 feet to the southwest corner of the Bobby Joe Lankford tract and more particularly shown on a survey entitled, "J. Spot Taylor Heirs Survey, Danbury Township, Stokes County, N.C.", by Grinski Surveying Company, dated June 1985, and filed in the State Property Office. The tract excluded from the State Nature and Historic Preserve under this subdivision is deleted from the State Parks System in accordance with G.S. 113-44.14.

(13) All lands and waters located within the boundaries of South Mountains State Park as of May 5, 2009, with the exception of the following tracts. The tracts excluded from the State Nature and Historic Preserve under this subdivision are deleted from the State Parks System in accordance with G.S. 113-44.14.

a, b. Repealed by Session Laws 2007-307, s. 1, effective July 28, 2007.

c. The portions of land at South Mountains State Park that lie south of the centerline of the CCC road as shown on the drawing entitled "Land Trade between South Mountains State Park and Adjacent Game Lands along CCC Road" prepared by the Division of Parks and Recreation, dated March 15, 1999, and filed in the State Property Office and that lie within: (i) the tract or property in Burke County, Lower Fork Township, described in Deed Book 495, Page 501; (ii) the tract or property in Burke County, Lower Fork and Upper Fork Townships, described in Deed Book 715, Page 719; or, (iii) within the tracts or property in Burke County, Upper Fork Township, described in Deed Book 860, Page 341, and Deed Book 884, Page 1640. The State of North Carolina may only exchange this land for other land for the expansion of South Mountains State Park or sell this land and use the proceeds for that purpose. The State may not otherwise sell or exchange this land.

d. Repealed by Session Laws 2007-307, s. 1, effective July 28, 2007.

(14) Repealed by Session Laws 2003-234, s. 1, effective June 19, 2003.

(15) All lands and waters within the boundaries of Jockey's Ridge State Park as of May 5, 2009, with the exception of the following tracts: The portion of those certain tracts or parcels of land at Jockey's Ridge State Park in Dare County, Nags Head Township, described in Deed Book 227, Page 499, and Deed Book 227, Page 501, and containing 33,901 square feet as shown on the survey prepared by Styons Surveying Services entitled "Raw Water Well Site 13 Jockey's Ridge State Park" dated March 7, 2001, and filed in the State Property Office; the portion of that certain tract or parcel of land at Jockey's Ridge State Park in Dare County, Nags Head Township, described in Deed Book 222, Page 726, and containing 42,909 square feet as shown on the survey prepared by Styons Surveying Services entitled "Raw Water Well Site 14 Jockey's Ridge State Park" dated March 7, 2001, and filed in the State Property Office; and the portion of that certain tract or parcel of land at Jockey's Ridge State Park in Dare County, Nags Head Township, described in Deed Book 224, Page 790, and Deed Book 224, Page 794, and containing 34,471 square feet as shown on

the survey prepared by Styons Surveying Services entitled "Raw Water Well Site 15 Jockey's Ridge State Park" dated March 7, 2001, and filed in the State Property Office.

(16) All lands and waters located within the boundaries of Mount Jefferson State Natural Area as of May 5, 2009. With respect to the communications tower site on the top of Mount Jefferson and located on that certain tract or parcel of land at Mount Jefferson State Natural Area in Ashe County, West Jefferson Township, described in Deed Book F-3, Page 94, the State may provide space at the communications tower site to State public safety and emergency management agencies for the placement of antennas, repeaters, and other communications devices for public communications purposes. Notwithstanding G.S. 146-29.2, the State may lease space at the communications tower site to local governments in Ashe County for the placement of antennas, repeaters, and other communications devices for public communications purposes. State agencies and local governments that are authorized to place communications devices at the communications tower site pursuant to this subdivision may also locate at or near the communications tower site communications equipment that is necessary for the proper operation of the communications devices. The use of the communications tower site pursuant to this subdivision is authorized by the General Assembly as a purpose other than the public purposes specified in Article XIV, Section 5, of the North Carolina Constitution, Article 25B of Chapter 143 of the General Statutes, and Article 2C of Chapter 113 of the General Statutes.

(17) All lands and waters within the Eno River State Park as of May 5, 2009, with the exception of the following tracts:

a. The portion of that certain tract or parcel of land at Eno River State Park in Durham County, Durham Outside Township, described in Deed Book 435, Page 673, and Plat Book 87, Page 66, containing 11,000 square feet and being the portion of Lot No. 2 shown as the existing scenic easement hereby removed on the drawing prepared by Sear-Brown entitled "Recombination Plat Eno Forest Subdivision" bearing the preparer's file name 00-208-07.dwg, and filed with State Property Office. The tract excluded from the State Nature and Historic Preserve under this subdivision is deleted from the State Parks System pursuant to G.S. 113-44.14. The State of North Carolina may only exchange this land for other land for the expansion of Eno River State Park or sell this land and use the proceeds for that purpose. The State may not otherwise sell or exchange this land.

b. The portion of that certain tract or parcel of land at Eno River State Park in Orange County, described in Deed Book 3878, Page 461, and Plat Book 98, Page 11, containing 5,313 square feet and required for the permanent easements for bridge replacement project B-4216 on SR 1002 (St. Mary's Road), as shown in the drawing entitled "Preliminary Plans, Project Reference No. B-4216" prepared for North Carolina Department of Transportation by Mulkey Engineers and Consultants dated March 10, 2009, and filed with the State Property Office. The tracts excluded from the State Nature and Historic Preserve under this section are deleted from the State Parks System pursuant to G.S. 113-44.14. The State of North Carolina may only exchange this land for other land for the expansion of Eno River State Park or sell this land and use the proceeds for that purpose. The State may not otherwise sell or exchange this land.

(18) All land and waters within the boundaries of Hemlock Bluffs State Natural Area as of May 5, 2009, with the exception of the following tracts: The portion of that certain tract or parcel of land at Hemlock Bluffs State Natural Area in Wake County, Swift Creek Township, described in Deed Book 2461, Page 037, containing 2,025 square feet and being the portion of this tract shown as proposed R/W on the drawing prepared by Titan Atlantic Group entitled "Right of Way Acquisition Map for Town of Cary Widening of Kildaire Farm Road (SR 1300) from Autumgate Drive to Palace Green" sheet 1 of 3 bearing the preparer's file name Town of Cary Case File No. TOC 01-37, dated 26 September 2003, and filed with the State Property Office; and the portion of those certain tracts or parcels of land at Hemlock Bluffs State Natural Area in Wake County, Swift Creek Township, described in Deed Book 4670, Page 420, containing 24,092 square feet and being the portion of these tracts shown as proposed R/W on the drawing prepared by Titan Atlantic Group entitled "Right of Way Acquisition Map for Town of Cary Widening of Kildaire Farm Road (SR 1300) from Autumgate Drive to Palace Green" sheet 3 of 3 bearing the preparer's file name Town of Cary Case File No. TOC 01-37, dated 26 September 2003, and filed with the State Property Office. The tracts excluded from the State Nature and Historic Preserve under this subdivision are deleted from the State Parks System pursuant to G.S. 113-44.14. The State of North Carolina may only exchange this land for other land for the expansion of Hemlock Bluffs State Natural Area or sell this land and use the proceeds for that purpose. The State may not otherwise sell or exchange this land.

(19) All lands and waters within the boundaries of Lake James State Park as of May 5, 2009, with the exception of the following tracts:

a. The portion of that certain tract or parcel of land at Lake James State Park containing 13.85 acres, and being 100 feet to the east and 150 feet to the west of a centerline shown on a survey by Witherspoon Surveying PLLC, dated February 9, 2007, and filed in the State Property Office. The State of North Carolina may grant a temporary easement to Duke Energy Corporation across this tract to facilitate the Catawba Dam Embankment Seismic Stability Improvements Project. The grant of the easement within Lake James State Park to Duke Energy Corporation under this sub-subdivision constitutes authorization by the General Assembly that the described tract of land may be used for a purpose other than the public purposes specified in Article XIV, Section 5, of the North Carolina Constitution, Article 25B of Chapter 143 of the General Statutes, and Article 2C of Chapter 113 of the General Statutes. The State of North Carolina may use the proceeds from the easement only for the expansion or improvement of Lake James State Park or another State park. The State may not otherwise sell or exchange this land.

b. The portion of that certain tract or parcel of land at Lake James State Park in McDowell County, Nebo Township, described in Deed Book 377, Page 423, and also shown as Tract B on the plat of survey prepared by Kenneth D. Suttles, RLS, dated December 4, 1987, entitled "Lake James State Park," Sheet 1 of 2, recorded in Plat Book 4, Page 275 of the McDowell County Registry, for a 40-foot right-of-way beginning at the southwest corner of Tract B and continuing along the southern boundary 86 38' 51" E for 400 feet to the now or former John D. Walker property. The State of North Carolina may grant an easement across this tract to extinguish prescriptive easements on Tract B to improve management of the State park property. The State may not otherwise sell or exchange this land. The easement excluded from the State Nature and Historic Preserve under this subdivision is deleted from the State Parks System pursuant to G.S. 113-44.14.

(20) All lands and waters within the boundaries of Lake Waccamaw State Park as of May 5, 2009, with the exception of the following tracts: The portions of that certain tract or parcel of land at Lake Waccamaw State Park in Columbus County described in Deed Book 835, Page 590, containing 48,210 square feet and being the portion of this tract shown as new R/W and permanent utility easement on drawing prepared by State of North Carolina Department of Transportation entitled "Map of Proposed Right of Way Property of State of North Carolina (Parks and Recreation) Columbus County" for Tip B-3830 on SR 1947 (Bella Coola Road) done by John E. Kaukola, PLS No. 3999 and compiled 1-18-2008, and filed with the State Property Office. The tracts excluded from the State Nature and Historic Preserve under this section are deleted from the State

Parks System pursuant to G.S. 113-44.14. The State of North Carolina may only exchange this land for other land for the expansion of Lake Waccamaw State Park or sell this land and use the proceeds for that purpose. The State may not otherwise sell or exchange this land.

(21) All lands and waters within the boundaries of Chimney Rock State Park as of May 5, 2009, with the exception of the following tract: The portion of that certain tract or parcel of land at Chimney Rock State Park in Rutherford County being a portion of Parcel 2 as described in Deed Book 933, Page 598, containing 346 square feet and being shown as proposed right-of-way for bridge replacement project B-4258 on U.S. 64 over the Broad River on drawing prepared by Kimley-Horn and Associates for the North Carolina Department of Transportation and revised October 26, 2007, and filed with the State Property Office. The tracts excluded from the State Nature and Historic Preserve under this section are deleted from the State Parks System pursuant to G.S. 113-44.14. The State of North Carolina may only exchange this land for other land for the expansion of Chimney Rock State Park or sell this land and use the proceeds for that purpose. The State may not otherwise sell or exchange this land.

(22) All State-owned land and waters within the boundaries of the Mountains-to-Sea Trail as of May 5, 2009, with the exception of the following tract: The portion of that certain tract or parcel in Johnston County described in Deed Book 3634, Page 278, containing 4.72 acres and being described as proposed easement area for Piedmont Natural Gas Company transmission line on drawing entitled "Easement Survey Prepared for Piedmont Natural Gas Company, Line 142, Easement to be Acquired from the State of North Carolina" by McKim & Creed and dated July 31, 2008, and revised March 11, 2009. The State of North Carolina may grant an easement to Piedmont Natural Gas Company across this tract to facilitate the transmission of natural gas. The grant of the easement within the Mountains-to-Sea Trail to Piedmont Natural Gas Company under this section constitutes authorization by the General Assembly that the described tract of land may be used for a purpose other than the public purposes specified in Section 5 of Article XIV of the North Carolina Constitution, Article 25B of Chapter 143 of the General Statutes, and Article 2C of Chapter 113 of the General Statutes. The State of North Carolina may use the proceeds from the easement only for the expansion or improvement of the Mountains-to-Sea Trail or another State park. The State may not otherwise sell or exchange this land. (1979, c. 498; 1989, Joint Res. 23; c. 146, s. 1; 1989 (Reg. Sess., 1990), c. 1004, s. 30; 1999-268, s. 2; 2001-217, s. 2; 2002-149, s. 1; 2003-234, s. 1; 2004-25, s. 2; 2007-307, s. 1; 2008-11, s. 1; 2009-503, s. 1.)

§§ 143-260.10A through 143-260.10B: Repealed by Session Laws 1989, c. 146, ss. 3, 4.

§ 143-260.10C. Removal of land in Hemlock Bluffs from the State Nature and Historic Preserve.

Notwithstanding the provisions of G.S. 143-260.10(1), the tract identified as a portion of the property legally described in Deed Book 3135, Page 937, Wake County Registry, containing 14.4 acres, as shown on a survey prepared by A. Roger Barnes (RLS) and entitled "Proposed Exchange of 14.4 Acres From the State of North Carolina to the Town of Cary," dated August 19, 1988, is removed from the State Nature and Historic Preserve.

The State of North Carolina may only exchange this land for other land to expand Hemlock Bluffs Natural Area or sell the land and use the proceeds for that purpose. The State of North Carolina may not otherwise sell or exchange this land.

The removal of the portion of Hemlock Bluffs under this section achieves the requirements and purposes of Article 2C of Chapter 113 of the General Statutes and constitutes a deletion from the State Parks System as required by G.S. 113-44.14. (1989, c. 384.)

§ 143-260.10D. Removal of land at Hammocks Beach State Park from the State Nature and Historic Preserve.

Notwithstanding the provisions of G.S. 143-260.10(1), the tract identified as a portion of the property legally described in Deed Book 414, Page 607, Onslow County Registry, containing 0.063 acres; beginning at a point located S 25°19'50" W, 60.86 feet, thence S 02°10'40" E, 33.61 feet from the southeast corner of above reference property, proceeding from said beginning point S 02°10'40" E, 32.73 feet, thence S 69°12'45" W, 176.47 feet to a point, thence N 59°47'25" E, 189.47 feet to the point of beginning; as shown on a survey prepared by John P. McLean Engineering Associates and entitled "Exhibit Map Showing Land Swap Between N.C. Park Service and Hammocks Point" dated June 29, 1990, is removed from the State Nature and Historic Preserve.

The State of North Carolina may only exchange this land for other land for inclusion in Hammocks Beach State Park or sell the land and use the proceeds for that purpose. The State of North Carolina may not otherwise sell or exchange this land.

The removal of the portion of Hammocks Beach State Park under this section achieves the requirements and purposes of Article 2C of Chapter 113 of the General Statutes and constitutes a deletion from the State Parks System as required by G.S. 113-44.14. (1991, c. 318; 1991, c. 318.)

§ 143-260.10E. Utility easement at William B. Umstead State Park.

(a) The State of North Carolina may grant a utility easement to Carolina Power and Light Company across a tract of land within William B. Umstead State Park. The easement shall be 100 feet wide, extending 50 feet on each side of the following-described survey line: Lying and being in Leesville township, Wake County, North Carolina; BEGINNING at point B2 as shown on the Drawing hereinafter referred to, the point B2 being located in a southern property line of Raleigh Durham Airport Authority (formerly Continental Mortgage Investors) and a northern property line of the State of North Carolina; the point B2 also being located North 87 degrees 01 minute 31 seconds West 834.04 feet from a concrete monument making a southeastern corner of Raleigh Durham Airport Authority (formerly Continental Mortgage Investors); and runs thence South 02 degrees 01 minute 53 seconds East 3508.00 feet to point A2 on the Drawing, the location of Point A2 having North Carolina Coordinates Y=773, 193.769 and X=2,069,162.420, the Point A2 being located at the terminus of Carolina Power and Light Company's existing 100 foot wide right-of-way strip, as shown and described on Carolina Power and Light Company Drawing No. RW-A-5246, dated September 1977, which Drawing also shows the respective complementing sidelines going to make up the easement.

(b) The State of North Carolina may only use the proceeds from the easement described in subsection (a) of this section to acquire property at any State park.

(c) The grant of the easement within William B. Umstead State Park to Carolina Power and Light Company under this section constitutes authorization by the General Assembly that the described tract of land may be used for a utility easement, which is a purpose other than the public purposes as specified in Article XIV, Section 5, of the Constitution, Article 25B of Chapter 143 of the

General Statutes, and Article 2C of Chapter 113 of the General Statutes. (1991 (Reg. Sess., 1992), c. 907, s. 1.)

§ 143-260.10F. Road right-of-way; Pilot Mountain State Park.

(a) Notwithstanding the provisions of G.S. 143-260.10, the State of North Carolina may convey a road right-of-way to the Department of Transportation across lands within Pilot Mountain State Park. The right-of-way for the road shall begin 71.9 feet S 70° 41' 12" E of park corner number 94 as shown on the June 1, 1968, Pilot Mountain State Park survey by Southern Mapping & Engineering Company. From point of beginning N 70° 41' 12" W for 71.9 feet, then following the centerline of the existing road SR 2068 N 02° 31' 21" E for 24.13 feet, then N 25° 17' 28" E for 225.06 feet, then N 35° 31'48" E for 139.35 feet, then with the northern boundary of the park S 55° 48' 51" E for 30.0 feet, then along new right-of-way line for approximately 350 feet as shown on Department of Transportation Plat of SR 2068, Shoals Road - McKinney Cut, Surry County, W.O. 6.742488 dated August 28, 1992, to point of beginning. The area of this right-of-way is approximately 17,850 square feet.

(b) The property described in subsection (a) of this section is removed from the State Nature and Historic Preserve and deleted from the State Parks System.

(c) The State shall only use the proceeds from this right-of-way to acquire lands for the expansion of Pilot Mountain State Park. (1993, c. 457.)

§ 143-260.10G. Removal of land in Crowders Mountain State Park from the State Nature and Historic Preserve.

(a) Notwithstanding the provisions of G.S. 143-260.10(6), the portion of that certain tract or parcel of property at Crowders Mountain State Park in Gaston County, Crowders Mountain Township, described in Deed Book 1240, Page 451, and containing 225 square feet and as shown in a survey by R&W Engineering and Surveying entitled "Conveyance of 0.0052 acres owned by Crowders Mountain State Park, Gaston Co., NC" and dated January 18, 1995, is removed from the State Nature and Historic Preserve.

(b) The property described in subsection (a) of the section is deleted from the State Parks System pursuant to G.S. 113-44.14.

(c) The State may only exchange this property for other property for the expansion of Crowders Mountain State Park or sell this land and use the proceeds for that purpose. The State shall not otherwise sell or exchange this land. (1995, c. 131, s. 1.)

Article 26.

State Education Commission.

§ 143-261. Appointment and membership; duties.

The Governor of North Carolina is hereby authorized to appoint a commission to be known as the State Education Commission, consisting of 18 members, six of whom shall be selected from educational groups within the State, and 12 of whom shall be selected from the agricultural, business, industrial, and professional life of the State. It shall be the duty of this Commission to study all educational problems to the end that a sound overall educational program may be developed in North Carolina, and to report their findings and make recommendations to the Governor and the General Assembly of 1949. (1947, c. 724, s. 1.)

§ 143-262. Organization meeting; election of officers; status of members.

After their appointment, the Commission shall meet in the office of the Governor of North Carolina not later than the fifteenth of May, 1947, and upon the recommendation of the Governor, elect a chairman and a full-time executive secretary. The secretary may or may not be a member of the Commission. Membership on the Commission herein authorized shall not constitute public office but shall be considered as a commissioner for a special purpose; and the Governor may appoint as ex officio member, or members, on said Commission any public official without violating the provisions of Article XIV, Sec. 7, of the State Constitution. (1947, c. 724, s. 2.)

§ 143-263. Comprehensive study of education problems.

This Commission shall make a comprehensive study of organization, administration, finance, teacher education, supervision, curriculum, standardization, consolidation, transportation, buildings, personnel, a merit rating system for teachers, vocational education, and any other problems related to the overall educational program of the State. (1947, c. 724, s. 3.)

§ 143-264. Per diem and travel allowances.

Each member of the Commission shall be entitled to per diem and travel the same as is paid to the State Board of Education, when attending any meeting of the Commission or while engaged in the performance of any duties of the Commission. (1947, c. 724, s. 4.)

§ 143-265. Salary of executive secretary.

The Commission is authorized to set the salary of a full-time executive secretary, with the approval of the Director of the Budget. (1947, c. 724, s. 5.)

§ 143-266. Powers of executive secretary.

The executive secretary of the Commission shall have the authority and power to subpoena witnesses and compel their attendance to testify and/or produce records at any hearing before the Commission, or any committee thereof, under the same provisions of the law as now apply to attendance of witnesses before legislative committees. (1947, c. 724, s. 6.)

Article 27.

Settlement of Affairs of Certain Inoperative Boards and Agencies.

§ 143-267. Release and payment of funds to State Treasurer; delivery of other assets to Secretary of Administration.

Whenever the statutes creating, or granting authority to, any licensing, regulatory, or examining board or agency have been or are hereafter repealed, or declared unconstitutional or invalid by the Supreme Court of North Carolina, every officer or other person responsible for or having control or custody of any funds, records, equipment or any other assets held or owned by any such board or agency which was theretofore authorized by any such statute to exercise licensing or regulatory powers or conduct examinations in respect to the right to practice any profession or engage in any trade, business, craft or calling, shall forthwith release and deliver all such funds to the State Treasurer of North Carolina, and shall forthwith release and deliver all other assets of every nature whatsoever to the Secretary of Administration for the State of North Carolina. (1949, c. 740, s. 1; 1975, c. 879, s. 46.)

§ 143-268. Official records turned over to Department of Cultural Resources; conversion of other assets into cash; allocation of assets to State agency or department.

The Secretary of Administration shall receive all such assets so delivered and, after they have served their purpose in the liquidation of the affairs of such board or agency, shall turn over all official records of such board or agency to the Department of Cultural Resources to be held pursuant to the statutes relating to such Department. The Secretary of Administration shall proceed to convert all other such assets into cash by public sale to the highest bidder, and shall deposit the net proceeds of any such sale with the State Treasurer: Provided, that the Secretary of Administration, in his discretion, may allocate to any State agency or department, the whole or any part of such assets, the sale of which is not required to discharge the obligations of the board or agency being liquidated. (1949, c. 740, s. 2; 1973, c. 476, s. 48; 1975, c. 879, s. 46.)

§ 143-269. Deposit of funds by State Treasurer.

The State Treasurer shall receive all funds delivered to him under this Article and shall deposit the same in a special fund for the account of the board or agency whose affairs are being liquidated, to be held and applied as hereinafter provided. (1949, c. 740, s. 3.)

§ 143-270. Statement of claims against board or agency; time limitation on presentation.

Any person having any claim or cause of action against any board or agency whose affairs are being liquidated under this Article, may present a verified statement of the same to the Secretary of Administration, who shall investigate and approve or disapprove such claim; any claim not presented to the Secretary of Administration within one year from the time such board or agency becomes inoperative by law shall be barred, and no claim shall be approved or paid which is barred by any statute of limitation or any statutory prohibition in respect to the payment of any claim, or the refund of any deposit, dues, assessment, or examination or license fee. (1949, c. 740, s. 4; 1975, c. 879, s. 46.)

§ 143-271. Claims certified to State Treasurer; payment; escheat of balance to University of North Carolina.

The Secretary of Administration shall certify to the State Treasurer a schedule of all claims approved or disapproved, and after one year from the time at which the board or agency became inoperative under the law, the State Treasurer shall, out of the funds in his hands for the account of such board or agency, pay all approved claims in full, or if such funds are insufficient for full payment, then he shall equally prorate said claims and make partial payment insofar as funds are available. Should any balance remain in the hands of the Treasurer after the payment of all approved claims, such balance shall escheat and be paid over to the University of North Carolina, to be held in accordance with the statutes governing escheats. (1949, c. 740, s. 5; 1975, c. 879, s. 46.)

§ 143-272. Audit of affairs of board or agency; payment for audit and other expenses.

Irrespective of the provisions of G.S. 143-271 of this Article, the State Treasurer is specifically authorized, in his discretion, to cause an audit to be made of the affairs of any such board or agency, and to immediately pay the cost of such audit, together with the expenses of transferring records and assets, and other necessary costs of liquidation, out of the first funds coming into his hands for the account of such board or agency. (1949, c. 740, s. 6.)

Article 28.

Communication Study Commission.

§§ 143-273 to 143-278. Expired.

Article 29.

Commission to Study the Care of the Aged and Handicapped.

§ 143-279. Establishment and designation of Commission.

A Commission is hereby established for the study of the problems relating to the care of the aged with especial reference to those failing mentally and the intellectually or physically handicapped of all ages and this Commission shall be known as "the Commission for the Study of Problems of the Care of the Aged and Intellectually or Physically Handicapped." (1949, c. 1211, s. 1.)

§ 143-280. Membership.

The Commission shall consist of three members from the Department of Health and Human Services, one member from the boards of county commissioners, one county superintendent of social services, one local health director, one clerk of the superior court. (1949, c. 1211, s. 2; 1957, c. 1357, s. 12; 1963, c. 1166, s. 10; 1969, c. 982; 1973, c. 476, ss. 128, 133, 138; 1997-443, s. 11A.95.)

§ 143-281. Appointment and removal of members.

The Governor shall appoint the members of this Commission, and may remove any member; he shall not be required to give any reason for the removal of any member. (1949, c. 1211, s. 3.)

§ 143-282. Duties of Commission; recommendations.

This Commission shall study the problems relating to the care of the aged with especial reference to those failing mentally and shall inquire into the methods of meeting and handling this problem in other states. It shall make a similar study of the problem of the care of the feebleminded, with especial attention to the custodial care of intellectually handicapped persons not teachable or trainable. It shall make a study of the problems relating to the care of the physically handicapped with a special reference to those whose physical handicap renders them incapable of self-support and shall inquire into the methods of meeting and handling this problem in other states.

It shall make recommendations to the Governor offering plans for dealing with the problem of the care needed for this group, and means of clarification of the responsibility of the State and respective counties. (1949, c. 1211, s. 4.)

§ 143-283. Compensation.

The members of the Commission shall receive for each day in actual performance of duties under this Article, a per diem of seven dollars ($7.00), and necessary travel and subsistence expenses, to be paid out of the contingency and emergency fund. (1949, c. 1211, s. 5.)

Article 29A.

Governor's Council on Employment of the Handicapped.

§ 143-283.1. Short title.

This Article may be cited as "The Governor's Council on Employment of the Handicapped Act." (1961, c. 981; 1973, c. 476, s. 179.)

§ 143-283.2. Purpose of Article; cooperation with President's Committee.

The purpose of this Article is to carry on a continuing program to promote the employment of the physically, mentally, emotionally, and otherwise handicapped citizens of North Carolina by creating statewide interest in the rehabilitation and employment of the handicapped, and by obtaining and maintaining cooperation with all public and private groups and individuals in this field. The Governor's Council shall work in close cooperation with the President's Committee on Employment of the Physically Handicapped to more effectively carry out the purpose of this Article, and with State and federal agencies having responsibilities for employment and rehabilitation of the handicapped. (1961, c. 981; 1973, c. 476, s. 179.)

§ 143-283.3. Celebration of National Employ the Physically Handicapped Week.

The Governor's Council shall, by proclamation, designate the first full week in October of each year as "National Employ the Physically Handicapped Week." The committee shall promote and encourage the holding of appropriate ceremonies throughout the State during said week, the purpose of which ceremonies shall be to enlist public support for and interest in the employment of the physically handicapped. The Governor shall, in his proclamation designating National Employ the Physically Handicapped Week, invite the mayors of all cities, heads of other instrumentalities of government, leaders of industry and business, educational and religious groups, labor, veterans, women, farm, scientific and professional, and all other organizations and individuals having an interest to participate in said ceremonies. (1961, c. 981; 1973, c. 476, s. 179.)

§§ 143-283.4 through 143-283.6. Repealed by Session Laws 1973, c. 476, s. 179.

§ 143-283.7: Repealed by Session Laws 1991, c. 45, s. 25.

§ 143-283.8. Governor's Council nonpartisan and nonprofit.

The Governor's Council shall be nonpartisan, nonprofit, and shall not be used for the dissemination of partisan principles, nor for the promotion of the candidacy of any person seeking public office or preferment. (1961, c. 981; 1973, c. 476, s. 179.)

§§ 143-283.9 through 143-283.10. Repealed by Session Laws 1973, c. 476, s. 179.

Article 29B.

Governor's Coordinating Council on Aging.

§§ 143-283.11 through 143-283.23. Repealed by Session Laws 1973, c. 476, s. 173.

Article 29C.

Youth Councils Act.

§§ 143-283.24 through 143-283.30. Repealed by Session Laws 1975, c. 879, s. 30.

§ 143-283.31. Repealed by Session Laws 1973, c. 797, s. 1.

§ 143-283.32. Repealed by Session Laws 1975, c. 879, s. 30.

§§ 143-283.33 through 143-283.40. Reserved for future codification purposes.

Article 29D.

Manpower Council.

§§ 143-283.41 through 143-283.48. Repealed by Session Laws 1975, c. 879, s. 42.

Article 30.

Nutbush Conservation Area.

§§ 143-284 through 143-286. Repealed by Session Laws 1973, c. 1262, s. 76.

§ 143-286.1. Nutbush Conservation Area.

The Department of Environment and Natural Resources is hereby authorized to enter into lease agreements with the proper agencies of the federal government covering the marginal land area of the John H. Kerr Reservoir or so much thereof as may be necessary or desirable in order to develop said area for park purposes and to carry on a program of conservation, forestry development and wildlife protection. The area so obtained shall be known as the Nutbush Conservation Area. The Department of Environment and Natural Resources is hereby authorized to control and develop the area so leased and to enter into sublease agreements on terms as may be authorized in the original lease agreement. All proceeds obtained from any sublease agreement shall be used exclusively for the further development of the Nutbush Conservation Area. (1953, c. 1312, s. 4; 1963, c. 612, s. 2; 1973, c. 1262, ss. 28, 76; 1977, c. 771, s. 4; 1989, c. 727, s. 218(114); 1997-443, s. 11A.119(a).)

§§ 143-287 through 143-288. Repealed by Session Laws 1973, c. 1262, s. 76.

§ 143-289. Contributions from certain counties and municipalities authorized; other grants or donations.

The boards of county commissioners of the Counties of Granville, Vance and Warren and the municipalities within these counties are authorized and empowered in their discretion to make annual contributions to the Department of Environment and Natural Resources for the purpose of defraying the necessary expenses of operation and the Department of Environment and Natural Resources is authorized and empowered to accept grants or donations from any interested citizens or from any State or federal agency. (1951, c. 444, s. 6;

1973, c. 1262, s. 76; 1977, c. 771, s. 4; 1989, c. 727, s. 218(115); 1997-443, s. 11A.119(a).)

§§ 143-290 through 143-290.1: Repealed by Session Laws 1973, c. 1262, s. 76.

Article 31.

Tort Claims against State Departments and Agencies.

§ 143-291. Industrial Commission constituted a court to hear and determine claims; damages; liability insurance in lieu of obligation under Article.

(a)   The North Carolina Industrial Commission is hereby constituted a court for the purpose of hearing and passing upon tort claims against the State Board of Education, the Board of Transportation, and all other departments, institutions and agencies of the State. The Industrial Commission shall determine whether or not each individual claim arose as a result of the negligence of any officer, employee, involuntary servant or agent of the State while acting within the scope of his office, employment, service, agency or authority, under circumstances where the State of North Carolina, if a private person, would be liable to the claimant in accordance with the laws of North Carolina. If the Commission finds that there was negligence on the part of an officer, employee, involuntary servant or agent of the State while acting within the scope of his office, employment, service, agency or authority that was the proximate cause of the injury and that there was no contributory negligence on the part of the claimant or the person in whose behalf the claim is asserted, the Commission shall determine the amount of damages that the claimant is entitled to be paid, including medical and other expenses, and by appropriate order direct the payment of damages as provided in subsection (a1) of this section, but in no event shall the amount of damages awarded exceed the amounts authorized in G.S. 143-299.2 cumulatively to all claimants on account of injury and damage to any one person arising out of a single occurrence. Community colleges and technical colleges shall be deemed State agencies for purposes of this Article. The fact that a claim may be brought under more than one Article under this Chapter shall not increase the foregoing maximum liability of the State.

(a1) The unit of State government that employed the employee at the time the cause of action arose shall pay the first one hundred fifty thousand dollars ($150,000) of liability, and the balance of any payment owed shall be paid in accordance with G.S. 143-299.4.

(b) If a State agency, otherwise authorized to purchase insurance, purchases a policy of commercial liability insurance providing coverage in an amount at least equal to the limits of the State Tort Claims Act, such insurance coverage shall be in lieu of the State's obligation for payment under this Article.

(c) The North Carolina High School Athletic Association, Inc., is a State agency for purposes of this Article, and its liability in tort shall be only under this Article. This subsection does not extend to any independent contractor of the Association. The Association shall be obligated for payments under this Article, through the purchase of commercial insurance or otherwise, in lieu of any responsibility of the State or The University of North Carolina for this payment. The Association shall be similarly obligated to reimburse or have reimbursed the Department of Justice for any expenses in defending any claim against the Association under this Article.

(d) Liability in tort of the State Health Plan for Teachers and State Employees for noncertifications as defined under G.S. 58-50-61 shall be only under this Article. (1951, c. 1059, s. 1; 1953, c. 1314; 1955, c. 400, s. 1; c. 1102, s. 1; c. 1361; 1957, c. 65, s. 11; 1965, c. 256, s. 1; 1967, c. 1206, s. 1; 1971, c. 893, s. 1; 1973, c. 507, s. 5; c. 1225, s. 1; 1977, c. 464, s. 34; c. 529, ss. 1, 2; 1979, c. 1053, s. 1; 1987, c. 684, s. 1; 1987 (Reg. Sess., 1988), c. 1087, s. 1; 1993 (Reg. Sess., 1994), c. 769, s. 19.33(a); c. 777, s. 5(a); 2000-67, ss. 7A(a), 7A(b); 2001-446, s. 5(f); 2007-323, s. 28.22A(o); 2007-345, s. 12.)

§ 143-291.1. Costs.

The Industrial Commission is authorized by such order to tax the costs against the loser in the same manner as costs are taxed by the superior court in civil actions. When a State department, institution, or agency appeals the decision rendered by the hearing commissioner to the full Commission, the State department, institution or agency shall furnish a copy of the transcript of the hearing to the appellee without cost therefor. The State department, institution or agency concerned is authorized and directed to pay such costs as may be taxed against it, including all costs heretofore taxed against such department, agency or institution. (1955, c. 1102, s. 2; 1971, c. 58.)

§ 143-291.2. Costs and fees.

(a) The Industrial Commission may by order tax the costs against the losing party in the same amount and the same manner as costs are taxed in the General Court of Justice. When a State department, institution, or agency appeals to the full commission the decision rendered by a hearing commissioner, the State department, institution, or agency shall furnish a copy of the transcript of the hearing to the appellee without cost. The State department, institution, or agency concerned may pay the costs taxed against it. When costs are not paid by a party from whom they are due, the Industrial Commission shall issue an execution for the costs and attach a bill of costs to each execution. The Sheriff shall levy upon the execution as provided in Chapter 6 of the General Statutes in civil actions.

(b) The Industrial Commission shall charge a filing fee for each affidavit initiating a claim filed under this Article in an amount equal to the filing fee charged for civil actions in the Superior Court Division of the General Court of Justice. No filing fee shall be required of indigent persons, provided each claim by an indigent complies with all statutory and administrative requirements applicable to the filing of civil actions by indigents in the Superior Court Division of the General Court of Justice. (1987 (Reg. Sess., 1988), c. 1087, s. 2.)

§ 143-291.3. Counterclaims by State.

The filing of a claim under this Article shall constitute consent by the plaintiff to the jurisdiction of the Industrial Commission to hear and determine any counterclaim of the maximum amount authorized for a claim in G.S. 143-299.2 or less that may be filed on behalf of a State department, institution or agency, or a county or city board of education. A final award of the Industrial Commission awarding damages on a counterclaim shall be filed with the clerk of the superior court of the county where the case was heard. These awards shall be docketed and shall be enforceable in the same manner as judgments of the General Court of Justice. Notwithstanding the provisions of Rule 12 of the Rules of Civil Procedure, nothing in this section shall require the filing of a counterclaim. (1987 (Reg. Sess., 1988), c. 1087, s. 3; 1995, c. 509, s. 82; 2000-67, s. 7A(c).)

§ 143-292. Notice of determination of claim; appeal to full Commission.

Upon determination of said claim the Commission shall notify all parties concerned in writing of its decision and either party shall have 15 days after receipt of such notice within which to file notice of appeal with the Industrial Commission. Such appeal, when so taken, shall be heard by the Industrial Commission, sitting as a full Commission, on the basis of the record in the matter and upon oral argument of the parties, and said full Commission may amend, set aside, or strike out the decision of the hearing commissioner and may issue its own findings of fact and conclusions of law. Upon determination of said claim by the Industrial Commission, sitting as a full Commission, the Commission shall notify all parties concerned in writing of its decision. Such determination by the Industrial Commission, sitting as a full Commission, upon claims in an amount of five hundred dollars ($500.00) or less, shall be final as to the State or any of its departments, institutions or agencies, and no appeal shall lie therefrom by the State or any of its departments, institutions or agencies. (1951, c. 1059, s. 2; 1955, c. 770; 1979, c. 581.)

§ 143-293. Appeals to Court of Appeals.

Either the claimant or the State may, within 30 days after receipt of the decision and order of the full Commission, to be sent by registered or certified mail, but not thereafter, appeal from the decision of the Commission to the Court of Appeals. Such appeal shall be for errors of law only under the same terms and conditions as govern appeals in ordinary civil actions, and the findings of fact of the Commission shall be conclusive if there is any competent evidence to support them. The appellant shall cause to be prepared a statement of the case as required by the rules of the Court of Appeals. A copy of this statement shall be served on the respondent within 45 days from the entry of the appeal taken; within 20 days after such service, the respondent shall return the copy with his approval or specified amendments endorsed or attached; if the case be approved by the respondent, it shall be filed with the clerk of the Court of Appeals as a part of the record; if not returned with objections within the time prescribed, it shall be deemed approved. The chairman of the Industrial

Commission shall have the power, in the exercise of his discretion, to enlarge the time in which to serve statement of case on appeal and exceptions thereto or counterstatement of case.

If the case on appeal is returned by the respondent with objections as prescribed, or if a countercase is served on appellant, the appellant shall immediately request the chairman of the Industrial Commission to fix a time and place for settling the case before him. If the appellant delays longer than 15 days after the respondent serves his countercase or exceptions to request the chairman to settle the case on appeal, and delays for such period to mail the case and countercase or exceptions to the chairman, then the exceptions filed by the respondent shall be allowed; or the countercase served by him shall constitute the case on appeal; but the time may be extended by agreement of counsel.

The chairman shall forthwith notify the attorneys of the parties to appear before him for that purpose at a certain time and place, which time shall not be more than 20 days from the receipt of the request. At the time and place stated, the chairman of the Industrial Commission or his designee shall settle and sign the case and deliver a copy to the attorneys of each party. The appellant shall within five days thereafter file it with the clerk of the Court of Appeals, and if he fails to do so the respondent may file his copy.

No appeal bond or supersedeas bond shall be required of State departments or agencies. (1951, c. 1059, s. 3; 1967, c. 655, s. 1; 1987 (Reg. Sess., 1988), c. 1087, s. 4.)

§ 143-294. Appeal to Court of Appeals to act as supersedeas.

The appeal from the decision of the Industrial Commission to the Court of Appeals shall act as a supersedeas, and the State department, institution or agency shall not be required to make payment of any judgment until the questions at issue therein shall have been finally determined as provided in this Article. (1951, c. 1059, s. 4; 1967, c. 655, s. 2.)

§ 143-295. Settlement of claims.

(a) Any claims except claims of minors pending or hereafter filed against the various departments, institutions and agencies of the State may be settled upon agreement between the claimant and the Attorney General for an amount not in excess of twenty-five thousand dollars ($25,000), without the approval of the Industrial Commission. The Attorney General may also make settlements by agreement for claims in excess of twenty-five thousand dollars ($25,000) and claims of infants or persons non sui juris, provided such claims have been subject to review and approval by the Industrial Commission.

(b) In settlements under twenty-five thousand dollars ($25,000), agreed upon between the Attorney General and the claimant, the filing of an affidavit as set forth in G.S. 143-297 shall not be required.

(c) Transfer of title of a motor vehicle acquired in behalf of the State in settlement of claim pursuant to the provisions of this Article may be transferred by the Attorney General in the same manner as provided for such transfer by an insurance company under the provisions of G.S. 20-75. (1951, c. 1059, s. 5; 1971, c. 1103, s.1; 1973, c. 699; 1975, c. 756; 1979, c. 877; 1981, c. 166; 1985, c. 693; 1989, c. 228, ss. 1, 2.)

§ 143-295.1. Settlement of small claims against institutions of the Department of Health and Human Services.

When the property of a resident of a State institution under the Department of Health and Human Services is lost, destroyed, or otherwise damaged through negligent handling by the institution, and the amount of damages is less than five hundred dollars ($500.00), the institution may make direct payment or provide replacement of the item to the resident without recourse to the procedures otherwise provided by this Article. (2003-285, s. 1.)

§ 143-296. Powers of Industrial Commission; deputies.

The members of the Industrial Commission, or a deputy thereof, shall have power to issue subpoenas, administer oaths, conduct hearings, take evidence, enter orders, opinions, and awards based thereon, punish for contempt, and issue writs of habeas corpus ad testificandum pursuant to G.S. 97-101.1. The Industrial Commission is authorized to appoint deputies and clerical assistants to carry out the purpose and intent of this Article, and such deputy or deputies are hereby vested with the same power and authority to hear and determine tort claims against State departments, institutions, and agencies as is by this Article vested in the members of the Industrial Commission. Such deputy or deputies shall also have and are hereby vested with the same power and authority to hear and determine cases arising under the Workers' Compensation Act when assigned to do so by the Industrial Commission. The Commission may order parties to participate in mediation, under rules substantially similar to those approved by the Supreme Court for use in the Superior Court division, except the Commission shall determine the manner in which payment of the costs of the mediated settlement conference is assessed. (1951, c. 1059, s. 6; 1979, c. 714, s. 2; 1993, c. 399, s. 2; c. 321, s. 25(b); 1995, c. 358, s. 8(a); c. 437, s. 6(a); c. 467, s. 5(a); c. 507, s. 25.13; 1998-217, s. 31.1(b).)

§ 143-297. Affidavit of claimant; docketing; venue; notice of hearing; answer, demurrer or other pleading to affidavit.

In all claims listed in Section 13 of Chapter 1059 of the Session Laws of 1951, and all claims which may hereafter be filed against the various departments, institutions, and agencies of the State, the claimant or the person in whose behalf the claim is made shall file with the Industrial Commission an affidavit in duplicate, setting forth the following information:

(1)   The name of the claimant;

(2)   The name of the department, institution or agency of the State against which the claim is asserted, and the name of the State employee upon whose alleged negligence the claim is based;

(3)   The amount of damages sought to be recovered;

(4)   The time and place where the injury occurred;

(5)   A brief statement of the facts and circumstances surrounding the injury and giving rise to the claim.

Upon receipt of such affidavit in duplicate, the Industrial Commission shall enter the case upon its hearing docket and shall hear and determine the matter in the county where the injury occurred unless the parties agree or the Industrial

Commission directs that the case may be heard in some other county. All parties shall be given reasonable notice of the date when and the place where the claim will be heard.

Immediately upon docketing the case, the Industrial Commission shall forward one copy of plaintiff's affidavit to the office of the Attorney General of North Carolina if the claim is asserted against any department, institution, or agency of the State.

The department, institution or agency of the State against whom the claim is asserted shall file answer, demurrer or other pleading to the affidavit within 30 days after receipt of copy of same setting forth any defense it proposes to make in the hearing or trial, and no defense may be asserted in the hearing or trial unless it is alleged in such answer, except such defenses as are not required by the Code of Civil Procedure or other laws to be alleged. (1951, c. 1059, s. 9; 1963, c. 1063; 1971, c. 893, s. 2; c. 1103, s. 2.)

§ 143-298. Duty of Attorney General; expenses; subpoenas.

It shall be the duty of the Attorney General to represent all departments, institutions, and agencies of the State in connection with claims asserted against them and to attend all hearings in connection therewith where the amount of the claim, in the opinion of the Attorney General, is of sufficient import to require and justify such appearance. In the event the amount appropriated to the Attorney General's office for travel and subsistence is insufficient to take care of the additional expense incident to attending these hearings, the Governor and Council of State are authorized to pay such additional travel expenses from the Contingency and Emergency Fund.

Subpoenas for any purpose authorized by G.S. 1A-1, Rule 45 may be issued by an Attorney of Record for either party in all proceedings under the State Tort Claims Act and served by the means specified in the North Carolina Rules of Civil Procedure or served by registered or certified mail, and service shall be proved by filing of the return receipt. (1951, c. 1059, s. 10; 1971, c. 1103, s. 3; 1987 (Reg. Sess., 1988), c. 1087, s. 5.)

§ 143-299. Limitation on claims.

All claims against any and all State departments, institutions, and agencies shall henceforth be forever barred unless a claim be filed with the Industrial Commission within three years after the accrual of such claim, or if death results from the accident, the claim for wrongful death shall be forever barred unless a claim be filed by the personal representative of the deceased with the Industrial Commission within two years after such death. (1951, c. 1059, s. 11; 1973, c. 659.)

§ 143-299.1. Contributory negligence a matter of defense; burden of proof.

Contributory negligence on the part of the claimant or the person in whose behalf the claim is asserted shall be deemed to be a matter of defense on the part of the State department, institution or agency against which the claim is asserted, and such State department, institution or agency shall have the burden of proving that the claimant or the person in whose behalf the claim is asserted was guilty of contributory negligence. (1955, c. 400, s. 1 1/4.)

§ 143-299.1A. Limit use of public duty doctrine as an affirmative defense.

(a) Except as provided in subsection (b) of this section, the public duty doctrine is an affirmative defense on the part of the State department, institution, or agency against which a claim is asserted if and only if the injury of the claimant is the result of any of the following:

(1) The alleged negligent failure to protect the claimant from the action of others or from an act of God by a law enforcement officer as defined in subsection (d) of this section.

(2) The alleged negligent failure of an officer, employee, involuntary servant or agent of the State to perform a health or safety inspection required by statute.

(b) Notwithstanding subsection (a) of this section, the affirmative defense of the public duty doctrine may not be asserted in any of the following instances:

(1) Where there is a special relationship between the claimant and the officer, employee, involuntary servant or agent of the State.

(2) When the State, through its officers, employees, involuntary servants or agents, has created a special duty owed to the claimant and the claimant's reliance on that duty is causally related to the injury suffered by the claimant.

(3) Where the alleged failure to perform a health or safety inspection required by statute was the result of gross negligence.

(c) This section does not apply to a unit of local government or its officers, employees, or agents.

(d) For purposes of this section, "law enforcement officer" means a full-time or part-time employee or agent of a State department, institution, or agency or an agent of the State operating under an agreement with a State department, institution, or agency of the State who is any of the following:

(1) Actively serving in a position with assigned primary duties and responsibilities for prevention and detection of crime or the general enforcement of the criminal laws of the State or serving civil processes.

(2) Possesses the power of arrest by virtue of an oath administered under the authority of the State.

(3) Is a juvenile justice officer, chief court counselor, or juvenile court counselor.

(4) Is a correctional officer performing duties of custody, supervision, and treatment to control and rehabilitate criminal offenders.

(5) Is a firefighter as defined in G.S. 106-955(1).

(6) Is a probation officer appointed under Article 20 of Chapter 15 of the General Statutes. (2008-170, s. 1; 2008-187, s. 47; 2009-570, s. 21.)

§ 143-299.2. Limitation on payments by the State.

(a) The maximum amount that the State may pay cumulatively to all claimants on account of injury and damage to any one person arising out of any one occurrence, whether the claim or claims are brought under this Article, or Article 31A or Article 31B of this Chapter, shall be one million dollars

($1,000,000), less any commercial liability insurance purchased by the State and applicable to the claim or claims under G.S. 143-291(b), 143-300.6(c), or 143-300.16(c).

(b) The fact that a claim or claims may be brought under more than one Article under this Chapter shall not increase the above maximum liability of the State. (1987 (Reg. Sess., 1988), c. 1087, s. 6; 1995, c. 509, s. 83; 2000-67, s. 7A(d); 2007-452, s. 1.)

§ 143-299.3. Use of State vehicles by North Carolina Amateur Sports; State to incur no liability.

(a) Notwithstanding G.S. 14-247 and G.S. 143-341(8)i, the Department of Administration or any other department of State government may allow North Carolina Amateur Sports to have the use of State trucks and vans for the 1989 and the 1990 State Games of North Carolina. There will not be any charge for use of vehicles under this section.

(b) The State of North Carolina shall incur no liability for any damages resulting from use of vehicles under this section and North Carolina Amateur Sports shall carry liability insurance of not less than $500,000 covering such vehicles while in its use. (1989, c. 242, s. 1(a), (b); 1991, c. 636, s. 17; 1993, c. 553, s. 5.)

§ 143-299.4. Payment of State excess liability.

For each claim payable during any fiscal year in excess of one hundred fifty thousand dollars ($150,000) per claim arising under this Article, or Article 31A or 31B of this Chapter, on account of injury or damage to any one person, each State agency shall transfer to the Office of State Budget and Management its proportionate share of that agency's estimated lapsed salaries, as determined by the Director of the Budget, and the Director of the Budget shall use these transferred funds to pay the balance of that claim in excess of one hundred fifty thousand dollars ($150,000). However, if the Director of the Budget determines that the agency liable for the claim has the resources to pay the full claim even though it exceeds one hundred fifty thousand dollars ($150,000), then the Director of the Budget may, in the Director's discretion, require the agency to pay the full claim. Additionally, the Director of the Budget may, in the Director's discretion, limit the number of agencies required to transfer funds to the agency liable for the claim to pay the balance of the claim. (2000-67, s. 7A(e); 2000-140, s. 93.1(i); 2001-424, s. 12.2(b); 2002-159, s. 43.)

§ 143-300. Rules and regulations of Industrial Commission; destruction of records.

The Industrial Commission is hereby authorized and empowered to adopt such rules and regulations as may, in the discretion of the Commission, be necessary to carry out the purpose and intent of this Article. The North Carolina Rules of Civil Procedure and Rules of Evidence, insofar as they are not in conflict with the provisions of this Article, shall be followed in proceedings under this Article. When any case or claim under this Article has been closed by proper order or award, all records concerning such case or claim may, after five years, in the discretion of the Industrial Commission with and by the authorization of the Department of Cultural Resources, be destroyed by burning or otherwise; provided, that no record pertaining to a case or claim of a minor shall be destroyed until the expiration of three years after such minor attains the age of 18 years. (1951, c. 1059, s. 12; 1957, c. 311; 1971, c. 1231, s. 1; 1973, c. 476, s. 48; 1987 (Reg. Sess., 1988), c. 1087, s. 7.)

§ 143-300.1. Claims against county and city boards of education for accidents involving school buses or school transportation service vehicles.

(a) The North Carolina Industrial Commission shall have jurisdiction to hear and determine tort claims against any county board of education or any city board of education, which claims arise as a result of any alleged mechanical defects or other defects which may affect the safe operation of a public school bus or school transportation service vehicle resulting from an alleged negligent act of maintenance personnel or as a result of any alleged negligent act or omission of the driver, transportation safety assistant, or monitor of a public school bus or school transportation service vehicle when:

(1) The driver is an employee of the county or city administrative unit of which that board is the governing body, and the driver is paid or authorized to be paid by that administrative unit,

(1a)   The monitor was appointed and acting in accordance with G.S. 115C-245(d),

(1b)   The transportation safety assistant was employed and acting in accordance with G.S. 115C-245(e), or

(2)   The driver is an unpaid school bus driver trainee under the supervision of an authorized employee of the Department of Transportation, Division of Motor Vehicles, or an authorized employee of that board or a county or city administrative unit thereof,

and which driver was at the time of the alleged negligent act or omission operating a public school bus or school transportation service vehicle in accordance with G.S. 115C-242 in the course of his employment by or training for that administrative unit or board, which monitor was at the time of the alleged negligent act or omission acting as such in the course of serving under G.S. 115C-245(d), or which transportation safety assistant was at the time of the alleged negligent act or omission acting as such in the course of serving under G.S. 115C-245(e). The liability of such county or city board of education, the defenses which may be asserted against such claim by such board, the amount of damages which may be awarded to the claimant, and the procedure for filing, hearing and determining such claim, the right of appeal from such determination, the effect of such appeal, and the procedure for taking, hearing and determining such appeal shall be the same in all respects as is provided in this Article with respect to tort claims against the State Board of Education except as hereinafter provided. Any claim filed against any county or city board of education pursuant to this section shall state the name and address of such board, the name of the employee upon whose alleged negligent act or omission the claim is based, and all other information required by G.S. 143-297 in the case of a claim against the State Board of Education. Immediately upon the docketing of a claim, the Industrial Commission shall forward one copy of the plaintiff's affidavit to the superintendent of the schools of the county or city administrative unit against the governing board of which such claim is made, one copy of the plaintiff's affidavit to the State Board of Education and one copy of the plaintiff's affidavit to the office of the Attorney General of North Carolina. All notices with respect to tort claims against any such county or city board of education shall be given to the superintendent of schools of the county or city administrative unit of which such board is a governing board, to the State Board of Education and also to the office of the Attorney General of North Carolina.

(b) The Attorney General shall be charged with the duty of representing the city or county board of education in connection with claims asserted against them pursuant to this section where the amount of the claim, in the opinion of the Attorney General, is of sufficient import to require and justify such appearance.

(c) In the event that the Industrial Commission awards damages against any county or city board of education under this section, the Attorney General shall draw a voucher for the amount required to pay the award. The funds necessary to cover the first one hundred fifty thousand dollars ($150,000) of liability per claim for claims against county and city boards of education for accidents involving school buses and school transportation service vehicles shall be made available from funds appropriated to the State Board of Education. The balance of any liability owed shall be paid in accordance with G.S. 143-299.4. Neither the county or city boards of education, or the county or city administrative unit shall be liable for the payment of any award made pursuant to the provisions of this section in excess of the amount paid upon a voucher by the Attorney General. Settlement and payment may be made by the Attorney General as provided in G.S. 143-295.

(d) Except as otherwise provided in this subsection, the Attorney General may, upon the request of an employee or former employee, defend any civil action brought against the driver, transportation safety assistant, or monitor of a public school bus or school transportation service vehicle or school bus maintenance mechanic when the driver or mechanic is employed and paid by the local school administrative unit, when the monitor is acting in accordance with G.S. 115C-245(d), when the transportation safety assistant is acting in accordance with G.S. 115C-245(e), or when the driver is an unpaid school bus driver trainee under the supervision of an authorized employee of the Department of Transportation, Division of Motor Vehicles, or an authorized employee of a county or city board of education or administrative unit. The Attorney General may afford this defense through the use of a member of his staff or, in his discretion, employ private counsel. The Attorney General is authorized to pay any judgment rendered in the civil action not to exceed the limit provided under the Tort Claims Act. The funds necessary to cover the first one hundred fifty thousand dollars ($150,000) of liability per claim shall be made available from funds appropriated to the State Board of Education. The balance of any liability owed shall be paid in accordance with G.S. 143-299.4. The Attorney General may compromise and settle any claim covered by this section to the extent that he finds the same to be valid, up to the limit provided in the Tort Claims Act, provided that the authority granted in this subsection shall be limited to only those claims that would be within the jurisdiction of the Industrial Commission under the Tort Claims Act.

The Attorney General shall refuse to provide for the defense of a civil action or proceeding brought against an employee or former employee if the Attorney General determines that:

(1)   The act or omission was not within the scope and course of his employment as a State employee; or

(2)   The employee or former employee acted or failed to act because of actual fraud, corruption, or actual malice on his part; or

(3)   Defense of the action or proceeding by the State would create a conflict of interest between the State and the employee or former employee; or

(4)   Defense of the action or proceeding would not be in the best interests of the State. (1955, c. 1283; 1961, c. 1102, ss. 1-3; 1967, c. 1032, s. 1; 1975, c. 589, s. 1; c. 916, ss. 1, 2; 1977, c. 935, s. 1; 1979, 2nd Sess., c. 1332, ss. 1, 2; 1983 (Reg. Sess., 1984), c. 1034, s. 30; 1998-212, s. 9.17(b); 2000-67, ss. 7A(f), 7A(g); 2001-424, s. 6.18.)

§ 143-300.1A. (See Editor's note on condition precedent) Claims arising from certain smallpox vaccinations of State employees.

The North Carolina Industrial Commission shall have jurisdiction to hear and determine claims in accordance with the procedures set forth in this Article made against the State by a person who is permanently or temporarily living in the home of a State employee who receives in employment vaccination against smallpox incident to the Administration of Smallpox Countermeasures by Health Professionals, section 304 of the Homeland Security Act, Pub. L. No. 107-296 (Nov. 25, 2002) (to be codified at 42 U.S.C. § 233(p)) when the person contracts an infection with smallpox or an infection with vaccinia or has any adverse medical reaction due to the vaccination received by the employee. A person covered by this section shall be entitled to recover from the State damages incurred by the person that are directly attributable to the vaccination of the employee under this section. No showing of negligence is required under this section. The provisions of G.S. 143-299.1 shall not apply to claims made under this section, and contributory negligence is not a defense for claims under this section. Damages awarded under this section shall be paid in accordance with G.S. 143-291(a1) and shall be subject to the same limits as those which apply to tort claims under this Article. (2003-169, s. 3.)

Article 31A.

Defense of State Employees, Medical Contractors and Local Sanitarians.

§ 143-300.2. Definitions.

Unless the context otherwise requires, the definitions contained in this section govern the construction of this Article.

(1) "Civil or criminal action or proceeding" includes any case, prosecution, special proceedings, or administrative proceeding in or before any court or agency of this State or any other state or the United States.

(2) "Employee" includes an officer, agent, or employee but does not include an independent contractor.

(3) "Employment" includes office, agency, or employment.

(4) "The State" includes all departments, agencies, boards, commissions, institutions, bureaus, and authorities of the State. Community colleges, technical colleges, and occupational licensing boards regulated by Chapter 93B of the General Statutes shall be deemed State agencies for purposes of this Article. (1967, c. 1092, s. 1; 1987, c. 684, s. 2; 2002-168, s. 2.)

§ 143-300.3. Defense of State employees.

Except as otherwise provided in G.S. 143-300.4, upon request of an employee or former employee, the State may provide for the defense of any civil or criminal action or proceeding brought against him in his official or individual capacity, or both, on account of an act done or omission made in the scope and course of his employment as a State employee. (1967, c. 1092, s. 1.)

§ 143-300.4. Grounds for refusal of defense.

(a) The State shall refuse to provide for the defense of a civil or criminal action or proceeding brought against an employee or former employee if the State determines that:

(1) The act or omission was not within the scope and course of his employment as a State employee; or

(2) The employee or former employee acted or failed to act because of actual fraud, corruption, or actual malice on his part; or

(3) Defense of the action or proceeding by the State would create a conflict of interest between the State and the employee or former employee; or

(4) Defense of the action or proceeding would not be in the best interests of the State.

(b) The determinations required by subsection (a) of this section shall be made by the Attorney General. The Attorney General may delegate his authority to make these determinations to the chief administrative authority of any agency, institution, board, or commission whose employees are to be defended as provided by subdivision (3) or (4) of G.S. 143-300.5. Approval of the request by an employee or former employee for provision of defense shall raise a presumption that the determination required by this section had been made and that no grounds for refusal to defend were discovered. (1967, c. 1092, s. 1.)

§ 143-300.5. Regulations for providing defense counsel.

The Governor may issue regulations for the defense of employees or former employees of the State pursuant to this Article through one or more of the following methods as may be appropriate to the employee or class of employees in question:

(1) By the Attorney General;

(2) By employing other counsel for this purpose as provided in G.S. 147-17;

(3) By authorizing the purchase of insurance which requires that the insurer provide or underwrite the cost of the defense; or

(4) By authorizing defense by counsel assigned to or employed by the department, agency, board, commission, institution, bureau, or authority which employed the person requesting the defense. (1967, c. 1092, s. 1.)

§ 143-300.6. Payments of judgments; compromise and settlement of claims.

(a) Payment of Judgments and Settlements. In an action to which this Article applies, the State shall pay (i) a final judgment awarded in a court of competent jurisdiction against a State employee or (ii) the amount due under a settlement of the action under this section. The unit of State government that employed the employee shall pay the first one hundred fifty thousand dollars ($150,000) of liability, and the balance of any payment owed shall be paid in accordance with G.S. 143-299.4. This section does not waive the sovereign immunity of the State with respect to any claim. A payment of a judgment or settlement of a claim against a State employee or several State employees as joint tort-feasors may not exceed the amount payable for one claim under the Tort Claims Act.

(b) Settlement of Claims. The Attorney General may compromise and settle any claim covered by this section to the extent he finds the claim valid. A settlement in excess of the limit provided in subsection (a) must be approved by the employee. In an action in which the Attorney General has stated in writing that private counsel should be provided the employee because of a conflict of interest between the employee and the State, a settlement in excess of the limit provided in subsection (a) must be approved by the private counsel.

(c) Other Insurance. The coverage afforded employees and former employees under this Article shall be excess coverage over any commercial liability insurance, other than insurance written under G.S. 58-32-15, up to the limit provided in subsection (a). (1973, c. 1372; 1975, c. 209, ss. 1, 2; 1979, c. 886; 1981, c. 1109, s. 2; 1991, c. 674, s. 2; 2000-67, s. 7A(h).)

§ 143-300.7. Defense of medical contractors.

Notwithstanding any other provisions of this Article, any person or professional association who at the request of the Division of Adult Correction of the Department of Public Safety provides medical and dental services to inmates in the custody of the Division of Adult Correction of the Department of Public Safety and who is sued pursuant to the Federal Civil Rights Act of 1871 may be defended by the Attorney General and shall be protected from liability for violations of civil rights in accordance with the provisions of this Article. (1979, c. 1053, s. 2; 2011-145, s. 19.1(h).)

§ 143-300.8. Defense of local sanitarians.

Any local health department sanitarian enforcing rules of the Commission for Public Health under the supervision of the Department of Health and Human Services pursuant to G.S. 130A-4 shall be defended by the Attorney General, subject to the provisions of G.S. 143-300.4, and shall be protected from liability in accordance with the provisions of this Article in any civil or criminal action or proceeding brought against the sanitarian in his official or individual capacity, or both, on account of an act done or omission made in the scope and course of enforcing the rules of the Commission for Public Health. The Department of Health and Human Services shall pay any judgment against the sanitarian, or any settlement made on his behalf, subject to the provisions of G.S. 143-300.6. (1987, c. 654, s. 2; 1989, c. 727, s. 219(36); 1997-443, s. 11A.96; 2006-202, s. 7; 2007-182, s. 2; 2011-145, s. 13.3(k); 2011-391, s. 27(b).)

§ 143-300.9. Payment of excess damages relating to unconstitutional taxes.

In an action to which this Article applies, the State shall pay the excess amount of a judgment or settlement under G.S. 143-300.6 for damages against a State employee for collecting or administering a tax that is held unconstitutional. The excess amount is the amount of the judgment or settlement over (i) the limit provided in G.S. 143-300.6(a) and (ii) any coverage under G.S. 58-32-15. This section does not waive the sovereign immunity of the State with respect to any claim. (1991, c. 674, s. 1.)

§ 143-300.10. Payment of excess damages relating to unconstitutional goals program.

In an action to which this Article applies, the State shall pay the excess amount of a judgment or settlement under G.S. 143-300.6 for damages against a State employee or member of a State board or commission for enforcing or administering a goals program promoting participation by disadvantaged businesses, minority businesses, and women businesses, in contracts let by a State department or agency that is held unconstitutional. The excess amount is the amount of the judgment or settlement over (i) the limit provided in G.S. 143-300.6(a) and (ii) any coverage under G.S. 58-32-15. This section does not waive the sovereign immunity of the State with respect to any claim. (1991 (Reg. Sess. 1992), c. 1044, s. 39(a).)

§ 143-300.11. Reserved for future codification purposes.

§ 143-300.12. Reserved for future codification purposes.

Article 31B.

Defense of Public School Employees.

§ 143-300.13. Definition of public school employee.

For the purpose of this Article, a public school employee is a person whose major responsibility is to teach or directly supervise teaching and who is employed in either a full-time or part-time capacity, including, but not limited to, the superintendent, assistant or associate superintendent, principal, assistant principal, classroom teacher, substitute teacher, supervisor, teacher aide, student teacher, or school nurse. (1979, c. 971, s. 2.)

§ 143-300.14. Defense of public school employees.

Except as provided in G.S. 143-300.15, the State shall provide defense counsel for the employee against whom a claim is made or civil action is commenced for personal injury on account of an act done or omission made in the course of the employee's duties under G.S. 115-146.1; provided that, no later than 30 days after the employee is notified of a claim or 10 days after the employee is served with complaint of the injured party, the employee gives written notice of the claim or action to the Attorney General which notice shall include:

(1)   The name and address of the claimant and his attorney;

(2)   A concise statement of the basis of the claim;

(3)   The name and address of any other employees involved; and

(4)   A copy of any correspondence received by the employee and legal documents served on the employee pertaining to the claim or civil action. (1979, c. 971, s. 2.)

§ 143-300.15. Refusal of defense.

The Attorney General may refuse to defend an employee for any of the reasons listed in G.S. 143-300.4(a). (1979, c. 971, s. 2.)

§ 143-300.16. Payment of judgments and settlement of claims.

(a)   Any final judgment awarded against an employee in an action that meets the requirements of G.S. 143-300.14, or any amount payable under a settlement of the action, shall be paid the State. The first one hundred fifty thousand dollars($150,000) of liability shall be paid from funds appropriated to the State Board of Education for the payment of State Tort Claims. The balance of any payment owed shall be paid in accordance with G.S. 143-299.4. No payment shall be made from either funds appropriated to the State Board of Education or funds transferred from State agencies under G.S. 143-299.4 for any judgment for punitive damages. Nothing in this section shall be deemed to waive the sovereign immunity of the State with respect to a claim covered under this section or authorize the payment of any judgment or settlement against a public school employee in excess of the limit provided in the Tort Claims Act.

(b)   The Attorney General may settle any claim to which this Article applies which he finds valid. In any case in which the Attorney General has stated in writing that private counsel ought to be provided because of a conflict with the interests of the State, any settlement shall be approved by the private counsel and the Attorney General.

(c) The coverage afforded an employee under this Article is excess coverage over any commercial insurance liability that the employee may have. (1979, c. 971, s. 2; 2000-67, s. 7A(i).)

§ 143-300.17. Employee's obligation for attorney fees.

If any employee has been defended by the Attorney General, or if the State has provided private counsel for an employee, and judgment rendered on the claim establishes that the act or omission complained of did not meet the requirements of G.S. 115-146.1, the judgment against the employee may provide for payment to the State of its costs including a reasonable attorney fee. (1979, c. 971, s. 2.)

§ 143-300.18. Protection is additional.

The protection to employees provided in this Article is in addition to any other protection provided in the General Statutes. (1979, c. 971, s. 2.)

§§ 143-300.19 through 143-300.29. Reserved for future codification purposes.

Article 31C.

Service on Certification Entity.

§ 143-300.30. Service on National Tobacco Grower Settlement Trust.

(a) (1) Philip Morris, Inc., Brown and Williamson Tobacco Corporation, Lorillard Tobacco Company, and R.J. Reynolds Tobacco Company (hereinafter, the "tobacco companies") have proposed to create a National Tobacco Grower Settlement Trust under which the tobacco companies will pay, during a 12-year period, a base amount of approximately five billion one hundred fifty million dollars ($5,150,000,000) into a trust to provide payments to tobacco growers and allotment holders in 14 grower states, including North Carolina, for the purposes of ameliorating potential adverse economic consequences of likely changes in the tobacco market on grower states.

(2)   The tobacco companies desire that the money paid into the trust be divided among tobacco producers and allotment holders in accordance with a plan designed and approved by a certification entity in each state.

(3)   The tobacco companies desire that in larger grower states, including North Carolina, the certification entity be a nonprofit corporation governed by a board of directors consisting of the following public officials and persons appointed by public officials: the Governor, who shall serve as chair of the board of directors; the Commissioner of Agriculture, who shall serve as vice-chair; the Attorney General, who shall serve as secretary; a State Senator appointed by the President Pro Tempore of the Senate; a State Representative appointed by the Speaker of the House of Representatives; two members of the North Carolina congressional delegation selected by the delegation; and four to seven citizens appointed by the Governor.

(4)   It is in the public interest that these officials and citizens serve on the board of directors and determine the distribution of these private trust funds to tobacco producers and allotment holders in North Carolina.

(b)   The Governor, the Speaker of the House of Representatives, and the President Pro Tempore of the Senate are authorized to appoint members of the board of directors of the certification entity as provided in Section 1.(a)(3), and the public officials referred to in Section 1.(a)(3) are authorized to serve on that board.

(c)   No member of the certification entity for the National Tobacco Grower Trust Fund is subject to civil liability for any act or omission arising out of the performance of the member's duties as a member or officer of the certification entity. This section does not apply to liability arising from willful or wanton misconduct, intentional wrongdoing, or the operation of a motor vehicle. (1999-333, s.1.)

§§ 143-300.31 through 143-300.34. Reserved for future codification purposes.

Article 31D.

State Employee Federal Remedy Restoration Act.

§ 143-300.35. State Employee Federal Remedy Restoration Act.

(a) The sovereign immunity of the State is waived for the limited purpose of allowing State employees, except for those in exempt policy-making positions designated pursuant to G.S. 126-5(d), to maintain lawsuits in State and federal courts and obtain and satisfy judgments against the State or any of its departments, institutions, or agencies under:

(1) The Fair Labor Standards Act, 29 U.S.C. § 201, et seq.

(2) The Age Discrimination in Employment Act, 29 U.S.C. § 621, et seq.

(3) The Family and Medical Leave Act, 29 U.S.C. § 2601, et seq.

(4) The Americans with Disabilities Act, 42 U.S.C. § 12101, et seq.

(b) The amount of monetary relief a State employee receives under subsection (a) of this section shall not exceed the amounts authorized under G.S. 143-299.2 or the amounts authorized under the applicable federal law under this section, whichever is less. (2001-467, s. 1.)

Article 32.

Payroll Savings Plan for State Employees.

§ 143-301: Repealed by Session Laws 2011-210, s. 1, effective June 23, 2011.

§ 143-302: Repealed by Session Laws 2011-210, s. 1, effective June 23, 2011.

§ 143-303: Repealed by Session Laws 2011-210, s. 1, effective June 23, 2011.

§ 143-304: Repealed by Session Laws 2011-210, s. 1, effective June 23, 2011.

§ 143-305: Repealed by Session Laws 2011-210, s. 1, effective June 23, 2011.

Article 33.

Judicial Review of Decisions of Certain Administrative Agencies.

§§ 143-306 through 143-316. Repealed by Session Laws 1973, c. 1331, s. 2, as amended by Session Laws 1975, c. 69, s. 4.

Article 33A.

Rules of Evidence in Administrative Proceedings before State Agencies.

§§ 143-317 through 143-318. Repealed by Session Laws 1973, c. 1331, s. 2, as amended by Session Laws 1975, c. 69, s. 4.

Article 33B.

Meetings of Governmental Bodies.

§§ 143-318.1 through 143-318.8. Repealed by Session Laws 1979, c. 655, s. 1.

Article 33C.

Meetings of Public Bodies.

§ 143-318.9. Public policy.

Whereas the public bodies that administer the legislative, policy-making, quasi-judicial, administrative, and advisory functions of North Carolina and its political subdivisions exist solely to conduct the people's business, it is the public policy of North Carolina that the hearings, deliberations, and actions of these bodies be conducted openly. (1979, c. 655, s. 1.)

§ 143-318.10. All official meetings of public bodies open to the public.

(a) Except as provided in G.S. 143-318.11, 143-318.14A, and 143-318.18, each official meeting of a public body shall be open to the public, and any person is entitled to attend such a meeting.

(b) As used in this Article, "public body" means any elected or appointed authority, board, commission, committee, council, or other body of the State, or of one or more counties, cities, school administrative units, constituent institutions of The University of North Carolina, or other political subdivisions or public corporations in the State that (i) is composed of two or more members and (ii) exercises or is authorized to exercise a legislative, policy-making, quasi-judicial, administrative, or advisory function. In addition, "public body" means the governing board of a "public hospital" as defined in G.S. 159-39 and the governing board of any nonprofit corporation to which a hospital facility has been sold or conveyed pursuant to G.S. 131E-8, any subsidiary of such nonprofit corporation, and any nonprofit corporation owning the corporation to which the hospital facility has been sold or conveyed.

(c) "Public body" does not include (i) a meeting solely among the professional staff of a public body, or (ii) the medical staff of a public hospital or the medical staff of a hospital that has been sold or conveyed pursuant to G.S. 131E-8.

(d) "Official meeting" means a meeting, assembly, or gathering together at any time or place or the simultaneous communication by conference telephone or other electronic means of a majority of the members of a public body for the purpose of conducting hearings, participating in deliberations, or voting upon or otherwise transacting the public business within the jurisdiction, real or apparent, of the public body. However, a social meeting or other informal assembly or gathering together of the members of a public body does not constitute an official meeting unless called or held to evade the spirit and purposes of this Article.

(e) Every public body shall keep full and accurate minutes of all official meetings, including any closed sessions held pursuant to G.S. 143-318.11. Such minutes may be in written form or, at the option of the public body, may be in the form of sound or video and sound recordings. When a public body meets in closed session, it shall keep a general account of the closed session so that a person not in attendance would have a reasonable understanding of what transpired. Such accounts may be a written narrative, or video or audio recordings. Such minutes and accounts shall be public records within the meaning of the Public Records Law, G.S. 132-1 et seq.; provided, however, that minutes or an account of a closed session conducted in compliance with G.S. 143-318.11 may be withheld from public inspection so long as public inspection would frustrate the purpose of a closed session. (1979, c. 655, s. 1; 1985 (Reg. Sess., 1986), c. 932, s. 4; 1991, c. 694, ss. 1, 2; 1993 (Reg. Sess., 1994), c. 570, s. 1; 1995, c. 509, s. 135.2(p); 1997-290, s. 1; 1997-456, s. 27; 2011-326, s. 8.)

§ 143-318.11. Closed sessions.

(a) Permitted Purposes. - It is the policy of this State that closed sessions shall be held only when required to permit a public body to act in the public interest as permitted in this section. A public body may hold a closed session and exclude the public only when a closed session is required:

(1) To prevent the disclosure of information that is privileged or confidential pursuant to the law of this State or of the United States, or not considered a public record within the meaning of Chapter 132 of the General Statutes.

(2) To prevent the premature disclosure of an honorary degree, scholarship, prize, or similar award.

(3) To consult with an attorney employed or retained by the public body in order to preserve the attorney-client privilege between the attorney and the public body, which privilege is hereby acknowledged. General policy matters may not be discussed in a closed session and nothing herein shall be construed to permit a public body to close a meeting that otherwise would be open merely because an attorney employed or retained by the public body is a participant. The public body may consider and give instructions to an attorney concerning the handling or settlement of a claim, judicial action, mediation, arbitration, or administrative procedure. If the public body has approved or considered a settlement, other than a malpractice settlement by or on behalf of a hospital, in closed session, the terms of that settlement shall be reported to the public body and entered into its minutes as soon as possible within a reasonable time after the settlement is concluded.

(4) To discuss matters relating to the location or expansion of industries or other businesses in the area served by the public body, including agreement on a tentative list of economic development incentives that may be offered by the public body in negotiations. The action approving the signing of an economic

development contract or commitment, or the action authorizing the payment of economic development expenditures, shall be taken in an open session.

(5) To establish, or to instruct the public body's staff or negotiating agents concerning the position to be taken by or on behalf of the public body in negotiating (i) the price and other material terms of a contract or proposed contract for the acquisition of real property by purchase, option, exchange, or lease; or (ii) the amount of compensation and other material terms of an employment contract or proposed employment contract.

(6) To consider the qualifications, competence, performance, character, fitness, conditions of appointment, or conditions of initial employment of an individual public officer or employee or prospective public officer or employee; or to hear or investigate a complaint, charge, or grievance by or against an individual public officer or employee. General personnel policy issues may not be considered in a closed session. A public body may not consider the qualifications, competence, performance, character, fitness, appointment, or removal of a member of the public body or another body and may not consider or fill a vacancy among its own membership except in an open meeting. Final action making an appointment or discharge or removal by a public body having final authority for the appointment or discharge or removal shall be taken in an open meeting.

(7) To plan, conduct, or hear reports concerning investigations of alleged criminal misconduct.

(8) To formulate plans by a local board of education relating to emergency response to incidents of school violence or to formulate and adopt the school safety components of school improvement plans by a local board of education or a school improvement team.

(9) To discuss and take action regarding plans to protect public safety as it relates to existing or potential terrorist activity and to receive briefings by staff members, legal counsel, or law enforcement or emergency service officials concerning actions taken or to be taken to respond to such activity.

(b) Repealed by Session Laws 1991, c. 694, s. 4.

(c) Calling a Closed Session. - A public body may hold a closed session only upon a motion duly made and adopted at an open meeting. Every motion to close a meeting shall cite one or more of the permissible purposes listed in subsection (a) of this section. A motion based on subdivision (a)(1) of this section shall also state the name or citation of the law that renders the information to be discussed privileged or confidential. A motion based on subdivision (a)(3) of this section shall identify the parties in each existing lawsuit concerning which the public body expects to receive advice during the closed session.

(d)   Repealed by Session Laws 1993 (Reg. Sess., 1994), c. 570, s. 2. (1979, c. 655, s. 1; 1981, c. 831; 1985 (Reg. Sess., 1986), c. 932, s. 5; 1991, c. 694, ss. 3, 4; 1993 (Reg. Sess., 1994), c. 570, s. 2; 1995, c. 509, s. 84; 1997-222, s. 2; 1997-290, s. 2; 2001-500, s. 2; 2003-180, s. 2; 2013-360, s. 8.41(b).)

§ 143-318.12. Public notice of official meetings.

(a)   If a public body has established, by ordinance, resolution, or otherwise, a schedule of regular meetings, it shall cause a current copy of that schedule, showing the time and place of regular meetings, to be kept on file as follows:

(1)   For public bodies that are part of State government, with the Secretary of State;

(2)   For the governing board and each other public body that is part of a county government, with the clerk to the board of county commissioners;

(3)   For the governing board and each other public body that is part of a city government, with the city clerk;

(4)   For each other public body, with its clerk or secretary, or, if the public body does not have a clerk or secretary, with the clerk to the board of county commissioners in the county in which the public body normally holds its meetings.

If a public body changes its schedule of regular meetings, it shall cause the revised schedule to be filed as provided in subdivisions (1) through (4) of this subsection at least seven calendar days before the day of the first meeting held pursuant to the revised schedule.

(b)   If a public body holds an official meeting at any time or place other than a time or place shown on the schedule filed pursuant to subsection (a) of this section, it shall give public notice of the time and place of that meeting as provided in this subsection.

(1)   If a public body recesses a regular, special, or emergency meeting held pursuant to public notice given in compliance with this subsection, and the time and place at which the meeting is to be continued is announced in open session, no further notice shall be required.

(2)   For any other meeting, except an emergency meeting, the public body shall cause written notice of the meeting stating its purpose (i) to be posted on the principal bulletin board of the public body or, if the public body has no such bulletin board, at the door of its usual meeting room, and (ii) to be mailed, e-mailed, or delivered to each newspaper, wire service, radio station, and television station that has filed a written request for notice with the clerk or secretary of the public body or with some other person designated by the public body. The public body shall also cause notice to be mailed, e-mailed, or delivered to any person, in addition to the representatives of the media listed above, who has filed a written request with the clerk, secretary, or other person designated by the public body. This notice shall be posted and mailed, e-mailed, or delivered at least 48 hours before the time of the meeting. The notice required to be posted on the principal bulletin board or at the door of its usual meeting room shall be posted on the door of the building or on the building in an area accessible to the public if the building containing the principal bulletin board or usual meeting room is closed to the public continuously for 48 hours before the time of the meeting. The public body may require each newspaper, wire service, radio station, and television station submitting a written request for notice to renew the request annually. The public body shall charge a fee to persons other than the media, who request notice, of ten dollars ($10.00) per calendar year, and may require them to renew their requests quarterly. No fee shall be charged for notices sent by e-mail.

(3)   For an emergency meeting, the public body shall cause notice of the meeting to be given to each local newspaper, local wire service, local radio station, and local television station that has filed a written request, which includes the newspaper's, wire service's, or station's telephone number, for emergency notice with the clerk or secretary of the public body or with some other person designated by the public body. This notice shall be given either by e-mail, by telephone, or by the same method used to notify the members of the public body and shall be given immediately after notice has been given to those members. This notice shall be given at the expense of the party notified. Only

business connected with the emergency may be considered at a meeting to which notice is given pursuant to this paragraph.

(c)   Repealed by Session Laws 1991, c. 694, s. 6.

(d)   If a public body has a Web site and has established a schedule of regular meetings, the public body shall post the schedule of regular meetings to the Web site.

(e)   If a public body has a Web site that one or more of its employees maintains, the public body shall post notice of any meeting held under subdivisions (b)(1) and (b)(2) of this section prior to the scheduled time of that meeting.

(f)   For purposes of this section, an "emergency meeting" is one called because of generally unexpected circumstances that require immediate consideration by the public body. (1979, c. 655, s. 1; 1991, c. 694, ss. 5, 6; 2009-350, s. 1.)

§ 143-318.13. Electronic meetings; written ballots; acting by reference.

(a)   Electronic Meetings. - If a public body holds an official meeting by use of conference telephone or other electronic means, it shall provide a location and means whereby members of the public may listen to the meeting and the notice of the meeting required by this Article shall specify that location. A fee of up to twenty-five dollars ($25.00) may be charged each such listener to defray in part the cost of providing the necessary location and equipment.

(b)   Written Ballots. - Except as provided in this subsection or by joint resolution of the General Assembly, a public body may not vote by secret or written ballot. If a public body decides to vote by written ballot, each member of the body so voting shall sign his or her ballot; and the minutes of the public body shall show the vote of each member voting. The ballots shall be available for public inspection in the office of the clerk or secretary to the public body immediately following the meeting at which the vote took place and until the minutes of that meeting are approved, at which time the ballots may be destroyed.

(c) Acting by Reference. - The members of a public body shall not deliberate, vote, or otherwise take action upon any matter by reference to a letter, number or other designation, or other secret device or method, with the intention of making it impossible for persons attending a meeting of the public body to understand what is being deliberated, voted, or acted upon. However, this subsection does not prohibit a public body from deliberating, voting, or otherwise taking action by reference to an agenda, if copies of the agenda, sufficiently worded to enable the public to understand what is being deliberated, voted, or acted upon, are available for public inspection at the meeting. (1979, c. 655, s. 1.)

§ 143-318.14. Broadcasting or recording meetings.

(a) Except as herein below provided, any radio or television station is entitled to broadcast all or any part of a meeting required to be open. Any person may photograph, film, tape-record, or otherwise reproduce any part of a meeting required to be open.

(b) A public body may regulate the placement and use of equipment necessary for broadcasting, photographing, filming, or recording a meeting, so as to prevent undue interference with the meeting. However, the public body must allow such equipment to be placed within the meeting room in such a way as to permit its intended use, and the ordinary use of such equipment shall not be declared to constitute undue interference; provided, however, that if the public body, in good faith, should determine that the size of the meeting room is such that all the members of the public body, members of the public present, and the equipment and personnel necessary for broadcasting, photographing, filming, and tape-recording the meeting cannot be accommodated in the meeting room without unduly interfering with the meeting and an adequate alternative meeting room is not readily available, then the public body, acting in good faith and consistent with the purposes of this Article, may require the pooling of such equipment and the personnel operating it; and provided further, if the news media, in order to facilitate news coverage, request an alternate site for the meeting, and the public body grants the request, then the news media making such request shall pay any costs incurred by the public body in securing an alternate meeting site. (1979, c. 655, s. 1.)

§ 143-318.14A. Legislative commissions, committees, and standing subcommittees.

(a) Except as provided in subsection (e) below, all official meetings of commissions, committees, and standing subcommittees of the General Assembly (including, without limitation, joint committees and study committees), shall be held in open session. For the purpose of this section, the following also shall be considered to be "commissions, committees, and standing subcommittees of the General Assembly":

(1) The Legislative Research Commission;

(2) The Legislative Services Commission;

(3) Repealed by Session Laws 2006-203, s. 93, effective July 1, 2007, and applicable to the budget for the 2007-2009 biennium and each subsequent biennium thereafter.

(4) Repealed by Session Laws 2011-291, s. 2.50, effective June 24, 2011;

(5) The Joint Legislative Commission on Governmental Operations;

(6) The Joint Legislative Commission [Committee] on Local Government;

(7) Repealed by Session Laws 1997, c. 443, s. 12.30, effective August 28, 1997.

(8) Repealed by Session Laws 2011-291, s. 2.50, effective June 24, 2011;

(9) The Environmental Review Commission;

(10) The Joint Legislative Transportation Oversight Committee;

(11) The Joint Legislative Education Oversight Committee;

(12) Repealed by Session Laws 2011-266, s. 1.28(b), effective July 1, 2011 and Session Laws 2011-291, s. 2.50, effective June 24, 2011;

(13) The Commission on Children with Special Needs;

(14) Repealed by Session Laws 2011-291, s. 2.50, effective June 24, 2011;

(15) The Agriculture and Forestry Awareness Study Commission; and

(16) Repealed by Session Laws 2011-291, s. 2.50, effective June 24, 2011;

(17) The standing Committees on Pensions and Retirement.

(b) Reasonable public notice of all meetings of commissions, committees, and standing subcommittees of the General Assembly shall be given. For purposes of this subsection, "reasonable public notice" includes, but is not limited to:

(1) Notice given openly at a session of the Senate or of the House; or

(2) Notice mailed or sent by electronic mail to those who have requested notice, and to the Legislative Services Office, which shall post the notice on the General Assembly web site.

G.S. 143-318.12 shall not apply to meetings of commissions, committees, and standing subcommittees of the General Assembly.

(c) A commission, committee, or standing subcommittee of the General Assembly may take final action only in an open meeting.

(d) A violation of this section by members of the General Assembly shall be punishable as prescribed by the rules of the House or the Senate.

(e) The following sections shall apply to meetings of commissions, committees, and standing subcommittees of the General Assembly: G.S. 143-318.10(e) and G.S. 143-318.11, G.S. 143-318.13 and G.S. 143-318.14, G.S. 143-318.16 through G.S. 143-318.17. (1991, c. 694, s. 7; 1991 (Reg. Sess., 1992), c. 785, s. 4; c. 1030, s. 42; 1993, c. 321, s. 169.2(f); 1997-443, s. 12.30; 2003-374, s. 1; 2006-203, s. 93; 2011-266, s. 1.28(b); 2011-291, s. 2.50.)

§ 143-318.15: Repealed by Session Laws 2006-203, s. 94, effective July 1, 2007, and applicable to the budget for the 2007-2009 biennium and each subsequent biennium thereafter.

§ 143-318.16. Injunctive relief against violations of Article.

(a) The General Court of Justice has jurisdiction to enter mandatory or prohibitory injunctions to enjoin (i) threatened violations of this Article, (ii) the recurrence of past violations of this Article, or (iii) continuing violations of this Article. Any person may bring an action in the appropriate division of the General Court of Justice seeking such an injunction; and the plaintiff need not allege or prove special damage different from that suffered by the public at large. It is not a defense to such an action that there is an adequate remedy at law.

(b) Any injunction entered pursuant to this section shall describe the acts enjoined with reference to the violations of this Article that have been proved in the action.

(c) Repealed by Session Laws 1985 (Reg. Sess., 1986), c. 932, s. 3, effective October 1, 1986. (1979, c. 655, s. 1; 1985 (Reg. Sess., 1986), c. 932, s. 3.)

§ 143-318.16A. Additional remedies for violations of Article.

(a) Any person may institute a suit in the superior court requesting the entry of a judgment declaring that any action of a public body was taken, considered, discussed, or deliberated in violation of this Article. Upon such a finding, the court may declare any such action null and void. Any person may seek such a declaratory judgment, and the plaintiff need not allege or prove special damage different from that suffered by the public at large. The public body whose action the suit seeks to set aside shall be made a party. The court may order other persons be made parties if they have or claim any right, title, or interest that would be directly affected by a declaratory judgment voiding the action that the suit seeks to set aside.

(b) A suit seeking declaratory relief under this section must be commenced within 45 days following the initial disclosure of the action that the suit seeks to have declared null and void; provided, however, that any suit for declaratory judgment brought pursuant to this section that seeks to set aside a bond order or bond referendum shall be commenced within the limitation periods prescribed by G.S. 159-59 and G.S. 159-62. If the challenged action is recorded in the minutes of the public body, its initial disclosure shall be deemed to have occurred on the date the minutes are first available for public inspection. If the challenged action is not recorded in the minutes of the public body, the date of its initial disclosure shall be determined by the court based on a finding as to when the plaintiff knew or should have known that the challenged action had been taken.

(c) In making the determination whether to declare the challenged action null and void, the court shall consider the following and any other relevant factors:

(1) The extent to which the violation affected the substance of the challenged action;

(2) The extent to which the violation thwarted or impaired access to meetings or proceedings that the public had a right to attend;

(3) The extent to which the violation prevented or impaired public knowledge or understanding of the people's business;

(4) Whether the violation was an isolated occurrence, or was a part of a continuing pattern of violations of this Article by the public body;

(5) The extent to which persons relied upon the validity of the challenged action, and the effect on such persons of declaring the challenged action void;

(6) Whether the violation was committed in bad faith for the purpose of evading or subverting the public policy embodied in this Article.

(d) A declaratory judgment pursuant to this section may be entered as an alternative to, or in combination with, an injunction entered pursuant to G.S. 143-318.16.

(e) The validity of any enacted law or joint resolution or passed simple resolution of either house of the General Assembly is not affected by this Article. (1985 (Reg. Sess., 1986), c. 932, s. 1; 1991, c. 694, s. 8.)

§ 143-318.16B. Assessments and awards of attorneys' fees.

When an action is brought pursuant to G.S. 143-318.16 or G.S. 143-318.16A, the court may make written findings specifying the prevailing party or parties, and may award the prevailing party or parties a reasonable attorney's fee, to be taxed against the losing party or parties as part of the costs. The court may order that all or any portion of any fee as assessed be paid personally by any individual member or members of the public body found by the court to have knowingly or intentionally committed the violation; provided, that no order against any individual member shall issue in any case where the public body or that individual member seeks the advice of an attorney, and such advice is followed. (1985 (Reg. Sess., 1986), c. 932, s. 2; 1993 (Reg. Sess., 1994), c. 570, s. 3.)

§ 143-318.16C. Accelerated hearing; priority.

Actions brought pursuant to G.S. 143-318.16 or G.S. 143-318.16A shall be set down for immediate hearing, and subsequent proceedings in such actions shall be accorded priority by the trial and appellate courts. (1993 (Reg. Sess., 1994), c. 570, s. 4.)

§ 143-318.16D. Local acts.

Any reference in any city charter or local act to an "executive session" is amended to read "closed session". (1993 (Reg. Sess., 1994), c. 570, s. 4.)

§ 143-318.17. Disruptions of official meetings.

A person who willfully interrupts, disturbs, or disrupts an official meeting and who, upon being directed to leave the meeting by the presiding officer, willfully refuses to leave the meeting is guilty of a Class 2 misdemeanor. (1979, c. 655, s. 1; 1993, c. 539, s. 1028; 1994, Ex. Sess., c. 24, s. 14(c).)

§ 143-318.18. Exceptions.

This Article does not apply to:

(1)   Grand and petit juries.

(2)   Any public body that is specifically authorized or directed by law to meet in executive or confidential session, to the extent of the authorization or direction.

(3)   The Judicial Standards Commission.

(3a)   The North Carolina Innocence Inquiry Commission.

(4)   Repealed by Session Laws 1991, c. 694, s. 9.

(4a)   The Legislative Ethics Committee.

(4b)   A conference committee of the General Assembly.

(4c)   A caucus by members of the General Assembly; however, no member of the General Assembly shall participate in a caucus which is called for the purpose of evading or subverting this Article.

(5)   Law enforcement agencies.

(6)   A public body authorized to investigate, examine, or determine the character and other qualifications of applicants for professional or occupational licenses or certificates or to take disciplinary actions against persons holding such licenses or certificates, (i) while preparing, approving, administering, or grading examinations or (ii) while meeting with respect to an individual applicant for or holder of such a license or certificate. This exception does not amend, repeal, or supersede any other statute that requires a public hearing or other practice and procedure in a proceeding before such a public body.

(7)   Any public body subject to the State Budget Act, Chapter 143C of the General Statutes and exercising quasi-judicial functions, during a meeting or session held solely for the purpose of making a decision in an adjudicatory action or proceeding.

(8)   The boards of trustees of endowment funds authorized by G.S. 116-36 or G.S. 116-238.

(9) Repealed by Session Laws 1991, c. 694, s. 9.

(10) Repealed by Session Laws 2013-234, s. 10, effective July 3, 2013.

(11) The General Court of Justice. (1979, c. 655, s. 1; 1985, c. 757, s. 206(e); 1991, c. 694, s. 9; 2006-184, s. 6; 2006-203, s. 95; 2010-171, s. 5; 2013-234, s. 10.)

Article 34.

Local Affairs.

§ 143-319: Repealed by Session Laws 1973, c. 1262, s. 51.

§ 143-320. Definitions.

As used in this Article, unless the context otherwise requires:

(1) "Department" means the Department of Environment and Natural Resources.

(2) "Secretary" means the Secretary of Environment and Natural Resources.

(3) "Recreation" means those interests that are diversionary in character and that aid in promoting entertainment, pleasure, relaxation, instruction, and other physical, mental, and cultural developments and experiences of a leisure nature, and includes all governmental, private nonprofit and commercial recreation forms of the recreation field and includes parks, conservation, recreation travel, the use of natural resources, wilderness and high density recreation types and the variety of recreation interests in areas and programs which are incorporated in this range. (1969, c. 1145, s. 1; 1973, c. 1262, s. 51; 1977, c. 771, ss. 4, 8; 1989, c. 727, s. 168; 1997-443, s. 11A.119(a).)

§§ 143-321 through 143-322. Repealed by Session Laws 1973, c. 1262, s. 51.

§ 143-323. Functions of Department of Environment and Natural Resources.

(a) Recreation. - The Department of Environment and Natural Resources shall have the following powers and duties with respect to recreation:

(1) To study and appraise the recreation needs of the State and to assemble and disseminate information relative to recreation.

(2) To cooperate in the promotion and organization of local recreation systems for counties, municipalities, and other political subdivisions of the State, to aid them in the administration, finance, planning, personnel, coordination and cooperation of recreation organizations and programs.

(3) To aid in recruiting, training, and placing recreation workers, and to promote recreation institutes and conferences.

(4) To establish and promote recreation standards.

(5) To cooperate with appropriate State, federal, and local agencies and private membership groups and commercial recreation interests in the promotion of recreation opportunities, and to represent the State in recreation conferences, study groups, and other matters of recreation concern.

(6) To accept gifts, devises, and endowments. The funds, if given as an endowment, shall be invested in securities designated by the donor, or if there is no such designation, in securities in which the State sinking fund may be invested. All such gifts and devises and all proceeds from such invested endowments shall be used for carrying out the purposes for which they were made.

(7) To advise agencies, departments, organizations and groups in the planning, application and use of federal and State funds which are assigned or administered by the State for recreation programs and services on land and water recreation areas and on which the State renders advisory or other recreation services or upon which the State exercises control.

(8) To act jointly, when advisable, with any other State, local or federal agency, institution, private individual or group in order to better carry out the Department's objectives and responsibilities.

(b) Repealed by Session Laws 1977, c. 70, s. 32.

(c) Repealed by Session Laws 1989, c. 751, s. 5.

(d) Federal Assistance. - The Department, with the approval of the Governor, may apply for and accept grants from the federal government and its agencies and from any foundation, corporation, association, or individual, and may comply with the terms, conditions, and limitations of the grant, in order to accomplish any of the purposes of the Department. Grant funds shall be expended pursuant to the Executive Budget Act.

(e) General. - The Department shall have the following general powers and duties.

(1) To study and to sponsor research on all aspects of local government and of relationships between the federal government, the State and local governments in North Carolina.

(2) To collect, collate, analyze, publish, and disseminate information necessary for the effective operation of the Department and useful to local government.

(3) To maintain an inventory of data and information, and to act as a clearinghouse of information and as a referral agency with respect to State, federal, and private services and programs available to local government; and to facilitate local participation in those programs by furnishing information, education, guidance, and technical assistance with respect to those programs.

(4) To assist in coordinating State and federal activities relating to local government.

(5) To assist local governments in the identification and solution of their problems.

(6) To assist local officials in bringing specific governmental problems to the attention of the appropriate State, federal, and private agencies.

(7) To advise and assist local governments with respect to intergovernmental contracts, joint service agreements, regional service arrangements, and other forms of intergovernmental cooperation.

(8) To inform and advise the Governor on the affairs and problems of local government and on the need for the administrative and legislative action with respect to local government. (1969, c. 1145, s. 1; 1973, c. 1262, s. 51; 1977, c. 70, s. 32; c. 771, s. 4; 1989, c. 727, s. 218(116); c. 751, s. 5; 1997-443, s. 11A.119(a); 2011-284, s. 92.)

§ 143-324. Repealed by Session Laws 1973, c. 1262, s. 51.

§ 143-325. Functions of committees.

(a) Repealed by Session Laws 1973, c. 1262, s. 51.

(b) Committee on Law and Order. - The Committee on Law and Order shall have policy-making and supervisory authority over the policies, programs, and activities of the Department in the field of the administration of criminal justice in assisting and participating with State and local law-enforcement agencies, at their request, to improve law enforcement and the administration of criminal justice.

(c) Repealed by Session Laws 1973, c. 1262, s. 51. (1969, c. 1145, s. 1; 1973, c. 1262, s. 51.)

§ 143-326. Transfer of functions, records, property, etc.

(a) All of the powers, duties, functions, records, property, supplies, equipment, personnel, funds, credits, appropriations, quarterly allotments, and executory contracts of the North Carolina Recreation Commission are transferred to the Department of Local Affairs, effective July 1, 1969. All statutory references to the "North Carolina Recreation Commission" or the "Recreation Commission" are amended to read "North Carolina Department of Local Affairs."

(b) All of the powers, duties, functions, records, property, supplies, equipment, personnel, funds, credits, appropriations, quarterly allotments, and executory contracts of the Governor's Committee on Law and Order are transferred to the Department of Local Affairs, effective July 1, 1969. All statutory references to the "Governor's Committee on Law and Order" are amended to read "North Carolina Department of Local Affairs."

(c) All of the powers, duties, functions, records, property, supplies, equipment, personnel, funds, credits, appropriations, quarterly allotments, and executory contracts of the Division of Community Planning of the Department of Conservation and Development are transferred to the Department of Local Affairs.

(d) Such portion of the powers, duties, functions, records, property, supplies, equipment, personnel, funds, credits, appropriations, quarterly allotments, and executory contracts of the State Planning Task Force Division of the Department of Administration as the Governor may designate is transferred to the Department of Local Affairs, effective July 1, 1969.

(e) The transfers directed by subsections (a) through (d), above shall be made under the supervision of the Governor, and he shall be the final arbiter of all differences or disputes arising incident to those transfers.

(f) No transfer of functions to the Department of Local Affairs provided for in this Article shall affect any action, suit, proceeding, prosecution, contract, lease, agreement, or other business transaction involving any of those functions that was initiated, undertaken, or entered into prior to or pending the time of the transfer, except that the Department shall be substituted for the agency from which the function was transferred, and as far as practicable the procedure provided for in this Article shall be employed in completing or disposing of the matter. All rules, regulations, and policies of the agencies from which powers, duties, and functions are herein transferred to the Department of Local Affairs shall continue in force as rules, regulations, and policies of the Department of Local Affairs until altered pursuant to G.S. 143-320(9). (1969, c. 1145, s. 1; 1973, c. 1262, s. 51.)

§ 143-327. Repealed by Session Laws 1973, c. 1262, s. 51.

§ 143-328. Reserved for future codification purposes.

Article 35.

Youth Service Commission.

§ 143-329: Expired.

§ 143-330: Expired.

§ 143-331: Expired.

§ 143-332: Expired.

§ 143-333: Expired.

Article 36.

Department of Administration.

Part 1. General Provisions.

§ 143-334. Short title.

This Article may be cited as the Department of Administration Act. (1957, c. 269, s. 1; 2000-140, s. 76(h).)

§ 143-335. Department of Administration created.

There is hereby created the Department of Administration. (1957, c. 269, s. 1.)

§ 143-336. Definitions.

As used in this Article:

"Agency" includes every agency, institution, board, commission, bureau, council, department, division, officer, and employee of the State, but does not include counties, municipal corporations, political subdivisions, county and city boards of education, and other local public bodies.

"Community college buildings" means all buildings, utilities, and other property developments located at a community college, which is defined in G.S. 115D-2(2).

"Department" means the Department of Administration, unless the context otherwise requires.

"Public buildings" means all buildings owned or maintained by the State in the City of Raleigh, but does not mean any building which a State agency other than the Department of Administration is required by law to care for and maintain.

"Public buildings and grounds" means all buildings and grounds owned or maintained by the State in the City of Raleigh, but does not mean any building or grounds which a State agency other than the Department of Administration is required by law to care for and maintain.

"Public grounds" means all grounds owned or maintained by the State in the City of Raleigh, but does not mean any grounds which a State agency other than the Department of Administration is required by law to care for and maintain.

"Secretary" means the Secretary of Administration, unless the context otherwise requires.

"State buildings" mean all State buildings, utilities, and other property developments except the State Legislative Building, railroads, highway structures, bridge structures, and any buildings, utilities, or property owned or leased by the North Carolina Global TransPark Authority.

But under no circumstances shall this Article or any part thereof apply to the judicial or to the legislative branches of the State. (1957, c. 215, s. 2; c. 269, s. 1; 1963, c. 1, s. 6; 1971, c. 1097, s. 1; 1975, c. 879, s. 46; 1989, c. 58, s. 1; 1991, c. 749, s. 5; 1993 (Reg. Sess., 1994), c. 777, s. 4(h); 2001, c. 442, ss. 5, 8.)

§§ 143-337 through 143-339. Repealed by Session Laws 1975, c. 879, s. 46.

§ 143-340. Powers and duties of Secretary.

The Secretary of Administration has the following powers and duties:

(1) To establish the State Employee Suggestion Program pursuant to Article 36A of this Chapter, with the authority to adopt all rules necessary to implement the program. The Secretary shall serve ex officio on all program committees and shall designate an executive secretary to administer the program.

(2) through (9) Repealed by Session Laws 1975, c. 879, s. 46.

(10) To require reports from any State agency at any time upon any matters within the scope of the responsibilities of the Secretary or the Department.

(11) Repealed by Session Laws 1975, c. 879, s. 46.

(12) To enter the premises of any State agency; to inspect its property; and to examine its books, papers, documents, and all other agency records and copy any of them; and any State agency shall permit such entry, examination, and copying, and upon demand shall produce without unnecessary delay all books, papers, documents, and other records in its office and furnish information respecting its records and other matters pertaining to that agency and related to the responsibilities of the Department.

(13) Repealed by Session Laws 1975, c. 879, s. 46.

(14) Repealed by Session Laws 1989, c. 239, s. 1.

(15), (16) Repealed by Session Laws 1975, c. 879, s. 46.

(17) To supervise the work of janitors appointed by the General Assembly to perform services in connection with the sessions of the General Assembly.

(18) To adopt reasonable rules and regulations with respect to the parking of automobiles on all public grounds, subject to the approval of the Governor and Council of State, and to enforce those rules and regulations. Any person who

violates a rule or regulation concerning parking on public grounds is guilty of a Class 1 misdemeanor. Upon the allocation of parking spaces to any agency pursuant to such rules and regulations, the agency shall adopt written guidelines governing the individual assignment of such parking spaces by the agency. Such guidelines shall give first priority treatment to the physically handicapped and to carpoolers and vanpoolers, however, first priority shall be given to those on call for duty at a time other than normal working hours. A copy of said guidelines shall be made available for inspection by any person upon request.

(19) Any motor vehicle parked in a State-owned parking lot, when such lot is clearly designated as such by a sign no smaller than 24 inches by 24 inches prominently displayed at the entrance thereto, in violation of the "Rules and Regulations Governing State-Owned Parking Lots" dated September, 1968 or as amended, may be removed from such lot to a place of storage and the registered owner of that vehicle shall become liable for removal and storage charges. Any person who removes a vehicle pursuant to this section shall not be held liable for damages for the removal of the vehicle to the owner, lienholder or other person legally entitled to the possession of the vehicle removed; however, any person who intentionally or negligently damages a vehicle in the removal of such vehicle, or intentionally or negligently inflicts injury upon any person in the removal of such vehicle, may be held liable for damages. Any motor vehicle parked without authorization on State-owned public grounds under the control of the Department of Administration other than a designated parking area may be removed from that property to a storage area and the registered owner of the vehicle shall be liable for removal and storage fees.

(20) To use at all times such means as, in his opinion, may be effective in protecting all public buildings and grounds from fire.

(21), (22) Repealed by Session Laws 2009-451, s. 17.3(b), effective July 1, 2009.

(23) Repealed by Session Laws 1975, c. 879, s. 46.

(24) To perform such additional duties as the Governor may direct.

(25) Repealed by Session Laws 1991, c. 542, s. 9.

(26) To establish the State Employees Combined Campaign in the Department of Administration to allow State employees the opportunity to contribute to charitable nonpartisan organizations in an orderly and uniform

process, with the authority to adopt all rules necessary to implement the campaign. (1957, c. 215, s. 2; c. 269, s. 1; 1969, c. 627; c. 1267, s. 4; 1971, c. 280; c. 1097, s. 2; 1975, c. 204; c. 879, s. 46; 1977, c. 119; c. 288, s. 2; 1979, c. 901, ss. 1, 2; c. 930; 1981, c. 696; 1981 (Reg. Sess., 1982), c. 1239, s. 4; 1983, c. 406; c. 420, s. 7; 1987, c. 274; 1989, c. 239, s. 1; c. 644, s. 5; 1991, c. 542, s. 9; 1993, c. 539, s. 1029; 1994, Ex. Sess., c. 24, s. 14(c); 1997-513, s. 3; 1999-250, s. 1; 2001-424, s. 7.2(a); 2009-451, s. 17.3(b); 2010-96, s. 41.3.)

§ 143-341. Powers and duties of Department.

The Department of Administration has the following powers and duties:

(1)   Repealed by Session Laws 1979, 2nd Session, c. 1137, s. 38.

(2)   Purchase and Contract:

a.   To exercise those powers and perform those duties which were, at the time of the ratification of this Article, conferred by statute upon the former Division of Purchase and Contract.

(3)   Architecture and Engineering:

a.   To examine and approve all plans and specifications for the construction or renovation of:

1.   All State buildings or buildings located on State lands, except those buildings over which a local building code inspection department has and exercises jurisdiction; and

2.   All community college buildings requiring the estimated expenditure for construction or repair work for which public bidding is required under G.S. 143-129 prior to the awarding of a contract for such work; and to examine and approve all changes in those plans and specifications made after the contract for such work has been awarded.

a1.   To organize and schedule, within three weeks of designer selection and before the design contract is let, a meeting of the stakeholders for each State capital improvement project to discuss plan review requirements and to define the terms of the memorandum of understanding developed by the State Building

Commission pursuant to G.S. 143-135.26(2). The stakeholders shall include the funded agency, each State agency having plan review responsibilities for the project, and the selected designer. Notwithstanding the foregoing, the meeting need not be scheduled if the funded agency so requests.

b. To assist, as necessary, all agencies in the preparation of requests for appropriations for the construction or renovation of all State buildings.

b1. To certify that a statement of needs pursuant to G.S. 143C-3-3, other than for a project of The University of North Carolina for which advance planning has not been completed, is feasible. For purposes of this sub-subdivision, "feasible" means that the proposed project is sufficiently defined in overall scope; building program; site development; detailed design, construction, and equipment budgets; and comprehensive project scheduling so as to reasonably ensure that it may be completed with the amount of funds requested. At the discretion of the General Assembly, advanced planning funds may be appropriated in support of this certification. This sub-subdivision shall not apply to requests for appropriations of less than one hundred thousand dollars ($100,000).

c. To supervise the letting of all contracts for the design, construction or renovation of all State buildings and all community college buildings whose plans and specifications must be examined and approved under a.2. of this subdivision.

d. To supervise and inspect all work done and materials used in the construction or renovation of all State buildings and all community college buildings whose plans and specifications must be examined and approved under a.2. of this subdivision; to act as the appropriate official inspector or inspection department for purposes of G.S. 143-143.2; and no such work may be accepted by the State or by any State agency until it has been approved by the Department.

e. To require all State agencies to use existing plans and specificiations for construction projects, where feasible. Prior to designing a project, State agencies shall consult with the Department of Administration on the availability of appropriate existing plans and specifications and the feasibility of using them for a project.

f. To provide written allocation of the deduction allowed under section 179D of the Code, as defined in G.S. 105-228.90, for designing energy efficient commercial building property that is installed on or in property owned by the State. The allocation must be made in accordance with section 179D of the Code.

Except for sub-subdivisions b., b1., e., and f. of this subdivision, this subdivision does not apply to the design, construction, or renovation of projects by The University of North Carolina pursuant to G.S. 116-31.11.

(4)   Real Property Control:

a.   To prepare and keep current a complete and accurate inventory of all land owned or leased by the State or by any State agency. This inventory shall show the location, acreage, description, source of title and current use of all land (including swamplands or marshlands) owned by the State or by any State agency, and the agency to which each tract is currently allocated. Surveys may be made where necessary to obtain information for the purposes of this inventory. Accurate plats or maps of all such land may be prepared, or copies obtained where such maps or plats are available.

b.   To prepare and keep current a complete and accurate inventory of all buildings owned or leased (in whole or in part) by the State or by any State agency. This inventory shall show the location, amount of floor space and floor plans of every building owned or leased by the State or by any State agency, and the agency to which each building, or space therein, is currently allocated. Floor plans of every such building shall be prepared or copies obtained where such floor plans are available, where needed for use in the allocation of space therein.

c.   To obtain and deposit with the Secretary of State the originals of all deeds and other conveyances of real property to the State or to any State agency, copies of all leases wherein the State or any State agency is lessor or lessee, and certified copies of wills, judgments, and other instruments whereby the State or any State agency has acquired title to real property. Where an original of a deed, lease, or other instrument cannot be found, but has been recorded in the registry of office of the clerk of superior court of any county, a certified copy of such deed, conveyance, or instrument shall be obtained and deposited with the Secretary of State.

d.   To acquire, whether by purchase, exercise of the power of eminent domain, lease, or rental, all land, buildings, and space in buildings for all State agencies, subject to the approval of the Governor and Council of State in each instance. The Governor, acting with the approval of the Council of State, may adopt rules (i) exempting from any or all of the requirements of this paragraph such classes of lease, rental, easement, and right-of-way transactions as he deems advisable; and (ii) authorizing any State agency to enter into and/or approve the classes of transactions thus exempted from the requirements of this paragraph; and (iii) delegating to any other State agency the authority to approve the severance of buildings and standing timber from State lands; upon such approval of severance, the buildings and timber so affected shall be treated, for the purposes of this Chapter, as personal property. Any contract entered into or any proceeding instituted contrary to the provisions of this paragraph is voidable in the discretion of the Governor and Council of State.

d1. To require all State departments, institutions, and agencies to use State-owned office space instead of negotiating or renegotiating leases for rental of office space. Any lease entered into contrary to the provisions of this paragraph is voidable in the discretion of the Governor and the Council of State.

The Department of Administration shall report to the Joint Legislative Commission on Governmental Operations and to the Fiscal Research Division no later than May 1 of each year on leased office space.

d2. To purchase or finance the purchase of buildings, utilities, structures, or other facilities or property developments, including streets and landscaping, the acquisition of land, equipment, machinery, and furnishings in connection therewith; additions, extensions, enlargements, renovations, and improvements to existing buildings, utilities, structures, or other facilities or property developments, including streets and landscaping; land or any interest in land; other infrastructure; furniture, fixtures, equipment, vehicles, machinery, and similar items; or any combination of the foregoing, through installment-purchase, lease-purchase, or other similar type installment financing agreements in the manner and to the extent provided in Article 9 of Chapter 142 of the General Statutes. Any contract entered into or any proceeding instituted contrary to the provisions of this paragraph is voidable in the discretion of the Council of State.

e. To make all sales of real property (including marshlands or swamplands) owned by the State or by any State agency, with the approval of the Governor and Council of State in each instance. All conveyances in fee by the State shall be executed in accordance with the provisions of G.S. 146-74 through 146-78. Any conveyance of land made or contract to convey land entered into without the approval of the Governor and Council of State is voidable in the discretion of the Governor and Council of State. The proceeds of all sales of swamplands or marshlands shall be dealt with in the manner required by the Constitution and statutes.

f.   With the approval of the Governor and Council of State, to make all leases and rentals of land or buildings owned by the State or by any State agency, and to sublease land or buildings leased by the State or by any State agency from another owner, where such land or building owned or leased by the State or by any State agency is not needed for current use. The Governor, acting with the approval of the Council of State, may adopt rules (i) exempting from any or all of the requirements of this paragraph such classes of lease or rental transactions as he deems advisable; and (ii) authorizing any State agency to enter into and/or approve the classes of transactions thus exempted from the requirements of this paragraph; and (iii) delegating to any other State agency the authority to approve the severance of buildings and standing timber from State lands; upon such approval of severance, the buildings and timber so affected shall be treated, for the purposes of this Chapter, as personal property. Any lease or rental agreement entered into contrary to the provisions of this paragraph is voidable in the discretion of the Governor and Council of State.

g.   To allocate and reallocate land, buildings, and space in buildings to the several State agencies, in accordance with rules adopted by the Governor with the approval of the Council of State; provided that if the proposed reallocation is of land with an appraised value of at least twenty-five thousand dollars ($25,000), the reallocation may only be made after consultation with the Joint Legislative Commission on Governmental Operations. The authority granted in this paragraph shall not apply to the State Legislative Building and grounds or to the Legislative Office Building and grounds.

h.   To require any State agency to make reports regarding the land and buildings owned by it or allocated to it at such times and in such form as the Department may deem necessary.

i.   To determine whether all deeds, judgments, and other instruments whereby title to real estate has been or may be acquired by the State or by any State agency have been properly recorded in the county wherein the real property is situated, and to make or cause to be made proper recordation of such instruments. The Department may have previously recorded instruments which conveyed title to or from the State or any State agency or officer reindexed, where necessary, to show the State of North Carolina or grantor or grantee, as the case may be, and the cost of such reindexing shall be paid from the State Land Fund.

j.   To call upon the Attorney General for advice and assistance in the performance of any of the foregoing duties.

k.   None of the provisions of this subdivision apply to highway or railroad rights-of-way or other interests or estates in land held for the same or similar purposes, or to the acquisition or disposition of such rights-of-way, interests, or estates in land.

l.   To manage and control the vacant and unappropriated lands, swamplands, lands acquired by the State by virtue of being sold for taxes, and submerged lands of the State, pursuant to Chapter 146 of the General Statutes.

m.   To contract for or approve all contracts for all appraisals and surveys of real property for all State agencies; provided, however, this provision shall not apply to appraisals and surveys obtained in connection with the acquisition of highway rights-of-way, borrow pits, or other interests or estates in land acquired for the same or similar purposes, or to the disposition thereof, by the Board of Transportation.

n.   To petition for the annexation of state-owned lands into any municipality.

o.   To provide that no fee, other than reimbursement of actual costs incurred and actual revenues lost by the State, shall be charged when State buildings are made available to a production company for a production. As used in this subdivision, the term "production company" has the meaning provided in G.S. 105-164.3.

(5)   Administrative Analysis:

a.   To study the organization, methods, and procedures of all State agencies, to formulate plans for improvements in the organization, methods, and procedures of any agency studied, and to advise and assist any agency studied in effecting improvements in its organization, methods, and procedures.

b.   To report to the Governor its findings and recommendations concerning improvements in the organization, methods, and procedures of any State agency, when such improvements cannot be effected by the cooperative efforts of the Department and the agency concerned.

c.   To submit to the Governor for transmittal to the General Assembly recommended legislation where such legislation is necessary to effect improvements in the organization, methods, and procedures of any State agency.

(6) State and Regional Planning:

a. To assist the Director of the Budget in reviewing the capital improvements needs and requests of all State agencies, and in preparing a coordinated biennial capital improvements budget and longer range capital improvements programs.

b. In cooperation with State agencies and other public and private agencies, to collect, analyze, and keep up-to-date a comprehensive collection of economic and social data pertinent to State planning, which shall be available to State and local governmental agencies and private agencies.

c. To coordinate and review all planning activity relative to federal government requirements for general statewide or regional comprehensive program planning.

d. To make economic analyses, studies, and projections and to advise the Governor on courses of action desirable for the maintenance of a sound economy.

e. To encourage and assist in the development of the planning process within State and local governmental agencies.

f. To assist State agencies by providing them with basic information and technical assistance needed in preparing their short-range and long-range programs.

g. To develop and maintain liaison and cooperative arrangements with federal, interstate, State, and private agencies and organizations in the interest of obtaining information and assistance with respect to State and regional planning.

h. To develop and maintain a comprehensive plan for the development of the State, representing the coordinated efforts and contributions of all participating planning groups.

i. In cooperation with the counties, the cities and towns, the federal government, multi-state commissions and private agencies and organizations, to develop a system of multi-county, regional planning districts to cover the entire State, and to assist in preparing for those districts comprehensive development plans coordinated with the comprehensive development plan for the State.

(7)   Development Programs:

a.   To participate in development programs, to enter into contracts, formulate plans and to do all things necessary to implement development programs in any area of the State.

b.   To accept, receive and disburse, in furtherance of its functions, any funds, grants and services made available by the federal government and its agencies, any county, municipality, private or civic sources.

(8)   General Services:

a.   To locate, maintain and care for public buildings and grounds; to establish, locate, maintain, and care for walks, driveways, trees, shrubs, flowers, fountains, monuments, memorials, markers, and tablets on public grounds; and to beautify the public grounds.

b.   To provide necessary and adequate cleaning and janitorial service, elevator operation service, and other operation or maintenance services for the public buildings and grounds.

c.   To provide necessary night watchmen for the public buildings and grounds.

d.   To make prompt repair of all public buildings and the equipment, furniture, and fixtures thereof; and to establish and operate shops for that purpose.

e.   To keep in repair, out of funds appropriated for that purpose, the furniture of the halls of the Senate and House of Representatives and the rooms of the Capitol used by the officers, clerks, and other employees of the General Assembly.

f.   Struck out by Session Laws 1959, c. 68, s. 3.

g. To establish and operate a mail service center that shall be used by all State agencies other than the Division of Employment Security (DES) of the Department of Commerce, and in connection therewith and in the discretion of the Secretary, to do all things necessary in connection with the maintenance of the mail service center. The Secretary shall allocate and charge against the respective departments and agencies their proportionate parts of the cost of the maintenance of the mail service center. The Secretary shall develop a plan for the efficient operation of the center that meets the needs of State agencies, ensures timely delivery of mail, and ensures no loss of federal funds.

h. To provide necessary and adequate messenger service for the State agencies served by the Department. However, this may not be construed as preventing the employment and control of messengers by any State agency when those messengers are compensated out of the funds of the employing agency.

i. To establish and operate a central motor pool and such subsidiary related facilities as the Secretary may deem necessary, and to that end:

1. To establish and operate central facilities for the maintenance, repair, and storage of state-owned passenger motor vehicles for the use of State agencies; to utilize any available State facilities for that purpose; and to establish such subsidiary facilities as the Secretary may deem necessary.

2. To acquire passenger motor vehicles by transfer from other State agencies and by purchase. All motor vehicles transferred to or purchased by the Department shall become part of a central motor pool.

2a. Every new motor vehicle transferred to or purchased by the Department that is designed to operate on diesel fuel shall be covered by an express manufacturer's warranty that allows the use of B-20 fuel, as defined in G.S. 143-58.4. This sub-sub-subdivision does not apply if the intended use, as determined by the Department, of the new motor vehicle requires a type of vehicle for which an express manufacturer's warranty allows the use of B-20 fuel is not available.

2b. As used in this sub-sub-subdivision, "fuel economy" and "class of comparable automobiles" have the same meaning as in Part 600 of Title 40 of the Code of Federal Regulations (July 1, 2008 Edition). As used in this sub-sub-subdivision, "passenger motor vehicle" has the same meaning as "private passenger vehicle" as defined in G.S. 20-4.01. Notwithstanding the requirements of sub-sub-subdivision 2a. of this sub-subdivision, every request for proposals for new passenger motor vehicles to be purchased by the Department shall state a preference for vehicles that have a fuel economy for the new vehicle's model year that is in the top fifteen percent (15%) of its class of comparable automobiles. The award for every new passenger motor vehicle that is purchased by the Department shall be based on the Department's evaluation of the best value for the State, taking into account fuel economy ratings and life cycle cost that reasonably consider both projected fuel costs and acquisition costs. This sub-sub-subdivision does not apply to vehicles used in law enforcement, emergency medical response, and firefighting. The Department shall report the number of new passenger motor vehicles that are purchased as required by this sub-sub-subdivision, the savings or costs for the purchase of vehicles to comply with this sub-sub-subdivision, and the quantity and cost of fuel saved for the previous fiscal year on or before October 1 of each year to the Joint Legislative Commission on Governmental Operations and the Environmental Review Commission.

2c. To participate in the energy credit banking and selling program under G.S. 143-58.4. The Division of Motor Fleet Management of the Department of Administration is eligible to receive proceeds from the Alternative Fuel Revolving Fund under G.S. 143-58.5 to purchase alternative fuel, develop alternative fuel refueling infrastructure, or purchase AFVs as defined in G.S. 143-58.4.

3. To require on a schedule determined by the Department all State agencies to transfer ownership, custody or control of any or all passenger motor vehicles within the ownership, custody or control of that agency to the Department, except those motor vehicles under the ownership, custody or control of the Highway Patrol, the State Bureau of Investigation, or the constituent institutions of The University of North Carolina which are used primarily for law-enforcement purposes.

4. To maintain, store, repair, dispose of, and replace state-owned motor vehicles under the control of the Department, using best management practices. The Department shall ensure that state-owned vehicles are replaced when most cost effective using a replacement formula developed by the Department and reviewed periodically for appropriateness of use. The Department shall report semiannually to the cochairs of the Joint Appropriations Subcommittee on General Government, on or before October 15 and March 15, on the effect of any new or revised replacement formula on the cost of operating the central

motor pool, including the amount of any savings from use of any new or revised replacement formula.

5. Upon proper requisition, proper showing of need for use on State business only, and proper showing of proof that all persons who will be driving the motor vehicle have valid drivers' licenses, to assign economically suitable transportation, either on a temporary or permanent basis, to any State employee or agency. An agency assigned a motor vehicle may not allow a person to operate that motor vehicle unless that person displays to the agency and allows the agency to copy that person's valid driver's license. Notwithstanding G.S. 20-30(6), persons or agencies requesting assignment of motor vehicles may photostat or otherwise reproduce drivers' licenses for purposes of complying with this subpart.

As used in this subpart, "economically suitable transportation" means the most cost-effective standard vehicle in the State motor fleet, unless special towing provisions are required by the agency. The Department may not assign any employee or agency a motor vehicle that is not economically suitable. The Department shall not approve requests for vehicle assignment or reassignment when the purpose of that assignment or reassignment is to provide any employee with a newer or lower mileage vehicle because of his or her rank, management authority, or length of service or because of any non-job-related reason. The Department shall not assign "special use" vehicles, such as four-wheel drive vehicles or law enforcement vehicles, to any agency or individual except upon written justification, verified by historical data, and accepted by the Secretary. The Department may provide law enforcement vehicles only to those agencies which have statutory pursuit authority.

6. To allocate and charge against each State agency to which transportation is furnished, on a basis of mileage or of rental, its proportionate part of the cost of maintenance and operation of the motor pool.

The amount allocated and charged by the Department of Administration to State agencies to which transportation is furnished shall be at least as follows:

I. Pursuit vehicles and full size four-wheel drive vehicles $.24ile.

II. Vans and compact four-wheel drive vehicles - $.22ile.

III. All other vehicles - $.20ile.

7. To adopt, with the approval of the Governor, reasonable rules for the efficient and economical operation, maintenance, repair, and replacement, as limited in paragraph 4. of this subdivision, of all state-owned motor vehicles under the control of the Department, and to enforce those rules; and to adopt, with the approval of the Governor, reasonable rules regulating the use of private motor vehicles upon State business by the officers and employees of State agencies, and to enforce those rules. The Department, with the approval of the Governor, may delegate to the respective heads of the agencies to which motor vehicles are permanently assigned by the Department the duty of enforcing the rules adopted by the Department pursuant to this paragraph. Any person who violates a rule adopted by the Department and approved by the Governor is guilty of a Class 1 misdemeanor.

7a. To adopt with the approval of the Governor and to enforce rules and to coordinate State policy regarding (i) the permanent assignment of state-owned passenger motor vehicles and (ii) the use of and reimbursement for those vehicles for the limited commuting permitted by this subdivision. For the purpose of this subdivision 7a, "state-owned passenger motor vehicle" includes any state-owned passenger motor vehicle, whether or not owned, maintained or controlled by the Department of Administration, and regardless of the source of the funds used to purchase it. Notwithstanding the provisions of G.S. 20-190 or any other provisions of law, all state-owned passenger motor vehicles are subject to the provisions of this subdivision 7a; no permanent assignment shall be made and no one shall be exempt from payment of reimbursement for commuting or from the other provisions of this subdivision 7a except as provided by this subdivision 7a. Commuting, as defined and regulated by this subdivision, is limited to those specific cases in which the Secretary has received and accepted written justification, verified by historical data. The Department shall not assign any state-owned motor vehicle that may be used for commuting other than those authorized by the procedure prescribed in this subdivision.

A State-owned passenger motor vehicle shall not be permanently assigned to an individual who is likely to drive it on official business at a rate of less than 3,150 miles per quarter unless (i) the individual's duties are routinely related to public safety or (ii) the individual's duties are likely to expose the individual routinely to life-threatening situations. A State-owned passenger motor vehicle shall also not be permanently assigned to an agency that is likely to drive it on official business at a rate of less than 3,150 miles per quarter unless the agency can justify to the Division of Motor Fleet Management the need for permanent assignment because of the unique use of the vehicle. Each agency, other than the Department of Transportation, that has a vehicle assigned to it or has an employee to whom a vehicle is assigned shall submit a quarterly report to the Division of Motor Fleet Management on the miles driven during the quarter by the assigned vehicle. The Division of Motor Fleet Management shall review the report to verify that each motor vehicle has been driven at the minimum allowable rate. If it has not and if the department by whom the individual to which the car is assigned is employed or the agency to which the car is assigned cannot justify the lower mileage for the quarter, the permanent assignment shall be revoked immediately. The Department of Transportation shall submit an annual report to the Division of Motor Fleet Management on the miles driven during the year by vehicles assigned to the Department or to employees of the Department. If a vehicle included in this report has not been driven at least 12,600 miles during the year, the Department of Transportation shall review the reasons for the lower mileage and decide whether to terminate the assignment. The Division of Motor Fleet Management may not revoke the assignment of a vehicle to the Department of Transportation or an employee of that Department for failure to meet the minimum mileage requirement unless the Department of Transportation consents to the revocation.

Every individual who uses a State-owned passenger motor vehicle, pickup truck, or van to drive between the individual's official work station and his or her home, shall reimburse the State for these trips at a rate computed by the Department. This rate shall approximate the benefit derived from the use of the vehicle as prescribed by federal law. Reimbursement shall be for 20 days per month regardless of how many days the individual uses the vehicle to commute during the month. Reimbursement shall be made by payroll deduction. Funds derived from reimbursement on vehicles owned by the Motor Fleet Management Division shall be deposited to the credit of the Division; funds derived from reimbursements on vehicles initially purchased with appropriations from the Highway Fund and not owned by the Division shall be deposited in a Special Depository Account in the Department of Transportation, which shall revert to the Highway Fund; funds derived from reimbursement on all other vehicles shall be deposited in a Special Depository Account in the Department of Administration which shall revert to the General Fund. Commuting, for purposes of this paragraph, does not include those individuals whose office is in their home, as determined by the Department of Administration, Division of Motor Fleet Management. Also, this paragraph does not apply to the following vehicles: (i) clearly marked police and fire vehicles, (ii) delivery trucks with seating only for the driver, (iii) flatbed trucks, (iv) cargo carriers with over a 14,000 pound capacity, (v) school and passenger buses with over 20 person capacities, (vi) ambulances, (vii) [Repealed]. (viii) bucket trucks, (ix) cranes and derricks, (x) forklifts, (xi) cement mixers, (xii) dump trucks, (xiii) garbage trucks, (xiv) specialized utility repair trucks (except vans and pickup trucks), (xv) tractors, (xvi) unmarked law-enforcement vehicles that are used in undercover work and are operated by full-time, fully sworn law-enforcement officers whose primary duties include carrying a firearm, executing search warrants, and making arrests, and (xvii) any other vehicle exempted under Section 274(d) of the Internal Revenue Code of 1954, and Federal Internal Revenue Services regulations based thereon. The Department of Administration, Division of Motor Fleet Management, shall report quarterly to the Joint Legislative Commission on Governmental Operations and to the Fiscal Research Division of the Legislative Services Office on individuals who use State-owned passenger motor vehicles, pickup trucks, or vans between their official work stations and their homes, who are not required to reimburse the State for these trips.

The Department of Administration shall revoke the assignment or require the Department owning the vehicle to revoke the assignment of a State-owned passenger motor vehicle, pickup truck or van to any individual who:

I.   Uses the vehicle for other than official business except in accordance with the commuting rules;

II. Fails to supply required reports to the Department of Administration, or supplies incomplete reports, or supplies reports in a form unacceptable to the Department of Administration and does not cure the deficiency within 30 days of receiving a request to do so;

III. Knowingly and willfully supplies false information to the Department of Administration on applications for permanent assignments, commuting reimbursement forms, or other required reports or forms;

IV. Does not personally sign all reports on forms submitted for vehicles permanently assigned to him or her and does not cure the deficiency within 30 days of receiving a request to do so;

V.   Abuses the vehicle; or

VI. Violates other rules or policy promulgated by the Department of Administration not in conflict with this act.

A new requisition shall not be honored until the Secretary of the Department of Administration is assured that the violation for which a vehicle was previously revoked will not recur.

The Department of Administration, with the approval of the Governor, may delegate, or conditionally delegate, to the respective heads of agencies which own passenger motor vehicles or to which passenger motor vehicles are permanently assigned by the Department, the duty of enforcing all or part of the rules adopted by the Department of Administration pursuant to this subdivision 7a. The Department of Administration, with the approval of the Governor, may revoke this delegation of authority.

Notwithstanding the provisions of this section and G.S. 14-247, the Department of Administration may allow the organization sanctioned by the Governor's Council on Physical Fitness to conduct the North Carolina State Games to use State trucks and vans for the State Games of North Carolina. The Department of Administration shall not charge any fees for the use of the vehicles for the State Games. The State shall incur no liability for any damages resulting from the use of vehicles under this provision. The organization that conducts the State Games shall carry liability insurance of not less than one million dollars ($1,000,000) covering such vehicles while in its use and shall be responsible for the full cost of repairs to these vehicles if they are damaged while used for the State Games.

8. To adopt and administer rules for the control of all state-owned passenger motor vehicles and to require State agencies to keep all records and make all reports regarding motor vehicle use as the Secretary deems necessary.

9. To acquire motor vehicle liability insurance on all State-owned motor vehicles under the control of the Department.

10. To contract with the appropriate State prison authorities for the furnishing, upon such conditions as may be agreed upon from time to time between such State prison authorities and the Secretary, of prison labor for use in connection with the operation of a central motor pool and related activities.

11. To report annually to the General Assembly on any rules adopted, amended or repealed under paragraphs 3, 7, or 7a of this subdivision.

j. To establish and operate central mimeographing and duplicating services, central stenographical and clerical pools, and other central services, if the Governor after appropriate investigation deems it advisable from the standpoint of efficiency and economy in operation to establish any or all such services. The Secretary may allocate and charge against the respective agencies their proportionate part of the cost of maintenance and operation of the central services which are established, in accordance with the rules adopted by him and approved by the Governor and Council of State pursuant to paragraph k, below. Upon the establishment of central mimeographing and duplicating services, the Secretary may, with the approval of the Governor, require any State agency to be served by those central services to transfer to the Department ownership, custody, and control of any or all mimeographing and duplicating equipment and supplies within the ownership, custody, or control of such agency.

k. To require the State agencies and their officers and employees to utilize the central facilities and services which are established; and to adopt, with the approval of the Governor and Council of State, reasonable rules and procedures requiring the utilization of such central facilities and services, and governing their operation and the charges to be made for their services.

l. To provide necessary information service for visitors to the Capitol.

m. To perform such additional duties and exercise such additional powers as may be assigned to it by statute or by the Governor.

(9) Repealed by Session Laws 1989, c. 239, s. 2.

(10) Block Grants. - To establish and maintain a block grants manual that will ensure uniform administration of block grant funds. The manual shall be a comprehensive source of reference for all general and statewide administrative procedures for block grant funds. The manual shall contain the applicable procedures for: the contents of an application, which shall be as simple as possible; the awarding of or contracting with block grant funds; auditing, which shall, to the extent possible, promote the use of single audits of grantees; the ensuring of civil rights compliance by grantees; and monitoring.

(11) Energy-related matters. - To exercise those powers and perform those duties prescribed in Article 1 of Chapter 113B and Part 1 of Article 3B of Chapter 143 of the General Statutes and Parts 2 and 3 of this Article. (1957, c. 215, s. 2; c. 269, s. 1; 1959, c. 683, ss. 2-4; c. 1326; 1963, c. 1, s. 5; 1965, c.

1023; 1969, c. 1144, s. 2; 1971, c. 1097, s. 3; 1975, c. 399, ss. 1, 2; c. 879, s. 46; 1979, c. 136, s. 1; c. 544; 1979, 2nd Sess., c. 1137, s. 38; 1981, c. 300; c. 859, ss. 48-51; 1981 (Reg. Sess., 1982), c. 1282, s. 62; 1983, c. 267, s. 1; c. 717, s. 74; c. 761, ss. 58, 151, 173, 174; c. 923, s. 217; 1983 (Reg. Sess., 1984), c. 1034, s. 122; 1985, c. 479, ss. 168, 170, 174; c. 757, ss. 174, 175, 177; c. 791, s. 51; 1985 (Reg. Sess., 1986), c. 955, ss. 94, 94.1; 1987, c. 738, ss. 43-45, 47(a); c. 827, s. 220; c. 874; 1987 (Reg. Sess., 1988), c. 1086, s. 34(b); 1989, c. 58, s. 2; c. 239, s. 2; 1991, c. 542, s. 10; c. 689, s. 22; 1993, c. 539, s. 1030; 1994, Ex. Sess., c. 24, s. 14(c); 1995, c. 97, s. 1; c. 402, s. 1; 1996, 2nd Ex. Sess., c. 18, s. 10.2; 1997-412, s. 6; 1998-45, s. 1; 2000-140, s. 76(g); 2000-153, s. 2; 2001-424, s. 7.4; 2001-496, s. 8(d); 2002-126, s. 19.2; 2003-177, s. 1; 2003-284, ss. 18.1, 46.3; 2003-314, s. 1.2; 2005-276, s. 6.25(b); 2005-300, s. 1; 2005-413, s. 3; 2006-203, ss. 96, 97; 2006-217, s. 1.1; 2007-420, s. 2; 2007-446, s. 5; 2009-241, s. 1; 2009-474, s. 5; 2010-167, s. 6; 2011-145, ss. 9.19, 19.1(g), 30.12(b); 2011-401, s. 5.1; 2013-360, s. 16B.4(c).)

§ 143-341.1: Repealed by Session Laws 2009-451, s. 17.3(c), effective July 1, 2009.

§ 143-342. Rules governing allocation of property and space.

The Governor, with the approval of the Council of State, shall adopt such reasonable rules, regulations, and procedures as he deems necessary concerning the allocation and reallocation by the Department of land, buildings, and space within buildings to and among the several State agencies. (1957, c. 269, s. 1.)

§ 143-342.1. State-owned office space; fees for use by self-supporting agencies.

The Department shall determine equitable fees for the use of State owned and operated office space, and it shall assess the Department of State Treasurer, the Department of Insurance, and all self-supporting agencies using any of this office space for payment of these fees. For the purposes of this section, self-supporting agencies are those agencies designated by the Director of the Budget as being primarily funded from sources other than State appropriations.

Fees assessed under this section shall be paid to the General Fund. (1977, 2nd Sess., c. 1219, s. 48; 1983, c. 717, ss. 76, 77; 1997-443, s. 27.4.)

§ 143-343. General Services Division.

If the Governor and Council of State at any time determine, pursuant to G.S. 129-11, that the General Services Division should be made a part of the Department of Administration, the powers and duties given the Director of General Services by statute shall thereafter be deemed a part of the statutory powers and duties of the Director of Administration, and the powers and duties given the General Services Division by statute shall thereafter be deemed a part of the statutory powers and duties of the Department of Administration. The head of the General Services Division shall thereafter be appointed and removed, and his salary shall be fixed, in the same manner prescribed for other division heads. Upon the accomplishment of such transfer, the General Services Division shall thereafter be in all respects a part of the Department of Administration and subject to the supervision and control of the Director of Administration. (1957, c. 269, s. 1.)

§ 143-344. Transfer of functions, property, records, etc.

(a) Repealed by Session Laws 1979, 2nd Session, c. 1137, s. 39.

(b) All of the powers, duties, functions, records, property, supplies, equipment, personnel, funds, credits, appropriations, quarterly allotments, and executory contracts of the Division of Purchase and Contract are hereby transferred to the Department of Administration, effective July 1, 1957. All statutory references to the "Division of Purchase and Contract" or the "Purchase and Contract Division" shall be deemed to refer to the Department of Administration.

(c) The transfers directed by subsections (a) and (b) above, shall be made under the supervision of the Governor, and he shall be the final arbiter of all differences or disputes arising incident to such transfers.

(d) Repealed by Session Laws 2006-203, s. 98, effective July 1, 2007, and applicable to the budget for the 2007-2009 biennium and each subsequent biennium thereafter. (1957, c. 269, s. 1; 1979, 2nd Sess., c. 1137, s. 39; 2006-203, s. 98.)

§ 143-345. Saving clause.

No transfer of functions to the Department of Administration provided for in this Article shall affect any action, suit, proceeding, prosecution, contract, lease, or other business transaction involving such a function which was initiated, undertaken, or entered into prior to or pending the time of the transfer, except that the Department shall be substituted for the agency from which the function was transferred, and so far as practicable the procedure provided for in this Article shall be employed in completing or disposing of the matter. (1957, c. 269, s. 1.)

§ 143-345.1. Rules and regulations.

The Governor, with the approval of the Council of State, shall adopt reasonable rules and regulations governing the use, care, protection, and maintenance of the public buildings and grounds (other than parking). Any person who violates a rule or regulation adopted by the Governor with the approval of the Council of State is guilty of a Class 1 misdemeanor. (1957, c. 215, s. 2; 1971, c. 1097, s. 4; 1993, c. 539, s. 1031; 1994, Ex. Sess., c. 24, s. 14(c).)

§ 143-345.2. Disorderly conduct in and injury to public buildings and grounds.

Any person who commits a nuisance or conducts himself in a disorderly manner in or around any public building or grounds, or defaces or injures any public building or grounds, is guilty of a Class 1 misdemeanor. (1957, c. 215, s. 2; 1971, c. 1097, s. 4; 1993, c. 539, s. 1032; 1994, Ex. Sess., c. 24, s. 14(c).)

§ 143-345.3. Construction and repair of public buildings; use of Contingency and Emergency Fund.

It is lawful to resort to the Contingency and Emergency Fund provided in the Appropriation Act for financial aid in the construction, alteration, renovation, or repair of any public building, when in the opinion of the Governor and Council of State it is necessary to construct, alter, renovate, or repair such building. (1957, c. 215, s. 2; 1971, c. 1097, s. 4.)

§ 143-345.4. Moore and Nash squares and other public lots.

The governing body of the City of Raleigh is authorized, at its own expense, to grade, to lay out in walks, to plant with trees, shrubbery, and flowers and otherwise to adorn Moore and Nash squares and to that end has the general charge and management of these squares. The governing body may manage and improve in like manner any of the vacant lots within the city limits which belong to the State and which are not otherwise appropriated, subject to the approval of the Governor and Council of State. The governing body may not prevent the free access of the public to such squares or lots during reasonable hours.

Whenever, in the opinion of the Secretary, the governing body is not properly keeping the squares or lots which it has taken in charge under this section, the Secretary shall call the matter to the attention of the governing body, and if the governing body then fails for a period of 60 days to begin to take proper care of the squares or lots, the Governor and Council of State may repossess them and proceed to manage and control them for the preservation of such property.

In the event that the use of these squares and lots is at any time needed by the State, the license of the City of Raleigh to control and manage them shall terminate six months after notice given by the Governor and Council of State to the governing body of the city, and possession shall be promptly surrendered to the State. (1957, c. 215, s. 2; 1971, c. 1097, s. 4; 1975, c. 879, s. 46.)

§ 143-345.5. Program for location and construction of future public buildings.

The Department of Administration is hereby authorized, empowered, and directed to formulate a long range building policy program and shall cooperate with the governing board of the City of Raleigh in zoning property adjacent to or in the vicinity of the Capitol Square when and if the City of Raleigh desires to zone said property. If the Department of Administration is of opinion that property adjacent to or in the vicinity of the Capitol Square will, in the future, be needed for State building purposes, it shall so advise the governing body of the City of Raleigh. At such times as the governing body of the City of Raleigh shall rezone property adjacent to or within four blocks of the State Capitol, it shall request an opinion from the Department of Administration as to whether the Department finds a future need for such property for State building purposes. In the event that the governing board of the City of Raleigh is informed by the Department of Administration that any property herein covered be needed for building purposes by the State in the future, the governing body of the City of Raleigh shall give full consideration to such opinion of the Department before making any rezoning order. Notwithstanding any other provision of law, no local zoning ordinance shall apply to any State-owned building built or to be built on any State-owned land within six blocks of the State Capitol without the consent of the Council of State. (1951, c. 1132; 1957, c. 215, s. 2; 1971, c. 1097, s. 4; 2007-482, s. 1.)

§ 143-345.6: Recodified as § 147-54.3 by Session Laws 1991, c. 689, s. 181(b).

§ 143-345.7. Repair and reconstruction of the Western Residence of the Governor.

If the Western Residence of the Governor in Asheville is damaged or destroyed by fire or other disaster, it shall be repaired or reconstructed. Funds from the Contingency and Emergency Fund may be used for this purpose with the approval of the Director of the Budget if insurance coverage on the property should be inadequate. Insurance on the Western Governor's mansion shall be as adequate as possible and used in case of a fire or devastation of the mansion for the purpose of rebuilding or repairing the mansion. (1983, c. 602.)

§ 143-345.8. North Carolina Purchase Directory.

The Division of Purchase and Contract of the Department of Administration shall electronically advertise information on contract and purchase requirements from the Division of Purchase and Contract, the Office of State Construction, the Department of Transportation, and other agencies of State government which make direct purchases from private suppliers. The Division shall coordinate with the other departments of State government to ensure that the electronic advertisement is meeting the goals of disseminating as widely as possible and in a timely manner information on those State contracts which are open for bids. A printed copy of any information that is electronically advertised shall be made available to any party upon request. The Secretary of the Department of Administration may adopt rules governing the routine and procedures to be followed in advertising information on contract and purchase opportunities, what contracts and purchases will be advertised, and under what conditions exceptions to the electronic advertisement may occur. (1983, c. 839; 1999-417, s. 1.)

§ 143-345.9. Official "Prisoner of War/Missing in Action" flag to be flown over the State Capitol.

The Department of Administration is authorized to fly the official "Prisoner of War/Missing in Action (POW/MIA)" flag over the State Capitol on Veterans Day, Memorial Day, Armed Forces Day, and all other national holidays honoring veterans. (1989, c. 613.)

§ 143-345.10. Parking of maintenance vehicles.

Maintenance vehicles of the Department of Administration may park without charge at any metered parking space located on the street blocks bordering the State's Capitol Square when performing work at or on the State's Capitol Square. No maintenance vehicle shall be parked upon the State's Capitol Square in a location that obstructs the view of or access to any monument on the Square, unless the vehicle itself is needed to perform some maintenance function or duty required by this Article. (2009-262, s. 1.)

§ 143-345.11. Secretary's approval of plans for State buildings required.

(a) No agency or other person authorized or directed by law to select a plan and erect a building for the use of the State or any State institution shall receive and approve of the plan until it is submitted to and approved by the Secretary as to State construction standards and at a minimum as to the safety of the proposed building from fire, including the property's occupants or contents.

(b) Any plan submitted to the Commissioner of Insurance and approved prior to October 1, 2009 shall be deemed to have been approved jointly by the Commissioner of Insurance and the Secretary.

(c) Except as provided in subsection (a) of this section, nothing in this section shall be construed to abrogate the authority of the Commissioner of Insurance under G.S. 58-31-40 or any other provision of law.

(d) The Secretary shall provide quarterly written reports on plans reviewed and approved under this section to the Commissioner of Insurance. The reports shall be made in a form approved by the Commissioner of Insurance and the Secretary. (2009-474, s. 2.)

§ 143-345.12. Reserved for future codification purposes.

Part 2. Stocks of Coal and Petroleum Fuels.

§ 143-345.13. Reporting of stocks of coal and petroleum fuels.

The Department of Administration may, with the prior express approval of the Energy Policy Council and the Governor, require that all coal and petroleum suppliers in North Carolina supplying coal, motor gasoline, middle distillates, residual oils, and propane for resale within the State, file with the Department of Administration, on forms prepared by the Department, accurate reports as to the stocks of coal and petroleum products and storage capacities maintained by the supplier, including the supplier's current inventory and stock of coal, motor gasoline, middle distillates, residual oils and propane, the expected time such supplies will last under ordinary distribution demand and the schedule for receiving additional or replacement stocks. The reports and the information contained therein shall be proprietary information available only to regular employees of the Department of Administration, except that aggregate tables or schedules consolidating information from the reports may be released if they do not reveal individual report data for any named supplier. It is further the intent of this section that no information shall be required from coal and petroleum suppliers, that is, at the time the reports are requested, already on file with any agency, commission, or department of State government.

It is the intent of this section that the reports be filed only at such times as the Energy Policy Council and the Governor determine that an energy crisis as defined in G.S. 113B-20 exists or may be imminent.

If any petroleum or coal supplier fails to file the accurate reports as may be required by this section for more than 10 days after the date on which any such report is due, the Secretary of Administration is authorized and empowered to petition the district court, Division of the General Court of Justice, in the county in which the principal office or place of business of the supplier is located, for a mandatory injunction compelling the supplier to file the report. (2000-140, s. 76(i).)

Vision Books Order Form

Fax Orders:	1-980-299-5965
Phone Orders:	1-704-898-0770
E-mail Orders:	www.visionbooks.org
Mail Orders:	Vision Books, LLC P.O. Box 42406 Charlotte, NC 28215

Shipp To:
Name_____
Address_____
City_____State_____Zip_____
Phone_____Fax_____
Email_____@_____

Bill To: We can bill a third party on your behalf.
Name_____
Address_____
City_____State_____Zip_____
Phone___(_____)_____Fax_____
Email_____@_____

Pamphlet Number ($15.00 Each)	Qty	Total Cost
_____	_____	_____
_____	_____	_____
_____	_____	_____
_____	_____	_____
_____	_____	_____
_____	_____	_____
_____	_____	_____
Full Volume Set 1-92	92 Pamphlets	1,380.00

Free Shipping & Handling on Full Volume Orders
Add $1.00 Shipping & Handling Per Pamphlet $_____

Total Cost $_____

Thank you for your support. Management!

DID YOU ENJOY THIS BOOK?

Vision Books, LLC would like to hear from you! If you or someone you know has been fasely imprisoned, we would like to hear your story. If the 'North Carolina Criminal Law and Procedure' has had an effect in your life or if you have suggestions, we would like to hear from you. Send your letters to:

Vision Books, LLC
Attn: Staff Writers
P.O. Box 42406
Charlotte, NC 28215
Email: staff@visionbooks.org

Order Additional Copies:

Fax Orders: 1-980-299-5965

Phone Orders: 1-704-898-0770

E-mail Orders: www.visionbooks.org

Mail Orders: Vision Books, LLC
                   P.O. Box 42406
                   Charlotte, NC 28215

www.ingramcontent.com/pod-product-compliance
Lightning Source LLC
Chambersburg PA
CBHW051629170526
45167CB00001B/123